BEST
NEW
HAMPSHIRE
DRIVES

BEST NEW HAMPSHIRE DRIVES

14 Tours
in the
Granite State

Kay and Bill Scheller

Jasper Heights Press   Waterville, Vermont

Best
New Hampshire
Drives

Contents

Introduction

Best New Hampshire Drives, the second volume in the Jasper Heights Press *Best New England Drives* series, offers a new approach to touring the Granite State. We've divided New Hampshire into 14 drives, ranging from 25 to 140 miles in length and encompassing virtually all of the state's scenic highlights, historical touchstones, and recreational opportunities.

Our goal throughout *Best New Hampshire Drives* has been to offer an informal, conversational approach. But we haven't forgotten that along with anecdotes, most travelers want tips on where to stay, where to eat, and what attractions are worth their while. Within the drive narratives, numbers precede each new area or major point of interest. At the end of each drive, an "Information" section lists all of the lodgings, restaurants, attractions, activities, and shops that appear in boldface type in the text. Each listing is preceded by a number in parentheses, corresponding to the numbers that accompany places in the text. This makes it easy to tell if an inn or restaurant, for example, is close to the point where you've chosen to break up a drive with a meal or a night's stay.

For all lodgings in the "Information" sections, we've indicated rate categories keyed to dollar sign symbols. Rates are based upon double occupancy: $ = $75 or less; $$ = $76-$150; $$$ = over $150.

These rates are for high season, which generally means summer, peak foliage season, and winter if there's a ski area nearby. Private bath is assumed, unless otherwise noted. We've also indicated where young children may not be welcome, but be sure to check. And book well ahead for foliage season -- just about every place fills up way in advance.

For restaurants and attractions, we've indicated only days closed; otherwise, assume that they are open daily. Still, it's always a good idea to phone ahead, as schedules often change from season to season. **All Area Codes are 603 except for toll-free numbers as indicated.**

Dollar sign symbols for restaurants are based on the average cost of appetizer, entrée and dessert, before tax, tip or drinks (if dinner is not served, the signs are based on breakfast and/or lunch): $ = less than $20; $$ = $21-$35; $$$ = $36 or more.

We've indicated lodgings that have restaurants with an (R), and restaurants that have lodgings with an (L).

Best New Hampshire Drives is not a mile-by-mile guide, and we have deliberately avoided instructions such as, "turn left 3.2 miles ahead" unless there is a chance of confusion. Before you head out on any of the drives, we recommend picking up a copy of New Hampshire's official road map, available free at information centers throughout the state. Hiking trail distances are for round trips, unless otherwise noted.

Happy driving!

Kay and Bill Scheller
June, 2001

For a free state guidebook, contact the New Hampshire Office of Travel & Tourism, Box 1856, Concord, NH 03302. For general information, call 1-800-FUN-IN-NH. Web site: www.visitnh.gov

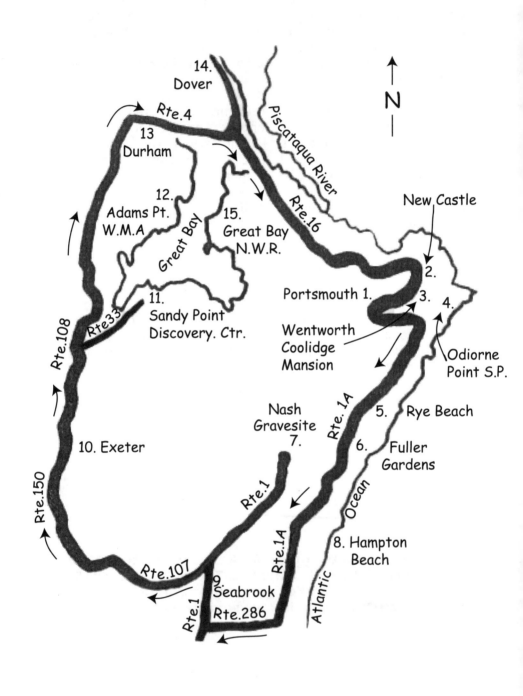

Drive 1

The Seacoast and the State's First Towns

55 miles

New Hampshire has the shortest seacoast in the United States -- a mere 18 miles -- and this drive takes in all of it. Start at Portsmouth, the splendidly preserved colonial capital, and head south along the ocean before turning inland to visit the three other towns -- Hampton, Dover, and Exeter, that constituted the entire colony of New Hampshire prior to 1675. The drive skirts a vast inland salt-water estuary, and returns to Portsmouth by way of Durham, home of the University of New Hampshire.

(1) Just off I-95, along the way toward downtown **Portsmouth**, the U.S.S. *Albacore* sits high and dry, with a dent in its nose and a permanent gangplank fixed to its side, at the **Port of Portsmouth Maritime Museum and Albacore Park**. The first blimp-shaped submarine, once the fastest in the world, was launched in Portsmouth in 1953, and decommissioned and returned here in 1985.

The *Albacore* is an altogether appropriate place to begin a tour of Portsmouth. Anyone who wishes to know the city should first come to terms with its nautical traditions, of which submarines are only the latest incarnation. Portsmouth is a city brought to life by the sea, by the pursuit of maritime commerce and naval defense. Now well into its fourth century, it successively has struggled through obscurity, grown rich on international trade, settled into genteel dilapidation and been born again as a paradigm of gentrification and New England prosperity. But down

11

through all of its years, it has been a seaport first and foremost.

It was at the future site of Portsmouth that an Englishman first dropped anchor in New Hampshire waters. The year was 1603 and the visitor was Captain Martin Pring, master of the vessels *Speedwell* and *Discover*, who made an unsuccessful visit to shore to look for sassafras. Pring didn't linger at the mouth of the Piscataqua, and neither did Samuel de Champlain, who stopped by in 1605 while exploring the coastline south of his Nova Scotia base of operations.

The first party of colonists to establish a settlement in the vicinity of Portsmouth was led by David Thompson, who arrived just south of the Piscataqua at Odiorne's Point (*see #4 below*) in 1623. Within a year, there was a small community on the south shore of the river's ample and well- protected harbor. These settlers, who had come to the New Hampshire coast under the auspices of Britain's royally-chartered Council for New England, were joined in 1631 by a group of Massachusetts planters who secured a charter for a community they called Piscataqua, but soon rechristened Strawberry Bank. ("Portsmouth" wasn't adopted until 1653.)

The old name is preserved today, in its 17th-century spelling, at the restored town-within-a-town of **Strawbery Banke**, a 10-acre living history museum that tells the story of the evolution of the city's oldest neighborhood from 1650 to 1950. Today's visitors can enter 10 furnished houses, ranging from gracious Georgian mansions to the modest homes of small tradesmen. There are also artisans' shops, where colonial-era crafts are demonstrated; period gardens; and a Piscataqua Gundalow, a flat-bottomed boat used from the mid-1600s to the mid-1800s to transport goods upriver from Portsmouth.

One of the major colonial-era crafts to thrive here was shipbuilding. Much of the hinterlands timber that became the colony's first staple crop found its way to

England and the shipyards of the Royal Navy. But it wasn't long before Portsmouth itself was an important shipbuilding center. Merchant and fishing vessels came first, but in 1690 the first man o' war slid down the ways into the mouth of the Piscataqua. This was the beginning of a tradition that was to last into the 1960s, when the last keels were laid at the **Portsmouth Naval Shipyard**. The greatest days of the naval shipyard came during World War II, when a new submarine was launched here every two weeks. The battle of the Atlantic was, in large part, won in Portsmouth harbor.

Portsmouth Naval Shipyard, actually located across the harbor in Kittery, Maine, survives today as an important naval maintenance facility. To passersby on the harbor bridges, though, its salient feature is the massive white naval prison that occupies the heights above the river's mouth: this is the largest brig on the East Coast.

During Portsmouth's halcyon years of shipbuilding, however, it was the merchants who made the city's economy and gave it the character it has so carefully burnished and preserved. During the mid-1700s, Portsmouth's yards were averaging 25 ships per year; a hundred years later, 10 new vessels were built annually -- but they were larger and faster ships, including more than 30 of the peerless Yankee clippers.

To this day, the homes and neighborhoods built by those long-ago merchant princes give Portsmouth so much of its character. Among them is the **Governor John Langdon House**. When he visited the five-year-old Georgian mansion in 1789, George Washington proclaimed it the "handsomest house in Portsmouth." John Moffatt, a sea captain turned shipowner, paid $12,000 to build the **Moffatt-Ladd House** as a wedding present for his son, Samuel. Although the elder Moffatt had also given Samuel a Harvard education, the young man didn't inherit his father's business sense. Within five years, he had to flee to the West Indies to escape his creditors. John Moffatt moved in, and lived in the house for the remainder of his 94 years. On the lawn is a horse chestnut tree planted by William Whipple, after he returned from signing the Declaration of Independence in 1776.

The **Wentworth Gardner House**, built as a gift from Madame Mark Hunking Wentworth to her son Thomas in 1760, is considered one of the finest examples of Georgian architecture in New England. New York's Metropolitan Museum of Art once owned the house and had plans to move it to Central Park. Fortunately, those plans fell through. The only place for a great house built by New England seafaring money is standing squarely on the banks of its harbor, forever looking for its ships to come in.

Among the other "must see" sights in Portsmouth: the 1758 National Historic Landmark **John Paul Jones House**; the 1807 **Rundlet-May House**; the state's oldest standing structure, the 1664 **Jackson House**; the 1716 **Warner House**; and the 1807 **St. John's Church**, which displays one of the oldest organs in the country, and a "Vinegar Bible" (so called because of a misprint of the word "vineyard"), one of only four in existence in the United States. The 1803 **Athenaeum**, across from the 1731 **North Church**, is one of the country's oldest subscription libraries. On the waterfront, the magnificently landscaped **Prescott Park**, the oldest and largest outdoor venue in New England, presents free events throughout the summer.

Many of the city's restaurants and shops are clustered on Ceres and Market streets.

Side Trip: The Isles of Shoals

"A heap of bare and splintery crags,
Tumbled about by lightning and frost,
With rifts and chasms, and storm-bleached jags,
That wait and growl for a ship to be lost."

This is how James Russell Lowell described the cluster of rocky and virtually treeless islands nine miles off the New Hampshire coast. They were "discovered" by Captain John Smith in 1614, but it is likely that Spanish, Portuguese and Basque fishermen were using them as cod-drying stations even before the venturesome Englishman honored them with his own name. In any event, the era of colonial settlement that followed Smith's exploration saw hundreds of fishermen come to live here, and to rename the islands because of the way fish "shoaled" or schooled in their vicinity.

In 1839 Thomas Laighton arrived with his family on White Island, where he had been engaged to serve as lighthouse keeper. Later he opened a hotel on Appledore Island to cater to the summer tourist trade. His daughter Celia Laighton Thaxter (1835-1894) returned to Appledore each summer throughout her adult life. Here she held her famous literary salons, attended by the likes of Whittier, Emerson, Lowell, and the elder Oliver Wendell Holmes. She also cultivated an exquisite flower garden, which she wrote about in her book *Among the Isles of Shoals*, and which was captured in a number of paintings by the American Impressionist Childe Hassam.. Today, the island is home to Cornell University's Shoals Marine Laboratory, which offers tours of the gardens by advance reservation.

Although Thomas Laighton's establishment burned down many years ago, the Isles' other great hostelry, the Oceanic Hotel on Star Island, survives as the center for a program of summer conferences held under the auspices of the Star Island Corporation, ranging from religious retreats to conferences on the arts.

The serenity of the Isles was almost lost in 1973 when Aristotle Onassis's scheme to build an enormous oil refinery at Durham, with a companion supertanker port at the Isles, was given the enthusiastic support of the state's governor, Meldrim Thompson. The citizens of Durham (*see Drive 1*) voted against the refinery at their annual town meeting.

Several companies in Portsmouth offer narrated boat tours of the Isles, including the Isles of Shoals Steamship Company, which also transports visitors to Star Island (day visitors are welcome); and Portsmouth Harbor Cruises.

----

(2) Follow Rte.1B along the shore out of Portsmouth to **New Castle**, actually a one-square-mile island connected to the mainland by bridges. This is where New Hampshiremen staged their famous raid on Fort William and Mary in December 1774, presaging the revolutionary battles of the following spring. Rebuilt in 1808 and renamed **Fort Constitution**, the old garrison still stands. Many of the saltbox-style fishermen's houses that cluster along New Castle's winding lanes were here well before Fort William and Mary fell, and have a look about them that suggests they will survive another century or two. Great Island Common, overlooking the ocean, is a delightful spot to picnic.

Continue on Rte. 1B past the grandest structure on the island, the Wentworth Hotel, a vast Victorian ark that once hosted delegates to the 1905 peace conference that produced the Treaty of Portsmouth and ended the Russo-Japanese War. Renovations are underway to return the hotel to its former glory, and it should be ready for guests in a few years.

(3) At the intersection of Rtes. 1B and 1A turn north on Rte. 1A, and take the right-hand turn onto Little Harbor Road to reach the **Wentworth-Coolidge Mansion**, home to Benning Wentworth, the Royal Governor of New Hampshire from 1741-67.

Henry Wadsworth Longfellow wrote of the 40-room mansion in his poem "Lady Wentworth":

It was a pleasant mansion, an abode
Near and yet hidden from the great highroad,
Sequestered among trees, a noble pile,
Baronial and colonial in its style.

Gables and dormer windows everywhere,
And stacks of chimneys rising high in air,
Pandaran pipes, on which all winds that blew
Made mournful music the whole winter through.

During the late 1800s, the mansion was the summer home of historian Francis Parkman. It now belongs to the state.

(4) Continue south on Rte. 1A. The promontory called Odiorne's Point is the setting for one of New Hampshire's loveliest parks, **Odiorne Point State Park and Seacoast Science Center**. Here is where Champlain and John Smith first spied the New Hampshire coast, and where David Thompson and his party built their trading post. Today, the site is dotted with the remnants of Fort Dearborn, a collection of observation bunkers and gun turrets built during World War II. There are also miles of wooded trails, as well as tidal pools and salt marshes teeming with bird, plant, and sea life.

South of here, Rte. 1A dips and turns alongside the rocky cliffs, past **Wallis Sands State Park** (swimming. bath house), **Rye Harbor State Park** (fishing, picnic area) and **Jenness Beach State Park** (swimming, bath house).

(5) It was next to the present site of the Rye Beach Motel at **Rye Beach** that the Atlantic Cable, "The Voice Beneath the Sea," was laid in 1874.   The telegraph cable stretched 2,500 miles to the Irish coast.

(6) Turn onto Chapel Rd. to **Fuller Gardens**, built in the 1920s for Massachusetts Governor Alvin T. Fuller. More than 1,500 rose bushes, a Japanese garden. and a conservatory with tropical and desert plants are among the highlights.

Side Trip

(7) Fans of poet-humorist Ogden Nash (the wit who gave us "Candy/is dandy/But liquor/is Quicker") can make a pilgrimage to his burial place in his family plot at Little River Cemetery. He was buried on October 2, 1971 next to his friend, Clarence Collins. Head west on Rte. 111, through North Hampton Center to the corner of Woodland Road and Atlantic Avenue. Look for his grave at the rear, near the stone wall.

Turn-of-the-century mansions overlook the sea at **Little Boar's Head** (one is the governor's official summer residence).   **North Hampton State Beach** offers excellent swimming and a two-mile path, lined with beach rose bushes, winding along the rocky ridge to the Rye Beach Club.

At **Great Boars Head**, look for John Greenleaf Whittier's "Grisley Head of the Boar... [which] tosses the foam from tusks of stone ... as it juts into the ocean." ("The Tent on the Beach.")

(8) The character of this seaside drive quickly changes at **Hampton Beach**, a throwback to an earlier species of oceanside resort. There's nothing the slightest bit chic about it: on one side of Rte. 1A is a long boardwalk, with steps leading down to the broad

strand of **Hampton Beach State Park**. On the other side is a Smithsonian-quality slice of honky-tonk, amusement-arcade, beachfront Americana. **Hampton Beach Casino** hosts a summer-long series of top entertainment, often causing major traffic jams.

Eunice Cole, a 17th-century resident of Hampton, was a self-proclaimed witch. One day a group of young people sailing down the Hampton River on a fishing ship passed by her shack. A girl climbed up on the ship's shrouds and shouted, "Fie on the witch." According to legend, Cole replied, "You are very brave today, but I hear the little waves laugh and tell me that your broth that awaits you at home will be very, very cold." Unfortunately, her prediction proved true: the ship sank in a storm off the Isles of Shoals later that day, and all were lost at sea. Several years later she was tried before the Quarter Sessions, which found "noe full proof" of witchcraft. But in deference to popular opinion, they decided to punish her anyway, taking her to jail and attaching a heavy shackle to her leg for several days. When she died a short time later, her neighbors dug a hole outside her hut, drove a stake into her corpse, and buried her with no marker for her grave.

----

(9) **Seabrook**, before 1976, was simply the name of a small town on Rte. 1, and not yet a rallying cry. That year, residents voted down a plan by the utility firm Public Service of New Hampshire to build a two-reactor nuclear generating facility in the town. The company had greater influence in state government than Aristotle Onassis did, though, and this time the town meeting vote did not close the issue. A coalition of anti-nuclear activists called the Clamshell Alliance launched increasingly larger protests at the construction site, culminating in a demonstration on April 30, 1977 that led to 1,000 arrests. The utility won (although only one of two planned units was

19

built), and Seabrook Station, on Seabrook Beach, has now been in operation for more than a decade.

Turn west off Rte. 1A onto Rte. 286 and continue through South Seabrook to Rte. 1N. Turn north onto Rte. 1, and then north onto Rte. 107, past **Seabrook Greyhound Park,** and then north onto Rte. 150, through Kensington, to Rte. 108. On 108, turn north toward Exeter.

(10) **Exeter**, one of New Hampshire's earliest settlements (only Portsmouth and Dover are older), was first settled by the Reverend John Wheelwright, a dissenter from the Puritan orthodoxy of Boston. He came here in 1638 and negotiated a deed for the surrounding territory from the sagamore of the Squamscott tribe, Wehanownowit. He was joined by only a handful of co-religionists at first, but by 1642 the town had grown sufficiently large to assume equal footing with its two predecessors.

Over the course of the 17th and 18th centuries, Exeter grew in political importance. Throughout most of the American Revolution it was the state's capital; on July 21, 1774, the first Provincial Congress met here, and on January 5, 1776 adopted a written constitution that effectively proclaimed New Hampshire's independence -- seven months before a messenger rode into town with the more famous declaration written by Thomas Jefferson and adopted in Philadelphia. The **American Independence Museum,** in the Ladd-Gilman House that served as the State's Treasury from 1775 to 1789 and the governor's mansion for 14 years, offers a glimpse of America's -- and Exeter's -- experience during the Revolutionary War.

Throughout the late 18th century Exeter grew in prosperity, with much of the area's industry dependent upon the power provided by Squamscott Falls. By 1800, Exeter's mills turned out everything from paper to snuff to chocolate to sailing ships: some of the country's finest frigates were built here.

Exeter's past two centuries have seen the water-powered mills fall silent, and a much more famous enterprise rise to prominence. The town is home to **Phillips Exeter Academy**, founded in 1783 by John Phillips, a successful Exeter merchant who had five years earlier established the other Phillips Academy in his native Andover, Massachusetts. Today Phillips Exeter, in the **Front Street Historic District**, is one of America's most prestigious college preparatory schools. Among its alumni were Robert Todd Lincoln, whose father, President Abraham Lincoln, visited him here; and Daniel Webster, remembered by his classmates as a "shy boy who could not make a declamation."

Exeter natives include Amos Tuck, founder of the American Republican Party, who in 1853 named all splinter groups opposed to slavery "Republicans;" and Dudley Leavitt, born here in 1772. With just three months of formal schooling, Leavitt became one of the most celebrated teachers of his day. He published "Leavitt's Farmer's Almanac" and, in the last issue in 1852, included a map of California because "so many of our people have gone there." One of his 11 children was the mother of the first white child born in Minnesota.

Head north out of Exeter on Rte. 85, through Newfields, originally part of Exeter.

Side Trip

(11) Great Bay Estuary and Reserve -- the largest inland body of salt water in New England -- covers 4,471 acres of tidal waters and mud flats, 48 acres of shoreline, and 800 acres of salt marshes, tidal creeks, woodlands, and open fields. Fed by numerous rivers and creeks, the reserve provides a fertile environment for a wide variety of birds (including nesting bald eagles in winter), other wildlife, and plant species, including many that are threatened or endangered. Sandy Point Discovery Center is the

Reserve's main headquarters for educational programs and exhibits. Gentle trails here lead to viewing areas, and, at low tide, into the mud flats.

The center offers four- to six- hour interpretive kayak trips for persons 18 years and older; advance reservations are highly recommended.

To get to the center, turn east (right) onto Rte. 33 and follow the brown and white N.H. Fish and Game Department signs onto Depot Road.

On Rte. 85, continue to the junction with Rte. 108, and then continue north on 108 to tiny **Newmarket**, at a falls on the Lamprey River. The water below the falls was deep enough at high tide to float large vessels, making it easy to bring heavy equipment and supplies to town. This, and its natural source of water power, contributed to the town's growth as an industrial center in the 19th century. Although it now exists primarily as a bedroom community for Portsmouth and Durham, its early mill days are preserved in the handsome, stone Rivermore Mill which now houses restaurants, craft shops, and offices.

(12) Turn right onto Bay/Lamprey Rd. and continue alongside Great Bay to **Adams Point Wildlife Management Area** and the trailhead for the Adams Point Trail, a 45-minute walk around the peninsula separating Little Bay from Great Bay. A trail guide brochure is available at the kiosk. The Jackson Laboratory, a University of New Hampshire estuarine research facility, is located here (for information, contact the Great Bay National Estuarine Research Reserve).

(13) Continue on Rte. 108, alongside the Oyster River, into **Durham**. The town's first colonists came from Dover, sailing into the Oyster River via the Piscataqua and the upper reaches of Great Bay (or Little Bay, as its narrow northern arm is called). They found the elbow room they were looking for, but paid

for it with vulnerability to Indian attacks. A raid here in 1675 marked the opening of hostilities in King Philip's War, while the 1694 sacking and burning of the town ranked as one of the worst atrocities of the era of French-English hostility. The attack was carried out by Indians, but planned in Quebec and led by a French soldier. More than 100 residents were killed or taken captive, and most of the town was reduced to ashes.

Like Exeter to the south, Durham was a hotbed of activity during the Revolution. It was Durham men who stole more than 100 barrels of gunpowder, cannon, and guns from the British at Fort William and Mary in Newcastle (*see #2 above*) and for two days chopped ice in the Oyster River so they could float the material downstream and hide it in town. The bridges across the Bellamy and Piscataqua rivers from Durham to Portsmouth are named for two local heroes of the Revolution: General Sullivan, who led the men on the raid at Newcastle; and Colonel Alexander Scammel, General Washington's adjutant general who died of wounds received at the Battle of Yorktown.

Today, Durham is home of the **University of New Hampshire**, the state's principal public institution of higher learning. The university started life as a state agricultural college in Hanover, but moved here in 1893 when a rich farmer's legacy became available on condition that the school be transplanted to the site of his Durham farm. Modern-day UNH, though, is more devoted to the liberal arts than to agriculture. That said, however, be sure to visit the Jesse Hepler Lilac Arboretum at Nesmith Hall.

Side Trip

(14) Continue north on Rte. 108 to Dover, a former mill town at Cocheco Falls which has reinvented itself as a service center for UNH. The self-guided Heritage Walking Trail provides an excellent overview of the

town's rich history. The major attraction, however, is the quirky and fascinating three-building Woodman Institute, whose main building houses several floors of "stuff" -- collections of war-related uniforms and guns, period furniture, family treasures, and old documents. Also on the grounds are the 1813 Hale House and the 1675 Damm Garrison.

In the 1600s, prominent merchant Richard Waldron cheated local Indians whenever he could. When buying beaver skins, he would use his fist as a balancing weight and claim it weighed a pound. He "forgot" to cross out paid accounts.

When a force of 130 English and 40 Indians came to Dover to subdue a group of Indians who had taken refuge with the Dover Indians after attacking settlers to the north, Waldron offered to join forces with the locals against the British. He had his men meet the lobsterbacks in a sham fight, and ordered a grand round of musketry. The Indians dutifully discharged their guns, but the English withheld fire and and took 200 "hostiles" into custody without bloodshed.

Twelve years later, in 1688, the Indians attacked and captured Waldron. According to lore, they tied him in the armchair where he had sat in judgment over the years. Then they stabbed him with their knives, saying with each stroke, "I cross out my account!"

Just out of town, turn east on Rte. 4 (Spaulding Turnpike) to head back to Portsmouth.

Side Trip

(15) **Pease Air Force Base**, which closed in 1989, has metamorphosed into **Pease International Tradeport**; but the 1,954-acre **Great Bay National Wildlife Refuge** on its border remains a prime habitat for nesting eagles (winter) and other bird species, including wild

24

turkey, kestrels, and great horned owls; and an abundance of animals, including coyote, fox, and white-tailed deer. There are two hiking trails: a two-mile loop to the bay; and a 1/2-mile walk to a nearby pond.

To get to the Refuge, take the Pease International Tradeport exit off Rte. 4 to the bottom of the ramp, turn right, and continue through the traffic light to the "T" intersection. Turn right onto Arboretum Drive and continue straight for about 2 1/2 miles to the refuge entrance.

Information

Exeter Chamber of Commerce (772-2411), 120 Water St., Exeter. www.exeterarea.org.

Greater Dover Chamber of Commerce (742-2218), 299 Central Ave., Dover 03820. www.dovernh.org

Greater Portsmouth Chamber of Commerce (436-1118), 500 Market St. (just off I-95), Box 239, Portsmouth 03802. www.portcity.org. Seasonal kiosk in Market Square.

Hampton Chamber of Commerce (800-438-2826 or 926-8717), P.O. Box 790S, 180 Ocean Blvd., Hampton Beach 03842. www.hamptonbeach.org

Lodging

(1) Sheraton Harborside (877-248-3794 or 431-2300), 250 Market St., Portsmouth 03801. In-town hotel /convention center has 203 rooms and condominium suites. Indoor pool, sauna and exercise room. $$-$$$ www.sheratonportsmouth.com.

(1) Bow Street Inn (431-7760), 121 Bow St., Portsmouth 03801. Converted brick brewery on the Piscataqua River has nine rooms and two suites, including a penthouse with kitchen; some water views. $$-$$$

(1) Sise Inn (800-267-0525 or 433-1200), 40 Court St, Portsmouth 03801. www.someplacesdifferent.com. Historic, in-town Queen Anne has 34 elegant rooms and suites with full bath or jacuzzi in the original section and a modern addition. $$-$$$

(2) Great Islander B & B (436-8536), 62 Main St., New Castle 03854. Three rooms (one with private bath) in traditional B & B overlooking the river. Lap pool. $$

(8)Ashworth by the Sea (800-345-6736 or 926-6762), 295 Ocean Blvd., Rte. 1A, Hampton Beach 03842. www.ashworthhotel.com. Year-round, oceanfront landmark has rooms with balconies overlooking the water and indoor/outdoor pool. Restaurant serves steak, lobster, and seafood. $$-$$$

(8) DW's Oceanside Inn & Cottages (926-3542), 365 Ocean Blvd., Hampton Beach 03842. www.oceansideinn.com. Oceanfront inn, cottages, apartments, and condo rentals; weekly in summer. $$

(10) The Inn by the Bandstand (877-239-3837), Four Front St., Exeter 03833. www.innbybandstand.com. Revolutionary-era home has nine elegantly furnished rooms (some with fireplaces) with private baths, phone, and TV. $$-$$$

(10) (R) The Inn of Exeter (800-782-8444 or 772-5901), Front St., Exeter 03833. www.exeterinn.com. The Academy's Georgian-style lodging has 46 Colonial rooms and suites furnished with antiques and period pieces (some fireplaces). The restaurant serves three meals, including a popular Sunday brunch. $$$

(13) New England Conference Center and Hotel (800-590-4334 or 862-2712), UNH Campus, 15 Strafford Ave., Durham 03824. www.necc.unh.edu. Conference/hotel complex has a total of 115 well-equipped guest rooms. $$

(13)(R) Three Chimneys Inn (888-399-9777 or 868-7800), 17 Newmarket Rd., Durham 03824. www.threechimneysinn.com. 1649 home is now a fine inn with 23 elegantly-furnished rooms with fireplaces and four poster canopy beds in the inn and carriage house. Restaurants include: Maples, with candlelight dining in a formal atmosphere (jackets required), ffrost Sawyer Tavern, and The Conservatory. $$$

(14) Highland Farm B & B (743-3399), 148 County Farm Rd., Dover 03820. Spacious, antiques-filled guest accommodations in large brick Victorian farmhouse on 75 acres among the Cocheco River. Breakfast served in the formal dining room. $$

Restaurants

(1) Dunfey's (433-3111), Harbour Place Marina, Portsmouth. Four levels of indoor/outdoor dining--from seafood to smokestack grill--aboard the converted, 1923 steam tugboat John Wanamaker. L, D, Sun. brunch. $$-$$$

(1) The Library Restaurant (431-5202), 401 State St., Portsmouth. Casual but elegant surroundings provide the setting for contemporary cuisine served in the former 1875 Rockingham House, once the city's premier hotel. L, D and Sun. brunch. $$-$$$

(1) Muddy River Smokehouse (430-9582), 21 Congress St., Portsmouth. BBQ, homemade chili, 24 beers on tap and a blues club downstairs. $

(1) Petey's Seafood Shack and Dining Room, Rte. 1A, between Portsmouth and Rye. May-mid-Oct. Fried seafood baskets. Closed Wed. $

(1) **The Portsmouth Brewery** (431-1115), 56 Market St., Portsmouth. New Hampshire's original brew pub serves pub grub daily; tours available. L, D. $-$$

(5) **Saunders at Rye Harbor** (964-6466), Rt. 1A, Rye Harbor. Harborfront landmark serves fine lobster, seafood, poultry, and prime beef. Live music on the deck Sun. July and Aug. L, D. $$-$$$

(8) **Little Jack's Seafood Restaurant** (926-8053), 539 Ocean Blvd., Hampton Beach. Baked, broiled, steamed and fried seafood and shore dinners overlooking the ocean. $-$$

(10) **Loaf and Ladle** (778-8955), 9 Water St., Exeter. Homemade soups, breads, sandwiches, and salads. $

(10) **Szechuan Taste** (772-8888), 42 Water St., Exeter. Fine Chinese fare, including a luncheon buffet. $-$$

(14) **Newick's Lobster House and Restaurant** (742-3205), Dover Point Rd., Dover. One of the most popular spots in the area for large portions of fresh seafood served in an informal atmosphere overlooking Great Bay. L, D. $$

(15) **The Redhook Ale Brewery** (430-8600), 35 Corporate Dr., Pease International Tradeport, Portsmouth. Tour the craft brewery ($), which brews in the tradition of *Rheinheitsgebot* -- and then have a casual lunch at the Cataqua Public House. $

Attractions

(1) The 1664 Jackson House, the oldest house in the state; the Langdon House; and the Rundlet-May House are owned by the Society for the Preservation of New England Antiquities (SPNEA); open June 1-Oct., Wed.-Sun., 1-5. $

(1) Albacore Park, Portsmouth (436-3680), 600 Market St., Portsmouth. May-Columbus Day. Tours. $

(1) The Children's Museum of Portsmouth (436-3853), 280 Marcy St., Portsmouth. Hands-on exhibits including dinosaurs and the human body. Closed Mon. except summer and school vacation $

(1) Portsmouth Athenaeum (431-2538), 9 Market Sq., Portsmouth. Tours Thurs. 1-4 check.

(1) Prescott Park (436-2848), PO. Box 4370, Marcy St., Portsmouth.

(1) Shoals Marine Laboratory: Celia Thaxter's Garden (607-254-2900), Cornell University, Ithaca, NY 14853. 2 1/2 hr. tours, via ferry, Wed. mid-June-Labor Day. $

(1) St. John's Episcopal Church (436-6902), Chapel St., Portsmouth.

(1) Strawbery Banke Museum (433-1106), 64 Marcy St., Portsmouth. Mid April-Oct. daily. #

(2) Fort Constitution State Historic Site, New Castle. Constructed in the 1600s for protection against pirates; raided by Sons of Liberty (local Portsmouth patriots) Dec., 1774 following warning by Paul Revere. Base of walls and interpretive panels.

(2) Fort Stark State Historic Site, New Castle. Mid-18th-century military fortification protected Little Harbor during each conflict from the American Revolution through WW II.

(4) Odiorne Point State Park/Seacoast Science Center (436-8043), 570 Ocean Boulevard, Rye. $

(6) Fuller Gardens (964-5414), Rte. 101D, North Hampton. $

(8) Hampton Beach State Park (926-3784), Rte. 1A, Hampton Beach. $

(9) Seabrook Greyhound Park (474-3065), Rte. 107, Seabrook. Year-round.

(10) American Independence Museum (772-0861), One Governors Lane, Exeter. May 1-Oct., Wed.-Sun. noon-5. $

(10) Gilman Garrison House (436-3205), 12 Water St., Exeter. One of the town's oldest buildings reflects mid-1700s life. The part constructed of logs in 1660 served as a garrison. June-mid-Oct., Tues., Thurs., Sat. and Sun., noon-5. $

(10) Moses-Kent House (772-2044), Pine and Linden Sts., Exeter. 1868 mansard-style home in the historic district has Victorian furnishings. June-Sept. $

(10) Phillips Exeter Academy, Rte. 111, Exeter.

(11) Great Bay National Estuarine Research Reserve (868-1095), 37 Concord Rd., Durham: Sandy Point Discovery Center (778-0015), 89 Depot Rd., Stratham. May-Sept., Wed.-Sun. 10-4 Oct., weekends 10-4; grounds open year round.

(13) Durham Historic Association (868-5436), Main St. and Newmarket Rd., Durham. June-Aug., Mon-Fri. 1-4; Sept.-May, Tues. and Thurs. 2-4.

(13) University of New Hampshire (862-1234): The Art Gallery, (862-3712), Paul Creative Arts Center, Durham. Sept.-May, daily except Fri. and holidays.

(14) Cochecho River Trail (749-4445), Strafford County Farm, Dover. One-mile loon trail across an old flood plain; trail maps at beginning.
(14) Woodman Institute (742-1038), 182 Central Ave., Dover. Tues.-Sat. 2-5.

(15) Great Bay National Wildlife Refuge (431-7511),

U.S. Fish and Wildlife Service, 601 Spaulding Turnpike, Suite 17, Portsmouth 03801.

Activities

(1) Ballet New England (430-03-0), 135 Daniel St., Portsmouth. Largest professional ballet troupe in N.H.

(1) Isles of Shoals Steamship Co. (800-441-4620 or 431-5500), 315 Market St., Portsmouth. Whale watches; lighthouse, harbor and Isles of Shoals cruises; Star Island picnics and explorations.

(1) The Music Hall (436-2400), 28 Chestnut St., Portsmouth. 1878 historic hall hosts music, theater, dance, and movies.

(1) Pontine (436-6660), 135 McDonough St., Portsmouth. Cutting-edge productions presented in an intimate, Soho-style performance space.

(1) Portsmouth Harbor Cruises (800-776-0915 or 436-8084), Ceres St. Dock, Portsmouth. Tours of harbor, Isles of Shoals, Great Bay, and the Cocheco River.

(1) Prescott Park Arts Festival (436-2848), Prescott Park, Portsmouth.

(1) Seacoast Repertory Theater (433-4793), 125 Bow St., Portsmouth. Year-long program of live theater.

(1) Water Country (427-1111), Rte. 1 S, Portsmouth. New England's largest water park has more than 20 acres of fun.

(5) Atlantic Fishing Fleet (964-5220), Rye Harbor State Marina, Rte. 1A, Rye Harbor. Half- and full-day fishing and whale watching cruises.
(5) Shoals Sailing Adventures (964-6446), P.O. Box 66, Rye Harbor. Sails to the Isles of Shoals.

(8) Al Gauron Deep Sea Fishing and Whale Watching

(800 905-7820 or 926-2469), State Pier, Hampton Beach. Two-hr. night, half, and full-day fishing trips and marathons; five- hr. whale watching cruises.

(8) Hampton Playhouse (926-3073), Rt. 101E, Winnacunnet Rd., Hampton. Summer repertory theater.

(10) Ioka Theater (772-2222), Exeter. The restored soda fountain in the lobby of this 1915 Art Deco theater is a delightful spot for an ice cream float. The theater shows classic films and hosts live performances.

(13) The Little Bay Buffalo Company (868-3300), 50 Langley Rd., Durham. Tours of a wildlife estate/bison farm; bison meat and bison products for sale. April-Oct.

Tours

(1) Ghostly Tours of Portsmouth (433-9999), 49 Pleasant St., Portsmouth.

(1) Portsmouth Harbor Trail (436-3988), Information Kiosk, Market Sq., Portsmouth. July 4-Columbus Day, Thurs.-Sun., 10:30 and 6.

Arts, Crafts and Antiques

(10) League of New Hampshire Craftsmen (778-8282), 61 Water St., Exeter. Juried crafts by more than 250 local artisans.

(14) Salmon Falls Stoneware (749-1467), Oak Street, Dover. Traditional New England salt-glaze pottery by local artisans.

Shopping

(1) The Book Guild of Portsmouth (436-1758), 58

State St., Portsmouth. Eight dealers. Open daily.

(10) Exeter Bookstore, 13 Spring St., Exeter. The academy's bookstore is well stocked with regional books.

(10) Water Street Bookstore (778-9731), Water St., Exeter.

(13) Emery Farm (742-8495), Rt. 4, Durham. Established in 1655, this may be the nation's oldest family farm. Pick your own berries or buy them ready-picked, along with peaches, local crafts, home-baked bread, and pottery. Easter - Christmas.

(14) The Christmas Dove (800-550-3683), jct. Rtes. 125 and 9, Dover. Year-round shopping for ornaments, candles, and other holiday-related products.

(14) Tuttle's Red Barn (742-4313), Dover Point Rd., Dover. Country's oldest continuously-operating family farm sells fresh local produce, baked goods, and cheeses.

<u>Off the Drive</u>

Kittery, Maine outlet stores

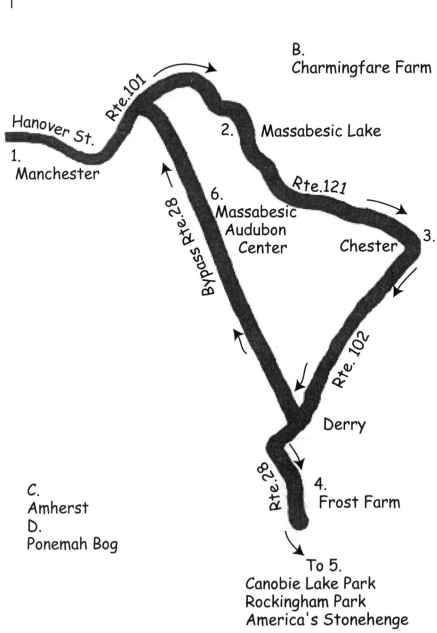

N

A.
Bear Brook S.P.

B.
Charmingfare Farm

Rte.101

Hanover St.

1.
Manchester

2. Massabesic Lake

Rte.121

6.
Massabesic
Audubon
Center

Chester

3.

Bypass Rte.28

Rte. 102

Derry

C.
Amherst
D.
Ponemah Bog

Rte.28

4.
Frost Farm

To 5.
Canobie Lake Park
Rockingham Park
America's Stonehenge

Drive 2

The Queen City
and Her Satellites

25 miles

This short drive actually covers quite a bit of territory, as it takes in New Hampshire's largest city. Visit the Manchester of yesterday and today, then head off to nearby places as varied as an old-fashioned amusement park, a famous poet's farm, and a mysterious prehistoric site.

Many of the roads in this most densely populated part of the state are quite heavily traveled, and aren't really "scenic drive" material. So, rather than tie together all of the region's attractions in this region into a drive, we've listed several of them as side trips.

(1) One day in 1810, Judge Samuel Blodgett stood at the Amoskeag Falls and said of the surrounding village (called Derryfield back then) that the area would be "the *Manchester* of New England." He was a likely character to predict that the town built along the river would someday rival the British textile city. He had spent a good part of his life promoting the idea of a canal around the Amoskeag Falls of the Merrimack, and had seen his dream become reality in 1807. With the new water link with Boston by way of the Middlesex Canal, and a ready supply of power right at the falls, Derryfield could begin to realize its destiny as a manufacturing center.

But it would be 27 years until a group of Boston capitalists -- already busy developing the mills of nearby Lowell, Massachusetts -- bought water power rights to the entire Merrimack River, and assembled a parcel of 15,000 acres along the Merrimack's east bank near the Amoskeag Falls. They then laid out and built the city of Manchester, and the Amoskeag Manufacturing Company was born. At its pinnacle of its size and power, in the early years of the 20th century, "the Amoskeag" was the world's largest textile enterprise, employing 17,000 workers to tend its 700,000 spindles and 23,000 looms in a complex of 30 major mills that turned raw cotton fiber into finished cloth. The mill buildings stretched for a mile along the river's eastern shore.

As Manchester's economy was determined by the Amoskeag, so was its social fabric. By the early 1900s this was largely an immigrant city. Although the predominant group was French-Canadian, all of the European nationalities that flocked to this country during the wide-open years of immigration were represented, and they were absorbed into as paternalistic a system of employment as ever existed in the United States, with the possible exception of wholly-owned corporate towns such as the sleeping-car manufacturing center of Pullman, Illinois.

Although only a small fraction of the workers actually lived in company-owned housing, the firm sponsored clubs and sports teams, published a magazine, and ran night schools that offered English as a second language. There was an Amoskeag playground for workers' children, a dental plan (during the company's later years), and even a mortgage assistance program. All of this largess was designed to keep organized labor out of the mills. But several strikes (1919, 1922, 1933, and 1934), coupled with a movement in the 1920s to shift the base of the American textile industry to the South where physical plants were newer and labor was cheaper, took their toll: the Amoskeag declared bankruptcy and shut its doors in 1935.

The history of Manchester since then has been the story of a city's attempts -- ultimately successful -- to fill the void left by the departure of such a giant.

Some three-quarters of the Amoskeag mill buildings are still standing: some are derelict, but a core have been revitalized as offices and manufacturing companies. Today the "Queen City," straddling the banks of the Merrimack River, is the largest in Northern New England. It has the state's finest art museum, an excellent symphony, and is the hub for eight area colleges.

Any visitor's approach to Manchester should begin where the city itself did, on the banks of the Merrimack River at the place the Indians called Amoskeag -- "place of good fishing." The present Amoskeag Bridge, at Canal and West Salmon streets, is approximately at the site. Near here at Amoskeag Falls, obscured now by a power dam, are the remains of the stone gatehouse that marked the place where Judge Blodgett's 1807 canal joined the Merrimack. You can watch fish climb up a concrete ladder on their way up the Merrimack to spawn, from an underwater window at **Amoskeag Fishways**, next to the TraveLodge on Fletcher St.

The millyard and central concentration of brick factory buildings of Amoskeag Manufacturing Company stand abut 15 blocks south of the falls and bridge. Begin a tour of the **Amoskeag Mill** and surroundings (note: Manchester covers several miles of north-south distance along the Merrimack, and consequently no attempt will be made here to recommend specific walking directions) at the **Manchester Historic Association**, where exhibits and educational programs interpret the social, cultural and industrial history of the city. Walking tour maps are available at the museum shop, or you can take an organized walking tour (see *Tours* below). Among the sites: the mills, workers' housing, and the city's ethnic neighborhoods. The association has a **Millyard Orientation Center** at Mill #3 at the corner of Commercial and Pleasant Streets.

Manchester's premier cultural attraction is the **Currier Gallery of Art**, frequently ranked among America's finest small museums. European paintings, sculptures and decorative art of the past six centuries, as well as an impressive American collection, are exhibited on two floors surrounding a central court, as well as on a lower level. Among artists represented are Picasso, Matisse, Monet, Sargent, Hopper, Wyeth, Calder, and O'Keeffe. A 19th-century furniture collection ranges from anonymous country pieces to the works of the Dunlop family, master cabinetmakers of late 18th-century New Hampshire. An off-site gem of the Currier's collection is the **Zimmerman House**, designed by Frank Lloyd Wright in 1950. Wright designed only five homes in New England, and this -- one of his compact "Usonian" designs -- is the only one open to the public. The house may be visited only by joining a shuttle-bus tour leaving from the gallery.

The **Franco-American Centre** exhibits works of French and Francophone artists and, with a library of more than 30,000 volumes, provides information about French culture, heritage and history in North America. Other downtown sites include the 1845 Gothic Revival, National Register of Historic Places City Hall; and the **New Hampshire Institute of Art**, with its fine gift shop.

Turn-of-the-century Manchester wasn't all work and no play. The Palace Theater, on Hanover St. near Elm St., was built in 1915 by Victor Charas, a Greek immigrant who made his fortune as a restaurateur and speculator. During his day there were nearly two dozen vaudeville and burlesque houses within a few city blocks. Charas, believing there was demand for high-quality productions, booked the best vaudeville, traveling repertory, and Broadway show companies into his 960-seat theater. The era of live performances at the Palace lasted until the 1930s, after which it served as a movie house for several decades. By the 1960s, however, it had sunk to X-rated ignominy. It was saved from demolition by a citizens' group called the New Hampshire Performing Arts Center, and now shines as one of the brightest cultural lights in New Hampshire: it's home to the

Manchester Chorale Society, the New Hampshire Symphony Orchestra, and the New Hampshire Opera League.

In 1775, a man named John Stark was working at his Derryfield sawmill (remember, the town wasn't yet called "Manchester" in those days) when he heard news of the "shot heard 'round the world" and the start of the American Revolution. He organized 1,500 men into the First New Hampshire Militia, and marched them to Bunker Hill to fight the British. At the beginning of the Battle of Bennington, fought on the New York-Vermont border in 1777, as Stark's troops faced British regulars and Hessian mercenaries, he stood on a fence and proclaimed, "Now, my men, over there are the Hessians. They were bought for seven pounds, 10 pence a man. Tonight the American flag floats over yonder hill or Molly Stark sleeps a widow." Stark is credited with repulsing the British, setting the stage for their defeat at Saratoga. But it was in a written response regretfully declining an invitation by a group of Bennington veterans to attend a banquet commemorating the battle that the 81-year-old commander gave posterity his most famous words. He wrote, "the lamp of life is almost spent ... I go to the country from whence no traveler returns. I must soon receive marching orders ... Live free or die. Death is not the worst of evils." "Live free or die" has for the past quarter-century been the motto on New Hampshire's license plates.

General Stark lived for another 13 years, and ended his days as the last surviving general of the Revolution. He was buried with full military honors on his land, which is now **John Stark State Park**. The family plot is just a short distance from a statue of him mounted on his horse, Hessian. About 1/2 mi. south of the park, his boyhood home, the **General John Stark House**, is open in summer months by appointment.

Side trips from Manchester

(A) Bear Brook State Park

Follow Rte. 28 north out of Manchester to the turn-off for the state's largest developed state park. In addition to hiking, biking, and swimming on almost 10,000 acres, there are canoe and rowboat rentals at Beaver and Catamount Ponds, fly fishing on Archery Pond, a special fishing pond for kids under the age of 12, and the only public archery ranges in the state. There's also a museum complex with a nature center, the New Hampshire Antique Snowmobile Museum, Old Allenstown Meeting House, a Museum of Family Camping, and a Civilian Conservation Corps Museum (most of the museums are in buildings built by the CCC).

Several of the 40 miles of trails wander past marshes and bogs, including the Hayes Farm Trail which passes by Hayes Marsh, home to great blue herons, muskrat, and beaver. The Catamount Trail climbs sharply to the summit of 721-ft. Catamount Hill.

(B) Head north on Rte. 28 to to Rte. 27 east to **Charmingfare Farm**, home to the state's largest collection of agricultural animals and North American wildlife. The 180-acre farm has more than 20 animals of 30 different species including wolves, cougars, wolverines, reindeer, and river otters. There are also traditional farm animals, pony rides, and hayrides.

(C) Although just eight miles from Manchester via Rte. 101 west, the prototypical New England hamlet of **Amherst** seems a hundred years and a hundred miles from the city. Once a busy stagecoach stop, today it's an upscale bedroom community whose beautifully preserved buildings and trim, pear-shaped Common might easily be recognized by native son Horace Greeley, founder of the *New York Tribune*. Stones in the town cemetery date back to the 1700s.

40

(D) If you're a bog fancier, and/or you're visiting in mid-May, rather than backtracking to Manchester take Rte. 122 south out of Amherst for a few miles and watch on the left for Stearns Rd. Continue to Rhodora Drive and New Hampshire Audubon Society's **Ponemah B o g**, where once a year a riot of magenta rhododendrons burst into bloom. The bog is a fascinating spot in any season. Visitors squish their way along a narrow boardwalk which "floats" above a mat of moss and foliage to the bog -- a dense, quaking mass of sphagnum moss. Watch for lady's slippers, pitcher plants, ferns, and, of course, rhododendrons.

41

Return to Rte. 122 and continue south less than a mile to Rte. 101A; then head east to Rte. 293 and north back to Manchester.

(2) Head east out of Manchester on Hanover Street (the **Chamber of Commerce** office is on the corner) to the intersection with Rte. 121. Turn east (right) onto Rte. 121, which follows alongside the eastern shore of 1,500-acre **Massabesic Lake**, Manchester's water supply and a prime trout fishing spot. The New Hampshire volume in the *American Guide Series* tells how the lake may have gotten its name: "William Graham, an old resident of Auburn, related this tale in 1860, when he was 84 years old: 'Indians plenty round the great pond. Deacon Leach of the Presbyterian church in Cheshire sold rum in those days. One little Indian came out from Great Island, called Deer Island, wanted some "occupee." "What for?" said the deacon. "Massa be sick, want it for him." ' "

More than 50 mi. of access roads line the lake, and a network of wooded trails are splendid for hiking and mountain biking.

(3) Continue east into **Chester**, a small town with several handsome 18th-century houses. Among the most famous residents was the wealthy eccentric "Lord" Timothy Dexter, who moved here in 1796. According to tradition, Dexter kept his own coffin in the vestibule of his house for years, and once staged a rehearsal of his own funeral. The bizarre event took an even stranger turn when Dexter beat his wife, because she failed to cry convincingly enough. Tombstones at the National Register of Historic Places **Chester Village Cemetery** date back to 1751, and many were carved by local stonemason Abel Webster, known for inscribing them with oval faces bearing scowls or smiles.

(4) In the center of town, turn west (right) onto Rte. 102, past Beaver Lake (smallmouth bass, bluegill, pickerel and horned pout) to **Derry Village** and the

intersection of Bypass Rte. 28. Turn south (left) onto Rte. 28 and continue a short distance to the **Robert Frost Farm**, where a two-story, white clapboard house was home to the poet and his family from 1900 to 1909. The farmstead was purchased by Frost's grandfather, William, who stipulated in his will that his grandson could have the 1880 house and 13 acres if he kept it for 10 years. He did: from 1900 to 1906 he raised poultry and wrote some of his finest poetry here; and then taught at nearby Pinkerton Academy until 1911. Years later, when his friend and fellow poet Robert P. Tristram Coffin asked Frost where he had been the happiest, he replied: "The happiest? Oh, I guess it was when I lived in Derry, New Hampshire. It was the only piece of real estate I ever owned."

In addition to the house, barn, interpretive displays and video, the Hyla Brook Trail Frost often strolled along has numbered markers with quotes from his poetry.

(5) Continue south on Rte. 28 roughly five miles to **Canobie Lake Park**, which has been drawing thrill seekers for just about a century. Among the attractions: an antique carousel, a 24-in. gauge steam train, a paddle wheel riverboat, games, shows, arcades, The Yankee Cannonball roller coaster, a log flume ride, and a lake cruise. One price covers everything except the cruise.

Rockingham Park, one of the oldest thoroughbred racetracks in New England, is just a few miles to the south on Rte. 28.

Backtrack to the intersection of Rte. 111, turn east (right), and watch for signs directing you to **America's Stonehenge**. The site's owners bill it as "one of the largest and possibly the oldest megalithic sites in North America ... built by ancient people well versed in astronomy and stone construction. It has been determined that the site is an accurate astronomically aligned calendar." It's a maze of man-made chambers, walls, and ceremonial meeting places which carbon dating has proven to be about 4,000 years old. Visitors can wander through the chambers and form their own opinions as to how what is possibly the oldest man-made construction in North America came to be.

Backtrack on Bypass Rte. 28 through Derry Village, and past Pinkerton Academy. Founded in 1814 for "the purpose of promoting piety and virtue, and for the education of youth in such of the liberal arts and sciences or languages as the Trustees hereinafter provided shall direct," the college preparatory school includes among its alumni the late Admiral Alan B. Shepard, Jr. (class of 1940), the first American in space.

(6) From here, it's a straight shot on Bypass Rte. 28 to the turn-off onto Spofford Rd., in **Auburn**, for 135-acre **Massabesic Audubon Center**. There are miles of hiking trails and a modern visitor and program center with a wildlife observation room that looks out over fields and streams; a nature center; and a gift shop. Watch for loons, osprey, and, in the winter, nesting eagles, as well as a wide variety of other birds and mammals.

Return to Manchester on Bypass Rte. 28.

Information

Derry Chamber of Commerce (432-8205), Derry 03038.

Greater Manchester Chamber of Commerce (666-6600), 889 Elm St., Manchester 03101. www.Manchester-Chamber.org.

Greater Nashua Chamber of Commerce (881-8333), 1 Tara Blvd., Suite 211, Nashua 03062.

Londonderry Chamber of Commerce (434-7438), Londonderry 03053. www.sai.com/londonderry/

Salem Chamber of Commerce (893-3177), Salem 03079.

Lodging

Note: Many of the major motel chains are represented in the Manchester area.

(1) Center of New Hampshire Holiday Inn (800-HOLIDAY or 625-1000), 700 Elm St., Manchester. Chain with whirlpool, sauna, restaurant, and indoor/outdoor heated pool. $$-$$$

(1) Derryfield B & B (627-2082), 1081 Bridge St. Extension, Manchester 03104. Three pleasant guest rooms; fireplaced living room; full breakfast served on fine china, overlooking the pool and woods. $

(1) The Highlander Inn (800-548-9248 or 625-6426), 2 Highlander Way, Manchester 03103. www.highlanderinn.com. Hotel on 33 acres has nicely-appointed guest rooms and jacuzzi suites; dining room, and lounge. $$

(1) The Rice-Hamilton (800-528-2029 or 627-7281), 123 Pleasant St., Manchester. Downtown, former mill workers' housing in three-story brick buildings has been renovated and now has 10 fully-equipped, non-smoking apartments. $

(D) Sheraton Nashua Hotel (888-9970), 11 Tara Boulevard, Nashua. Tudor Castle-style hotel has 336 rooms, a healthy facility with indoor and outdoor pools, and a concierge's level. $$-$$$

(5) Park View Inn (898-5632), Rt. 29N, Salem. Nicely landscaped motel across from Rockingham Park and a mile from Canobie Lake Park has spacious, well-appointed guest rooms. $-$$

Not on Drive

(R) Bedford Village Inn (800-852-1166 or 472-2001), Two Village Inn Lane (off Rt. 101), Bedford. www.bedfordvillageinn.com. Multi-million dollar estate restoration of a working farm has created an award-winning property with 14 luxury guest rooms in the barn; 8 intimate dining rooms in the original residence. MAP available. $$$

Restaurants

(1) Cafe Pavoné (622-5488), 75 Arms Park Dr., Manchester. Millyard restaurant associated with the College Culinary Arts School offers varied, creative dishes in ample portions; patio. D. $-$$

(1) Down 'n Dirty (624-2224), 168 Amory St., Manchester. Genuine Southern pit barbecue. L,D except Mon. $

(1) Fratello's Ristorante Italiano (624-2022), 155 Dow St., Manchester. Traditional Italian cuisine. L, D. $-$$

(1) Red Arrow Lunch (624-2221), 61 Lowell St., Manchester. Popular diner open around the clock has been serving up American fare--and local gossip-- for almost 100 years. $

(1) Richard's Bistro (644-1180), 36 Lowell St., Manchester. House special shellfish chowder; creative salads, sandwiches, and dinner entreés, and homemade desserts. L, D, and Sun. brunch. $-$$

(1) Siam Orchid (228-1529), 158 North Main St., Manchester. Classic fare including satays, Pad Thai, and Hot and Crazy Noodles. L Mon-Fri., D nightly. $

(1) Stark Mill Brewery (622-0000), 500 Commercial St. (Mill #5), Manchester. Local brewery offers homemade brew, local entertainment, and good pub fare. $

(D) Ya Mama's (883-2264), 41 Canal St., Nashua. One of the region's hottest new restaurants serves northern and southern Italian dishes in a small, informal storefront dining room. $-$$

(4) The Green Forest Inn (434-8600), 3 Manchester Rd., Rte. 28, Derry. French and American classic fare served in a beautifully- restored farmhouse with an open hearth. L, D. $-$$

Off the Drive

Londonderry Homestead Restaurant (437-2022), Jct. Rts. 102 and Mammoth Rd., Londonderry. Classic American fare served in ample portions in a country farm house. L, D. $-$$

Attractions

(1) Amoskeag Falls Scenic Overlook: mid-April-Oct., 8-6:30. Observation deck.

(1) Amoskeag Fishways (626-3474), Amoskeag Dam, 6 Fletcher St., Manchester. Mon.-Sat. 9:30-5. Exhibits on the natural and cultural history of the Merrimac River Watershed; fish ladder in May and June.

(1) Currier Gallery of Art (669-6144), 192 Orange St., Manchester. Closed Tues. (free adm. Sat. 10-1). $

(1) Franco-American Centre (669-4045), 52 Concord St., Manchester. Mon.-Fri. 8:30-5.

(1) General John Stark House (647-6088), 2000 Elm St., Manchester. Owned by Molly Stark Chapter of the Daughters of the American Revolution; open by appt.

(1) Lawrence L. Lee Scouting Museum & Max I. Silber Scouting Library (669-8919), Bodwell Rd., Manchester. Extensive display of scouting books and memorabilia; founder Lord Baden-Powell's collection. July-Aug., daily; Sept.-June, Sat.

(1) Manchester Historic Association (622-7531), 129 Amherst St., Manchester. Tues. to Friday, 9-4; Sat. 10-4. Orientation Center open Mon.-Fri. 8-5.

(1) NH Institute of Art (623-0313), 148 Concord St., Manchester. Six galleries with changing exhibitions of regional and national artists. Closed Sun.

(1) SEE Science Center (669-0400), 200 Bedford St., Manchester. Bubble making to space and momentum in more than 70 hands-on exhibits. Daily. $

(1) The Zimmerman House (669-6144), 201 Myrtle Way, Manchester. Tours Thurs., Fri. and Mon.at 2 pm.; Sat. and Sun. at 1 pm, leaving from The Currier Gallery by museum van. $.

(A) Bear Brook State Park (485-9874), 157 Deerfield Rd., Allenstown. $

(B) Charmingfare Farm (483-5623), 774 High St., Candia. Early May -mid-Oct., Wed.-Sun. $

(D) Ponemah Bog, New Hampshire Audubon Society (224-9909), 3 Silk Farm Rd, Concord 03301.

(2) Lake Massabesic, Manchester Water Works (624-6482).

(4) Robert Frost Farm (432-3091), Rt. 28, P.O. Box 1075, Derry. Grounds always open. Farmhouse and barn Memorial Day-Columbus Day, Sat. and Sun.; June-Labor Day, daily; tours on the hour. $

(4) Taylor Up and Down Sawmill (271-3556), Island Pond Rd., Derry. State's only operating up and down mill. Water powered with wooden gears. Call for hrs.

(5) America's Stonehenge (893-8300), Island Pond Rd., Salem. Year-round, call for hours. $

(5) Canobie Lake Park (893-3506), I-93 Exit 2, Salem.Weekends mid-April-May, daily Memorial Day-Labor Day. $

(6) Massabesic Audubon Center (668-2045), 26 Audubon Way, Auburn. Year round.

Activities

(1) Dana Center at Saint Anselm College (641-7700), 100 Saint Anselm Dr., Manchester. Plays, concerts, and lectures from Sept.-May.

(1) Manchester Chorale Society (800-639-2928), P.O. Box 4182, Manchester. Community choral group.

(1) "Music at the Heart of It" (668-3800), Hampshire Plaza, 1000 Elm St., Manchester. Free, outdoor lunchtime concerts on the plaza Thurs. from early July-late Aug.

(1) New Hampshire Philharmonic Orchestra (647-6476), 83 Hanover St., 4th Floor, Manchester. Concert and ensemble performances include symphonic and pops.

(1) New Hampshire Symphony Orchestra (800-639-3559 or 639-9320), Manchester. Classical and pops series.

(1) Palace Theater (668-5588), 80 Hanover St., Manchester.

(1) Queen City Speedway (644-RACE), 87 Elm St., Manchester. State's largest slot car racing track.

(3) Folsom's Sugar House (887-3672), 130 Candia Rd., Chester. Open during sugar season (late Feb.-early April).

(4) Music and Drama Company (434-2180), Memorial Opera House, Derry. Year-round performances.

49

(4) Operafest (425-2845), 6 West Broadway, Derry. Musical performances at the turn-of-the-century Adams Memorial Opera House.

Not on Drive

Bedford Golfland (624-0503), 549 Donald St., Bedford. 18-hole miniature golf course and driving range.

Splash & Dash Hot Air Ballooning (483-5503), 25 Maple Farm Rd., Auburn. Hot air balloon rides.

Tours

(1) Aurore Eaton, Local History Tours & Talks (625-4826). History and architecture of Manchester.

(1) Heritage Walking Tours (625-4827), P.O. Box 3402, Manchester. Tours of Amoskeag Mill Yard and ethnic neighborhoods by local historians through the Historical Society. 1 1/2-2 hr. tours cost $5/person.

Galleries/Antiques

(1) Hands to Work Folk Art (669-1977), 1077 Elm St., Manchester. Works by traditional craftspeople from around the country.

(1) Art 3 Gallery (668-6650), 44 West Brook St., Manchester. Exhibits works of regional, national and international artists. Mon.-Fri. 9-1.

Shopping

(1) Mall of New Hampshire, Exit 1 off I-293, Willow St. 122 stores.

(1) McQuades (625-5451), 844 Elm St., Manchester. Old-fashioned department store with super bargain basement.

(4) Broadway Books (437-3418), 21 East Broadway, Derry. Out-of-print books and collector postcards.

Not on Drive

Mack's Apples/Moose Hill Orchard (432-3456), 230 Mammoth Rd., Londonderry. U-pick apples and pumpkins, ice cream, walking trails.

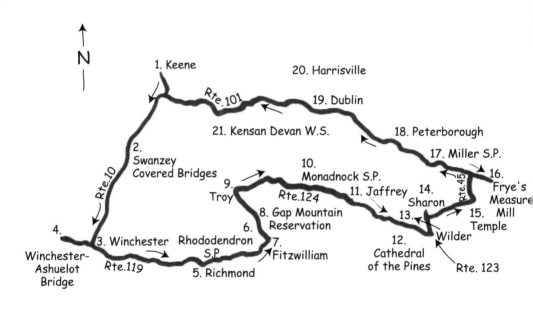

N

1. Keene

20. Harrisville

Rte.101

19. Dublin

21. Kensan Devan W.S.

18. Peterborough

17. Miller S.P.

2. Swanzey Covered Bridges

Rte.10

10. Monadnock S.P.

16. Frye's Measure

9. Troy

Rte.124

11. Jaffrey

14. Sharon

Rte.45

8. Gap Mountain Reservation

13.

15. Mill Temple

4.

6. Rhododendron S.P.

12. Cathedral of the Pines

Wilder

Winchester-Ashuelot Bridge

3. Winchester

7. Fitzwilliam

Rte. 123

Rte.119

5. Richmond

Drive 3

Mt. Monadnock and Surrounding Villages

70 miles

This jaunt through New Hampshire's southwestern corner begins in the college town of Keene, then winds through a countryside rich in covered bridges, rhododendrons, and mountain trails. The region's most distinctive peak and an open-air "cathedral" stand along the route, which also takes in a town that has assumed mythic proportions on the American stage.

(1) Begin in **Keene**, founded in the 1730s, abandoned a few years afterward because of Indian attacks, and resettled in the 1750s. Throughout its history, Keene has been a mill town: two of the town's prominent families opened Faulkner and Colony Mill in 1838 to weave wool gathered from surrounding sheep farms. When it finally shut down its looms in 1953, it was one of the oldest continuously operating mills in the country under its original management. Other products made in Keene over the years include chairs, shoes, glassware, and even golf tees.

Today, most of the mills have closed and the city on the Ashuelot River serves primarily as a market center for surrounding communities, and as the home of **Keene State College**. But many old factories, such as the Faulkner and Colony mills, have been restored and now house shops and restaurants: the sprawling **Colony Mill Marketplace** is one of the state's most successful renewal projects. Among its tenants are several multi-dealer antique shops.

In 1770 the trustees of Dartmouth College held their first meeting at a Main Street tavern built by Captain Isaac Wyman eight years earlier. On an April day five years later, 29 Minutemen under the command of Capt. Wyman set out from the tavern for Lexington and Concord. The restored **Wyman Tavern Museum** documents Keene's history from 1770 to 1820. The **Colony House Museum**, headquarters for the Historical Society of Cheshire County, is in the 1819 home of the city's first mayor, Horatio Colony. The 1806 Federal-style home of his grandson is now the **Horatio Colony House Museum**. The United Church of Christ, with its graceful wedding-cake spire gracing the northern end of Main St., was built in 1787.

(2) Head south out of Keene on Rte. 10. There are two Town lattice truss covered bridges in rural **Swanzey**. (This style of bridge was named not because it was used in towns, but because its lattice framework was devised by architect Ithiel Town in the early 1800s.) Bridge #6, which spans the Ashuelot River, was built in 1859 and is two miles off Rte. 10 (turn left at the covered bridge marker). The next, #5, right alongside Rte. 10 a little farther south, has a handsome outside walkway (there were originally two) and was built by Zadoc Taft in 1832 for $523.27. On Rte. 10, just past this bridge, is the **Swanzey Historical Museum**, whose exhibits include a 1901 steam fire pumper, a stage coach, and a 1930 Ford. Several antique centers and flea markets dot the road between here and the intersection with Rte. 119.

(3) Just before the junction of Rte. 119 in **Winchester** watch for the Evergreen Cemetery. It's the burial place of P.E.F. Albee, the first Avon Lady (1836-1914). She was hired by Daniel H. McConnell, Sr., who founded the California Perfume Company in 1883 and needed help with sales. Ms. Albee took to the road with her sample case, and began knocking on doors. The firm, which became Avon Products, dubbed her the "Mother of the Company" and named its highest sales award after her. Her stone is near the front of the cemetery.

Winchester itself is a workaday village whose major point of interest is a plaque on one of the town's 19th-century brick buildings (continue on Rte. 10 just past the intersection with Rte. 119). It marks the birthplace of Major General Leonard Wood, who was born here in 1860. Gen. Wood was a hero of the Spanish-American War, and went on to serve as Governor of Cuba and Chief of Staff of the U.S. Army.

Side Trip

(4) Before you turn left (east) onto Rte. 119, detour a few miles west on that road to this drive's most handsome covered bridge. The Town lattice Winchester-Ashuelot Bridge, built in 1864, has been described as "pure American Gothic architecture adapted to bridge building."
----

(5) Continue east on Rte. 119 through **Richmond**, where the 4-Corner Store advertises free advice and good coffee. There are lots of antique shops on the side roads between here and Fitzwilliam.

(6) Turn left onto Rhododendron Rd. and follow signs to 494-acre **Rhododendron State Park**, where a wooded wildflower trail winds for a mile up Little Monadnock Mountain. The park is lovely at any time, but if you're here in mid-July, you're in for a treat: that's prime blossom time for the 16 acres of *Rhododendron maximum* -- the largest stand of wild rhododendrons north of the Allegheny Mountains and east of the Mississippi. Many of the shrubs grow as high as 20 ft. The site is a National Natural Landmark.

(7) Back on Rte. 119, continue into **Fitzwilliam**, a gracious 18th-century village with a lovely green lined with Federal-style houses. The Historical Society's 1837 **Amos J. Blake House** was the home of a 19th-century attorney whose office remains here, intact. The 1796 **Fitzwilliam Inn** offers overnight lodging. The entrance to the town hall, built in 1817 as a

Congregational church, is framed by a two-story pedimented portico supported at each end by Ionic columns resting on locally-quarried granite blocks. The four-story steeple has a square clock tower, belfry, and a bell cast by Paul Revere.

Fitzwilliam has a number of antique shops, including the 40-dealer **Fitzwilliam Antique Center** and **Red Barn Antiques** in back of the Fitzwilliam Inn. At **Bloomin' Antiques,** three mi. south on Rte. 12 at the intersection with Rte. 119, 35 dealers display 18th- and 19th-century furniture, accessories, clocks, toys, and more.

(8) At the intersection of Rtes. 119 and 12, turn north on Rte. 12. You're approaching 1,107-acre **Gap Mountain Reservation**. On the outskirts of Troy, watch on the right for Quarry Rd. Turn here and continue past the high tension lines. When the road forks, take a hard left to the parking lot. The hike to the 1,862 ft. summit is fairly easy, and if you're here early enough in blueberry season (July and/or August), you might be able to find some berries on the bushes that thrive on the mountainside. There are terrific views of Mt. Monadnock to the north. Numerous hiking trails crisscross the mountain, including the 160-mi. Metacomet-Monadnock Trail which begins in Meriden, CT and ends at Grand Monadnock. For information, contact Monadnock State Park (see "Attractions" below).

(9) **Troy**, on the western flank of Mt. Monadnock, is home to Troy Woolen Mills, one of the oldest blanket manufacturers in the country. The mills began operation in 1857, and still dominate the town's landscape. Another major industry was quarrying: the steps of Washington's Congressional Library were made from Troy granite.

After visiting Troy, backtrack a short distance on Rte. 12 and turn left onto Monadnock/Jaffrey Rd. (if you don't go into Troy, the turn will be on the right as you come into town). Drive past Troy Mills. Up ahead, the view of Mt. Monadnock from the back lawn at **The Inn**

at East Hill Farm is spectacular.   Continue to the junction of Rte. 124 and turn east (right) onto Rte. 124 toward Jaffrey.

(10) The Toll Road at **Monadnock State Park** (seasonal parking) once provided access to a series of hotels on the mountain.   The earliest, the Grand Monadnock Hotel, was built on the summit in 1823. The last, the Halfway House, closed its doors in the 1960s.   Several trailheads begin here.

Just past the Toll Road turn-off, turn left at the sign for the main entrance to Monadnock State Park and hiking trails to the top of Mt. Monadnock ("one that stands alone").   Last year more than 130,000 people hiked America's most often-climbed mountain -- as many as 6,000 on one day. Why the popularity?   The peak is close to several large metropolitan areas, and Monadnock is a very "climbable" mountain.   There are 36 trails of varying difficulty; the shortest and easiest is the four-mi. White Dot Trail (we tackled it in full hiking gear one day alongside two six-year-old girls dancing along in black patent leather shoes).

The six-state view from the 3,165 ft. summit is sublime.   Ralph Waldo Emerson wrote of it,

Every morn I lift my head,
See New England underspread
South from St. Lawrence to the Sound,
From Katskill east to the sea-bound.

(11) Continue into **Jaffrey**. On the outskirts of town, in Jaffrey Center, is the town's original Meeting House, raised on the day of the Battle of Bunker Hill in 1775. In back of the church, in the Old Burying Ground, are interred former slave Amos Fortune (see sidebar, below), and the novelist Willa Cather, who, in 1918, worked on *My Antonia* and the Pulitzer Prize-winning *One of Ours* here.   An inscription from *My Antonia* is engraved on Cather's headstone, in the far southwest corner of the cemetery: "The truth and charity of her

57

great spirit will live on in the work which is her enduring gift to her country and all its people."

Amos Fortune, who settled in Jaffrey in the late 18th century and became a wealthy tanner, made a generous bequest to the town's school. When the building was abandoned in 1927, townspeople voted to use the money for a public speaking contest. Since that year the Amos Fortune Forum has presented a lecture series on subjects of public interest and importance to the Monadnock community. Seven free lectures are presented Friday evenings in July and August at 8 pm in the Jaffrey Center Meeting House. On Mr. Fortune's tombstone is the inscription: "Lived reputably, died hopefully."

Approximately 75,000 acres of the land within **Jaffrey's** borders are protected by state and local agencies, giving the one-time mill town slowly making the transition into a white collar community somewhat of a feeling of a diamond in the rough. Both the **Melville Academy Museum** and the Jaffrey Civic Center exhibit a wealth of historical memorabilia.

Continue out of town on Rte. 124 past **Silver Ranch Farm Ice Cream and Restaurant** and **Silver Ranch Air Park.** The air park offers scenic flights for as little as $60 for up to three people (20 minute flight). Longer tours are also available.

(12) Turn right onto Prescott Rd. and continue for several miles to **Cathedral of the Pines.** The sanctuary, "where all people can come and worship, each in his own way ..." is in a stand of pines overlooking Mt. Monadnock. It's dedicated to the memory of Lt. Sanderson ("Sandy") Sloane, an American aviator shot down over Germany in 1944, who had planned to build his home here after the war. The cross here is of New Hampshire granite; the Altar

58

of Nations, containing stones from every state in the Union, and the Memorial Bell Tower, are dedicated to America's war dead. Services are held Sundays at 9:15 a.m. from May through Oct. Outdoor organ meditations are held Monday through Friday from 10 a.m. to 2 p.m., weather permitting. Easter sunrise service begins at 5:45 a.m.

Back on Rte. 124, continuing east, look for a plaque on the left side of the road marking the site where a toll gate stood between 1803-1822 to collect tariffs from drivers herding cattle along the third New Hampshire turnpike.

(13) Continue through tiny **Wilder Village;** a marker indicates the site of Wilder's Chair Factory, which in the early 1800s manufactured more than 25,000 spindle-backed chairs in more than 40 designs. In 1869 a freshet washed out the mill dam; deprived of water power, the factory closed. Today the chairs are highly collectible antiques.

At the intersection of Rtes. 124 and 123, turn north (left) on Rte. 123 toward Sharon.

(14) Continue on Rte. 123 to the **Sharon Arts Center**, which exhibits and sells works of regional and international artists, and exhibits works by faculty and students. The center hosts a year-round series of films, lectures, and concerts, and has a shop-gallery in Peterborough (see *Arts, Crafts, and Galleries* below).

(15) Backtrack on Rte. 123 to Nashua/West Rd., turn left, and head over Spofford Gap. At the intersection, turn left (north) onto Rte. 45 into **Temple,** home of the state's first glassmaking factory, which opened here in 1780; and Temple Band, possibly the oldest in the country, which performs at venues including the Sharon Arts Center and the bandstand in Jaffrey. The Congregational Church facing the Town Common was built in 1842. The Old Burying Ground is dedicated to the "wives and mothers of 1776."

Little has changed at the circa 1800 **Birchwood Inn** since Henry David Thoreau spent a night here. The dining room in the National Register of Historic places inn possesses a superb mural by Rufus Porter, an itinerant painter who worked throughout New England during the early 19th century; and a reputation as one of the best lodging places and restaurants in the area. Dinner is served by candlelight; reservations are recommended.

Continue north on Rte. 45, past the entrance for Temple Mountain Ski Area, to the intersection of Rte. 101. Turn west (left) onto Rte. 101.

Side Trip

(16) At the junction of Rtes. 101 and 45, cross over Rte. 101 and continue approximately 4 1/2 mi. to Frye's Measure Mill, which has been making Colonial and Shaker boxes -- originally intended to provide accurate measurement of goods such as nails -- since 1858. It's one of few remaining water-powered mills, and the country's only active measure mill. There's a fine seven-room gift shop selling crafts, folk art by some of the country's finest artisans, and antiques (be sure to visit the markdown section). Old fire trucks and firefighting apparatus are on display in the mill's garage. There are blacksmithing and tinsmithing demonstrations in summer and fall; during those seasons, 1 1/2-hour tours are given daily. Reservations are recommended.

----

(17) Head west on Rte. 101. Ahead, at 489-acre **Miller State Park** (New Hampshire's first state park, opened in 1891), a 1 1/2-mile paved road winds steeply to the summit of 2,288-ft. Pack Monadnock. On clear days, Manchester and Boston are visible. The 21 mi. (one way) Wapack Trail, which follows the ridge of the Wapack Range from Watatic Mountain in Ashburnham, Massachusetts to the Pack Monadnocks, crosses here.

(18) Continue into **Peterborough**, which calls itself "a Good Town to Live In." It was immortalized in the 1930s by Thornton Wilder, who used it as the model for Grover's Corners in his play *Our Town*. The best way to see Peterborough's many historic sites is with a copy of the **Chamber of Commerce's** "A Walking Tour of Peterborough" brochure. Among places of interest: the Bulfinch-designed, 1825 National Historic Register Unitarian Universalist Church; the **Historical Society's** three-building complex (they also offer a tour of several restored mill houses); and the town's 1833 library, the first in the world to be supported by town funds. The **Peterborough Players,** a professional summer theater company since 1933, was the first to perform *Our Town*. Head south on Rte. 202 a short distance alongside the Contoocook River to **Noone's Mill**. The original structure, built in the early 1800s for carding wool and dressing home-woven cloth, was destroyed by the floods of 1936 and 1938, and closed for good in the 1970s. It now houses several retail businesses, including Van Campen's, which fashions museum-quality furniture; and **Noone Falls Café** (grab a table on the deck).

Just south of town on Rte. 123 is **Rosaly's Garden**, one of the state's largest certified organic gardens. Overlooking Mt. Monadnock, it's a grand place to stock up on local produce, flowers, and herbs.

American composer Edward MacDowell (1861-1908) wrote more than 50 compositions, including "Woodland Sketches," "Keltic Sonatas," and "New England Idylls." One of the founders of the American Academy of Arts and Letters, he became in 1960 the second musician ever to be elected to the Hall of Fame for Great Americans. In 1896 MacDowell and his wife, pianist Marian Nevins MacDowell, purchased an estate in Peterborough and began to spend summers here. MacDowell planned to open his estate to other artists to provide them with a tranquil and inspiring place to work, but he became terminally ill before he could realize his dream. His wife started

the MacDowell Colony in 1907; artists who have come to work here over the years have included Stephen Vincent Benet, Edwin Arlington Robinson, Thornton Wilder, and James Baldwin.

In 1937 a sign at the entrance announced, "Visitors Most Welcome, Save on Sunday". Today, visitors are not welcome, save one day each year, usually in mid-August, when the Edward MacDowell Medal is awarded to an artist who has made an outstanding contribution to American culture. That day, all are invited to come for a picnic lunch, tour the artists' studios, and attend the Medal presentation. The MacDowell Colony is on High St. off Main St., Peterborough

----

(19) Head west out of town on Rte. 101 to **Dublin**, home of *Yankee* Magazine (parent of the *Old Farmer's Almanac*, the oldest continuously published periodical in the country). With the help of a flagpole in the center of town, Dublin has the highest village center in the state. Though it was first settled by Scotch-Irish families in 1753, the pioneers were defeated by dense woods and returned to Peterborough, leaving behind only the name. It would be another 18 years before settlers would finally stay long enough to incorporate. Gold was discovered on the eastern end of town in 1875, but the diggings closed down after a year. But local business people struck a mother lode far more lucrative than that thin yellow vein: tourists. By 1879, 10 houses had opened their doors to travelers who flocked here each summer. The challenging, nine-mile Pumpelly Trail to the summit of Mt. Monadnock, cut by scientist and explorer Raphael Pumpelly, begins on Lake St.

----

(20) The National Historic Landmark 19th-century industrial community of Harrisville may be the state's best preserved and most photographed village.

Although the last mill shut down its looms in 1970, the buildings themselves are preserved in a park-like setting around a millpond perched above Goose Creek Ravine. One now houses Harrisville Designs, operated by a descendent of the Colony Mill in Keene. The folks at Harrisville Squires' Inn are extremely knowledgeable about the area: their inn is on the 47-mi. Monadnock-Sunapee Greenway Trail which stretches from Mt. Monadnock to Sunapee. They organize self-guided hiking and bicycling tours, and offer a shuttle service. Harrisville is 2 1/2 mi. north of Dublin, via Dublin Rd. off Rte. 101.

Continue on Rte. 101 and continue west past the **Friendly Farm** and **Leighton State Forest** into Marlborough.

Side Trip

(21) Turn south onto Rte. 124, drive 2.3 miles, and turn left onto Meetinghouse Pond Rd. Continue 1/2 mile to the New Hampshire Audubon Society's 400-acre Kensan Devan Wildlife Sanctuary (road not plowed in winter), which encompasses Meetinghouse Pond and the Rocky Ridge Trail. There are stands of northern hardwoods, white pine and hemlock, and views of Grand Monadnock. If you have a canoe, be sure to explore the floating bog mat.

Back on Rte. 101, continue west to return to Keene.

Information

Greater Keene Chamber of Commerce (352-1303), 48 Central Sq., Keene 03431. Closed Sat. and Sun.

Greater Peterborough Chamber of Commerce (924-7234), jct. Rtes. 101 and 202, P.O. Box 401, Peterborough. Closed Sun., Sat., winter and spring.

Jaffrey Chamber of Commerce (532-549), P.O Box 1, Jaffrey 03452.

Monadnock/Sunapee Greenway: Society for the Protection of NH Forests(224-9945), 54 Portsmouth St., Concord 03301.

Monadnock Travel Council (800-HEART NH), P.O Box 358, Keene 03431; www.MonadnockTravel.com.

Rindge Chamber of Commerce (899-5051), P.O. Box 911, Rindge 03461.

Lodging

Monadnock Lodging Association, P.O. Box 1088, Keene 03431: www.nhlodging.org. Links to inns and B&Bs throughout region.

(1) Wright Mansion (800-352-5890 or 355-2288), 695 Court St., Keene. www.wrightmansioninn.com. Elegant, 1930, three-story, brick Georgian home built for the grandson of the founder of J.A. Wright Silver Polish Co. has six guest rooms (four with private bath; two with fireplaces). Tennis. Student rates avail. $-$$

(7) Amos A. Parker House (585-6540), Rt. 119, Box 202, Fitzwilliam 03447. Four guest rooms (including two suites) in a c.1780, graciously appointed inn. Some have woodburning fireplaces. Breakfast is served by candlelight, and the grounds, with gardens and a lily pond, are magnificent. No credit cards. $$

(7) (R) The Fitzwilliam Inn (585-9000), Fitzwilliam 03447. In-town, 1830 Greek Revival has 25 nicely furnished guest rooms (12 with private bath), an outdoor pool, and a pub. Menu features fine continental fare. $$

(9) The Inn at East Hill Farm (800-242-6495 or 242-6495), 460 Monadnock St., Troy 03465. www.east-hill-farm.com. 150-acre resort/working farm offers cottages and inn rooms, mountain views, and a full roster of resort amenities including indoor and outdoor pools, whirlpools, sauna, tennis and horseback riding and winter activities; children's programs. FAP. $$$

(11) Benjamin Prescott Inn (532-6637), Rte.124 East, Jaffrey 03452. 1850s Greek Revival farmhouse adjacent to a dairy farm has 10 rooms (including two suites) with private baths. Children welcome. $-$$ www.virtualcities.com/ons/nh/m/nhm4601.htm.

(12) Cathedral House B&B (899-6790), 63 Cathedral Entrance, Rindge 03461. 1850s farmhouse on the cathedral grounds has five guest rooms and a fireplaced common room. $-$$

(15) (R) The Birchwood Inn (878-3285), Rte. 45, Temple 03084. Seven guest rooms (five with private bath). Breakfast (included in room rate) served Tues.-Sun.; dinner nightly except Sun. No credit cards. $

(15) Auk's Nest (878-3443), East Rd., Temple (mail: R.F.D. 1, Wilton 03086). Both children and pets are welcome (call in advance) at this comfortable B&B with three cozy guest rooms. $

(18) Apple Gate B & B (924-6543), 199 Upland Farm Rd., Peterborough 03458. Four rooms with private baths in an 1832 white clapboard Colonial across from an apple orchard two miles out of town. Candlelight breakfast. Dog and cat in residence. $-$$

(18) Peterborough Manor B&B (924-9832), 50 Summer St., Peterborough 03458. Seven guest rooms with private baths in an 1890s Victorian mansion. Guest kitchen available. $ www.monadnocktravel.com/peterboroughmanor.

(20) The Harrisville Squires' Inn (827-3925), Keene Rd., P.O. Box 19, Harrisville 03450. www.harrisvilesquiresinn.com. National Register of Historical Places 1842 refurbished inn has five spacious rooms with private baths, a hot tub, and gardens. $$

Not on Drive

(R) The Hancock Inn (800-525-1789 outside NH or 525-3318), 33 Main St., P.O. Box 96, Hancock 03449. www.hancockinn.com. New Hampshire's oldest inn, since 1789, has 11 guest rooms with a four-poster or canopy bed, and private baths; some gas wood stoves. There are several murals by Rufus Porter (if you're a real fan, you might want to stay in the Rufus Porter Room). Costumed waitstaff in the candlelit restaurant. $$-$$$

Restaurants

(1) 176 Main (357-3100), 176 Main St., Keene. Good American cuisine, large portions, and a good selection of imported as well as local brews. $-$$

(1) Elm City Restaurant & Brewery (355-3335), Colony Mill Marketplace, Keene. Solid fare, and hand-crafted ales & lagers. $-$$

(1) Nicola's Trattoria (355-5242), 39 Central Sq., Keene. Creative Italian specialties include Osso Buco, Cioppino, and a host of risottos. L, D Tues.-Sat.

(1) Tolman's Table (355-8923), Emerald St., Keene. Family-friendly restaurant serves fine home cooking. $-$$

(2) Tempestas, Rte. 10, W. Swanzey 352-0200. Pizza, pasta, and other Italian specialties. $

(3) Mt. Pisgah Diner (239-4101), 10 Main St., Winchester. 1940 Worcester-style diner. $

(9) Gap Mountain Bakery (242-3284), on the Common, Rte. 12, Troy. Home baked goodies, subs, pizza, and homemade soups. $

(11) Good 'n Baked, Main St., Jaffrey. Homemade baked goods. $

(12) Lilly's on the Pond (899-3322), Rte. 202 (north of the junction of Rte. 119), Rindge. Creative continental fare in a renovated, 1790s sawmill overlooking a mill pond. L, D Tues.-Sun. $-$$

(18) Noone Falls Café (924-6818), 50 Jaffrey Rd., Rte. 202S, Peterborough. Lunch features homemade soups and sandwiches, dinner entreés include Chicken Boursin. Homemade breads and pastries; wine and beer. 9 a.m.-8 p.m. Mon.-Sat. $-$$

(18) Peterborough Diner (924-6202), 10 Depot St., Peterborough. A classic with traditional diner fare. $

(19) Del Rossi's Trattoria (563-7195), Rte. 137, Dublin. Italian trattoria in Yankee surroundings; salads, homemade pastas, and seafood. Folk music Fri. and Sat. nights. Tues.-Sat., lunch and dinner. $-$$

Off the Drive

Pickity Place (878-1151), 2 mi. off Rte. 31, Nutting Hill Rd., Mason. 1786 cottage used for "Grandmother's House" by Elizabeth Orton Jones, illustrator of "Little Red Riding Hood, is now a restaurant serving herbal-themed, five-course lunches. There are five acres of herb and perennial gardens, and gift and garden shops. Lunch 10 a.m.-5 p.m.; reservations essential.

Attractions

(1) Historical Society (352-1895), 246 Main St., Keene. Mon-Fri. 9-4; Wed. evening til 9; Sat. 9-noon. Closed Sun. Free.

(1) Horatio Colony House Museum (352-0460), 199 Main St., Keene. May-mid-Oct., Wed.-Sun. 11-4. Free.

(1) Horatio Colony Trust, off Daniels Road, Keene. 450-acre bird and animal preserve.

(1) Monadnock Children's Museum (357-5161), 147 Washington St., Keene. Hands-on science and art exhibits. $

(1) Thorne-Sagendorph Gallery at Keene State College (358-2720), Wyman Way. Collection includes 19th-century landscapes. Daily noon-4 during academic year; until 7 Thurs. and Fri.; summer, Wed.-Sun. noon-4.

(1) Wyman Tavern Museum (357-3855), 339 Main St., Keene. June -Labor Day, Tues.--Sat. $

(2) Swanzey Historical Museum (352-4579), Rte. 10, W. Swanzey. Covered bridge information; local exhibits include a Concord Coach and Amoskeag steam fire pumper. June-Oct., daily.

(6) Rhododendron State Park (532-8862), Fitzwilliam. Mailing address: Monadnock State Park, P.O. Box 181, Jaffrey 03452. $

(7) Fitzwilliam Historical Society (585-7742), Fitzwilliam. Period antiques-furnished home, an early schoolroom and a 1779 fire engine. Memorial Day weekend-Columbus Day Weekend, Sat. 1-4.

(10) Monadnock State Park (532-8862), Jaffrey. Park Office/Visitor Center off Route 12 (Dublin Rd.), Jaffrey Center. Mailing address: P.O. Box 181, Jaffrey 03452. No dogs. $

(11) 1773 Meetinghouse (site of Amos Fortune Forum Series): for information, contact Jaffrey Chamber of Commerce (see *Information* above)

(11) **Melville Academy Museum** (532-7455), Thorndike Pond Rd., Jaffrey. 1833 Greek Revival schoolhouse. Call for hrs.

(12) **Cathedral of the Pines** (899-3300), 75 Cathedral Entrance, Rindge. May-Oct.

(14) **Sharon Arts Center** (924-7256), 457 Rte. 123, Sharon 03458.

(16) **Frye's Measure Mill** (654-6581), 12 Frye Rd., Wilton. Closed Mon. in season; closed Sun.-Tues. in winter.

(17) **Miller State Park** (924-7433), Rte. 101, Peterborough. Mid-April- mid-Nov., daily. $

(17) **Wapack National Wildlife Refuge** (off Rte. 101 at Miller State Park). 1,672 acres on North Pack Monadnock Mt.: watch for hawks.

(18) **Edward MacDowell Lake** (924-3431), 75 Wilder St., Peterborough. 1,198-acre U.S. Army Corps of Engineers dam offers swimming, picnic area, barbecue grills, hiking trails, and fishing for largemouth bass, pickerel, yellow perch, and horned pout.

(18) **MacDowell Colony** (924-3886). 100 High St., Peterborough.

(18) **Peterborough Historical Society** (924-3235), 19 Grove St., Peterborough. Mon.- Fri. 1-4. Free.

(18) **Shieling State Forest** (271-2214), Old Street Rd., Peterborough. For information: New Hampshire Division of Forests and Lands (271-3456), P.O Box 856, Concord 03302. 45 acres of tree-covered ridges and valleys encompass wildflower trails for hiking, skiing and walking the dog (on a leash). Self-guided nature trail.

(20) **Historic Harrisville** (827-3722).

(20) Monadnock-Sunapee Greenway Trail (357-2115 or 225-7274), P.O. Box 164, Marlow, 03456.

(21) Kensan Devan Wildlife Sanctuary, off Rte. 124, Marlborough. For information: Audubon Society of New Hampshire, 3 Silk Farm Rd., Concord 03301; tel. 224-9909).

Activities

(1) Summers Back Country Outfitters (357-5107), Keene. Kayak and canoe rentals and sales.

(9) Monadnock Berries (242-6417), 545 West Hill Rd., Troy. Pick your own berries.

(11) Contoocook Lake Beach, Quantum Road, Jaffrey. Sand beach. $

(11) Jaffrey Bandstand. Wednesday evenings in summer: contact Chamber of Commerce (*see "Information" above*).

(11) Moonlight Maples (532-8496), 43 Hunt Rd., Jaffrey. Maple syrup house: tours and sugar on snow.

(11) Sciatic Park Beach, Thorndike Pond (near entrance to Monadnock State Park), Jaffrey. $

(11) Silver Ranch Airpark (532-8870), Rte. 124, Jaffrey.

(15) Temple Band (878-2829)

(18) Monadnock Music (924-7610). Free chamber music concerts throughout the region, and a ticketed series in the Peterborough Town House.

(18) Peterborough Players (924-7585), Hadley Rd. off Middle Hancock Rd. Five to seven plays each summer in a renovated, air-conditioned, 19th- century barn.

(18) Spokes & Slopes (924-9961), 109 Grove St., Peterborough. Mountain and road bike rentals.

(19) Friendly Farm (563-8444), Rte. 101, Dublin. Five acres of rolling hills and farm animals. May-Labor Day, daily; weekends until Oct. $

(20) Monadnock Bicycle Touring Center (827-3925), 797 Chesham Rd., Harrisville. Custom-planned on- and off-road bicycle tours.

(21) Maple Homestead Farm (476-3838), 60 Richardson Rd., Marlborough. 4,000 taps.

Crafts, Galleries and Antiques

(1) Antiques at Colony Mill (358-6343), 222 West St., Keene. 240 dealers.

(1) Country Artisans (352-6980), Colony Mill Marketplace, 222 West St., Keene. 400+ juried American artisans display and sell their works.

(7) Bloomin' Antiques (585-6688), Rte. 12, Fitzwilliam.

(7) Fitzwilliam Antique Center (585-9092), Jct. Rtes. 12 & 119, Fitzwilliam.

(7) Red Barn Antiques (585-3134), 58 Richmond Rd., Fitzwilliam. Paint and finished country furniture, smalls and accessories.

(11) Sir Richard's (532-7945), 10 Old Fitzwilliam Rd., Jaffrey. Antique walking sticks, weapons, carved furniture and more.

(18) The Cobbs (924-9361), 83 Grove St., Peterborough. American and European art, primitive, country, formal and painted furniture, rugs, folk art, and more.

(18) Peterboro Basket Company Factory Outlet (924-3861), 130 Grove St., Peterborough. Family-owned company since 1854. The factory/outlet has some real bargains.

(18) Sharon Arts Downtown (924-2787), 7 School St., Depot Sq., Peterborough. Fine craft and art galleries selling jewelry, glass, pottery, weaving, silks, iron, wood and more, as well as regional fine art.

(18) Shepard Gallery (924-6020), 10 Main St., Peterborough. Watercolors and Limited Edition prints of Gary Shepard.

(19) Seaver & McLellan Antiques, Inc. (563-7144), Rte. 101 at Rte. 137, Dublin. Antiques and fine and decorative arts. Tues.-Sat.

(19) William Lary Antiques (563-8603), Gold Mine Rd. off Rte. 101, Dublin. 18th- and early-19th-century country and formal furniture; Shaker and folk art.

(20) Harrisville Designs (800-338 9415 or 827-3333; Main St., Harrisville. pinning mill and shop.

Shopping

(1) Colony Mill Marketplace (357-1240), 222 West St., Keene.

(1) Cohen & Sons Oriental Rugs (800-339-5122 or 357-5152), 443 Winchester St., Keene. One of, if not the, largest selection of Oriental rugs in Northern New England.

(1) Eagle Books (357-8721), 19 West St., Keene. General stock, New England and local history. Closed Sun.; Mon.-Tues. by chance or appt.

(1) Hannah Grimes Marketplace (352-6862), 46 Main St., Keene. Crafts, farm produce, antiques, artwork, and tea room.

(1) **Rainy Day Books** (585-3448), 37 Rt. 119 W., Fitzwilliam. General stock, radio, broadcasting, electrical science, cookbooks, town histories, and more. Daily exc. Wed. April 1-Nov. 15; rest of year by chance or appt.

(11) **Bacon's Sugar House** (532-8836), Dublin Rd., Jaffrey. Inventor Charles Bacon introduced the country's first plastic jug on his family's 1780 family farm in 1973.

(11) **Herb Barn** (532-8486), 80 Main St., Jaffrey. Fine gardens and large selection of herbs. Tea by reservation. Weekends 10-4.

(12) **Ed's Country Auction House** (899-6654), behind Lilly's on the Pond Restaurant, Rindge. Auctions Sat. night year-round.

(18) **Rosaly's Garden** (924-7774), Rte. 123S, Peterborough. Late Spring-Oct.

(18) **Toadstool Bookshop** (924-3543), Depot Sq., Peterborough. New and used books; Aesops Table serves sandwiches and other light fare.

(19) **Dublin General Store**, Dublin. Classic New England country store.

(19) **Morning Star Maple** (563-9218), Rte. 101, Dublin. Sugarhouse and gift shop sells products made on the premises. Open daily, but call ahead on Sunday.

(21) **Homestead Bookshop** (876-4213), Rte. 101, Marlborough. Used books, including local town histories and fiction.

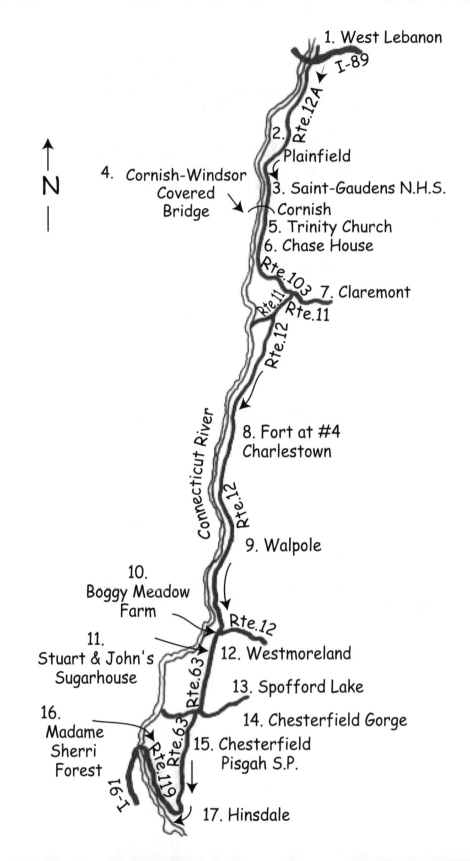

N

1. West Lebanon
I-89
Rte.12A
2. Plainfield
4. Cornish-Windsor Covered Bridge
3. Saint-Gaudens N.H.S.
Cornish
5. Trinity Church
6. Chase House
Rte.103
Rte.11
Rte.11
7. Claremont
Rte.12
8. Fort at #4 Charlestown
Connecticut River
Rte.12
9. Walpole
10. Boggy Meadow Farm
11. Stuart & John's Sugarhouse
Rte.12
Rte.63
12. Westmoreland
13. Spofford Lake
16. Madame Sherri Forest
Rte.63
14. Chesterfield Gorge
15. Chesterfield Pisgah S.P.
Rte.119
I-91
17. Hinsdale

Drive 4

The Southern Connecticut River Valley

72 miles

This drive follows the Connecticut River valley, never straying far from the river itself, from West Lebanon to the border country where New Hampshire, Vermont, and Massachusetts meet. There are stops at the home and studio of a great sculptor, at an improbably long covered bridge, and at the reconstruction of a fort built to defend what was once New England's wild frontier.

(1) From **West Lebanon** and I-89, head south on Rte. 12A. The first few miles will take you past a sprawl of big box stores, fast food restaurants, and malls. There are more than 40 shops and several restaurants at **Power House Mall**, a renovated electric powerhouse.

(2) As you leave the Lebanon area behind and approach **Plainfield**, the surroundings become more rural. The backdrop that one-time resident Maxfield Parrish painted for the **Plainfield Town Hall** portrays the area's largest mountain -- 3,320 ft. Mt. Ascutney, to the west in Vermont -- and the hills and valleys that surround it. Parrish built a home and studio in town in 1898, at the age of 28, and died there 68 years later, just as the popularity of his luminously vivid, fantasy-inspired work was coming back into vogue. His ashes are buried in the cemetery 1/4 mi. out of town.

The old building on the left just outside Plainfield's village center was named for Blow-Me-Down Brook, a

75

corruption of the name "Blomidon" bestowed on it by Charles C. Beamann. He was a New York lawyer who bought a summer home in Plainfield over a century ago, and continued to purchase property until, at one point, he owned 23 homes. He sent out the word that it was a good climate for artists and writers: among the first to arrive was Augustus Saint-Gaudens (*see #3 below*).

South of town, turn left at the state bridge sign to reach the Cornish Blow-Me-Down multiple kingpost truss covered bridge, built by illiterate bridge engineer James Tasker in 1877 for $528.

(3) Continue south on Rte. 12A to the **Augustus Saint-Gaudens National Historic Site**. The sculptor of pieces including the *Standing Lincoln*, Madison Square Garden's *Diana*, and the Robert Gould Shaw Memorial on Boston Common lived here year-round from 1900 until his death, at age 59, in 1907. The story has it that he first was steered toward New Hampshire while researching his *Standing Lincoln*. A New York friend told the sculptor that he would find "plenty of Lincoln-shaped men in the Granite State to use as models."

Whether or not he found any appropriate Lincolns, he did find beautiful sunsets over Mt. Ascutney and an old brick tavern on a hilltop to watch them from. He named his estate "Aspet" after his father's native village in France, and remodeled it into the imposing mansion now preserved, along with his gardens and studios, on the grounds of the national historic site. Be sure to save time to stroll along the wooded trails and garden paths. The honey locust in front of Gaudens' house is the largest of its type in the state.

Cornish native Winston Churchill (1871-1947) was the author of numerous novels including *Coniston*, based on his experiences in state politics. Mr. Churchill did much of his writing at Harlakenden House, which President Woodrow Wilson used as his summer White House in 1914 and 1915. The home burned in 1923.

Churchill was to be overshadowed in history by another man with the same name -- no relation -- born three years later. In his day, though, he was quite a popular author, and was one of the guiding lights of one of America's leading colonies of artists and writers -- the Cornish Colony, an informal gathering of artists and writers who summered in and around the town between 1885 and 1935. The group included Saint-Gaudens, Parrish, the poet Percy MacKaye, dramatists Langdon Mitchell and Louise Evans Shipman, sculptor Herbert Adams, and architect Charles A. Platt.

Cornish is also the home of the American literary figure least likely to be part of a "colony," coterie, or chowder society of any kind: novelist and short-story writer J. D. Salinger. Don't ask where he lives; the locals all know that he does not appreciate visitors.

(4) The longest two-span covered bridge in the world, the **Cornish-Windsor bridge**, connects New Hampshire with Windsor, Vermont. The 449 ft. 5 in. Town lattice wooden span (see Drive 3), built in 1866 for $9,000, is the fourth on this site. The first, which opened on November 8, 1796, was described that year in the local newspaper, *Rising Sun*: "...[i]t embraces the Connecticut River with two most beautiful arches, each 184 ft. 4 in. long, with a pier in the center. ... it comes sufficiently above high water mark so as to defend and break off the ice." Unfortunately, the newspaper was being overly optimistic: the bridge was destroyed by a flood in 1824, as were successor spans in 1848 and 1866. A 10¢ toll was collected as recently as the 1940s. In *New Hampshire's Covered Bridges* Thedia Cox Kenyon relates that back when bars in Cornish sold liquor and Windsor was "dry," the toll collector charged 2¢ to enter New Hampshire, but 3¢ to return to Vermont.

Side Trip: Two Covered Bridges

Just past the Cornish-Windsor Bridge, turn left at the state sign to see two more of James Tasker's multiple

kingpost truss design bridges. The closer of the two, Dingletown Hill bridge, was built in 1882. A few miles up the road, the Blacksmith Shop bridge (closed to traffic) was constructed in 1881.

----

(5) Just past the bridge turn-off, watch on the left for the **Trinity Church of Cornish**, built by Philip Tabor between 1803 and 1808, and reconstructed by Peter Hoesburling in 1984-85. The cemetery in back is a trove of fascinating headstones. Among them: one with a finger pointed upward bearing only the inscription, "My Mother's Grave." Another reads, "In Memory of Mr. John Smith, who died Nov. 1793, aged 43 years. His honest vertue and not his belief in any particular theological Docum enabled him to meet death, that King of Terror to the multitude, with a serene countenance and unruffled mind."

(6) A roadside marker in front of the sprawling, white Federal style, 1775 **Chase House B&B** marks the birthplace of Salmon P. Chase (1808-1873), a founder of the Republican Party, governor of Ohio, leader in the anti-slavery movement, President Lincoln's Secretary of the Treasury, and Chief Justice of the United States. The home was moved here in the 1840s from a short distance away.

(7) At the junction of Rtes. 12A and 103, turn east (left) onto Rte. 103 to head through West Claremont (once the site of a paper company that made the tissue paper found in dress patterns) and into **Claremont**, the only sizable city (approximately 15,000) in New Hampshire's lower Connecticut Valley. Long an industrial center, it manufactured the drill bits that opened the gold fields of the South African Transvaal. The aptly-named "Precision Valley" city still turns out machine tools made to exacting standards.

The Sugar River, which starts at Lake Sunapee (*see Drive 5*) runs through town; its 300-ft. falls provided power for the textile and woolen mills that once fueled the city's economy. Today, as in many of New

78

England's one-time industrial centers, the mill buildings are being converted to housing and shopping malls, and offer visitors both a glimpse into the past and a place to browse for souvenirs.

Thanks to its years of industrial prosperity, Claremont boasts an inordinate number of fine public buildings and private homes. It also has some of the state's oldest churches, including the brick, Roman Catholic St. Mary's Church, erected between 1823 and 1825. The Ball House, 31 Myrtle St., was the home of Albert Ball, who invented the Springfield rifle as well as the Transvaal drill bit mentioned above. Don't miss the newly-renovated gilded-age **Opera House** in the 1896 Town Hall. Pick up a smoked meat sub to go at **Todafrali's New York Style Deli** and head to Moody Park for a picnic. The **Chamber of Commerce** has a walking tour brochure.

(8) Head south out of town on Rte. 12 toward Charlestown. The mountain to the west, across the river, is Vermont's Mt. Ascutney. Turn west onto Rte. 11 (toward I-91) to **The Fort at #4.** In 1740, 12 families came here from Massachusetts to establish New England's northwesternmost white settlement. In 1744, During King George's War, they built a fort as a defense against hostile Abenaki Indians and the French. In 1747, the small group of settlers held off a far superior attacking force for three days, assuring continued English rule in northern New England. During the French and Indian War, Colonial troops massed here and marched to Crown Point to help Lord Jeffrey Amherst win the day; in 1777, General Stark, from nearby Derryfield, recruited 15,000 militiamen and marched south from the fort to participate in -- and help win -- the Battle of Bennington. This carefully-produced replica of the original fort recalls those precarious early days in New Hampshire's history.

Charlestown's mile-long Main Street, lined with historic homes and commercial buildings, was designated a National Historic Landmark in 1987. The Unitarian

Church and several of the homes were designed by the great-grandfather of renowned American Impressionist artist Childe Hassam. Richard Upjohn, popularizer of Gothic Revival architecture, designed St. Luke's Episcopal Church, built in 1863. Four stained glass window in St. Catherine's Church were designed by Louis Comfort Tiffany. Main Street itself was used as a training ground for General Stark's men on their way to Bennington. The *Historic Charlestown Walkabout* brochure, available at stores in town, provides an excellent historical account.

A bronze plaque on Main Street marks the Site of the Johnson House, attacked by Indians one August dawn in 1754. Seven people, including the pregnant Mrs. Johnson, were taken captive. The Indians, en route to Canada with their prisoners, made camp the first night in Felchville, Vermont. Mrs. Johnson later told of the ordeal:

"The men were made secure in having their legs put in split sticks, somewhat like stocks, and tied to the limbs of trees too high to be reached. My sister must lie between two Indians, with a cord thrown over her, and passing under each of them. ... I was taken with the pangs of child-birth. The Indians signified that we must go on to a brook. When we got there they showed some humanity by making a booth for me ... my children were crying at a distance, where they were held by their masters, and only my husband and sister to attend me -- none but a mother can figure to themselves my unhappy posture. The Indians were employed in making a bier for the prisoners to carry me on and another booth for my lodging during the night."

Mrs. Johnson returned to Charlestown 40 years later.

Between Charlestown and Walpole, the Connecticut reaches one of its widest points -- sometimes as much as two miles across.

In 1784, Colonel Enoch Hale built the first bridge over the Connecticut River to link New Hampshire with Bellows Falls, Vermont. The *Massachusetts Spy*, February 10, 1785, said of it: "This bridge is thought to exceed any ever built in America in strength, elegance, and public utility, as it is in the direct way from Boston, through New Hampshire and Vermont, to Canada." The toll was 3¢ for a man on horseback, double if he crossed in a chaise, and a chaise with two horses cost 20¢. Col. Hale had to borrow money from one Rudolph Geyer to build his bridge, and Mr. Geyer held the mortgage, which stated that if the monthly payment was not in time, ownership would revert to Geyer. When he saw how much money the bridge was netting Col. Hale, Geyer wanted the bridge.

One day Col. Hale's son set out by stage from Bellows Falls for Boston to make the mortgage payment. He put up for the night at an inn, where he met up with his estranged wife. They had a lovely *rapprochement* that night, but the young man missed the early morning stage that would deliver him to Boston in time to make the payment. That day the bridge became the property of Rudolph Geyer.

---

(9) It's a pleasant shock to drive into the tiny village of **Walpole** (just off Rte. 12) after wading through the industrial sprawl that lines the road south of Charlestown. Founded in 1752, this is one of New Hampshire's loveliest villages, a classic New England melange of pre- and post-Colonial public buildings and private homes representing a variety of architectural styles. One of the most impressive stands on the northern outskirts of town: the 1762 **Walpole Inn,** built by Col. Benjamin Bellows, one of the town's founders (he's buried in the village cemetery). Col. Bellows built the home to replace the log cabin he erected upon arriving in the area in 1752. Among the other standouts: Walpole's first house, a circa 1760 saltbox which still has its original hand-

made wood shingles and clapboards; an 1840 Greek Revival with a two-story portico; an 1867 classic Victorian with Moorish arches and double Gothic windows; and the 1792 Gen. Benjamin Bellows house, a Georgian/Federal design with full pilasters at the corners, dentilled cornice and frieze, and seven fireplaces.

A self-guided tour brochure is available at the Bridge Memorial Library on Main Street; or at the **Walpole Historical Society**, housed in the 1831 Academy, with its two-story Greek portico, fanned center entrance, and octagonal bell tower. The building, used as a school until 1950, now houses the society's trove of historic memorabilia. The Academy Ravine walk in back of the building follows alongside a brook to Louisa May Alcott Falls, named for the writer who summered in Walpole. Documentary filmmaker Ken Burns makes his home here.

Back on Rte. 12, continue south. Two fine used bookstores are housed on the right in the 1835 Major Leonard Keep house.

Side Trip

(10) Follow signs off Rte. 12, and head along the river to **Boggy Meadow Farm**, where the Cabot family has been making cheese since 1822. One of the specialties here is Fannie Mason Swiss cheese, but all are delicious. There's a retail shop at the factory.
----

(11) If, on an early spring day, you see white smoke as you come to the intersection of Rtes. 12 and 63 South (bear right onto Rte. 63) it means that the folks at **Stuart & John's Sugarhouse and Pancake Restaurant** are boiling sap to make maple syrup. If you're passing by on a spring or fall weekend between 7 a.m. and 3 p.m., be sure to stop in for a heaping plate of their plain or blueberry pancakes or chocolate chip waffles with, of course, freshly made syrup (they

also serve donuts, French toast, maple sundaes, and corn fritters). The store sells syrup year round: if there's nobody there, knock at the house next door -- someone is usually around.

(12) Continue south on Rte. 63. Just south of the restaurant is one of those surprises that makes drives like these so rewarding: a tiny development called Park Hill which is the oldest section of **Westmoreland**. The architectural standout here is the church, built between 1762 and 1764 near the cemetery north of town and moved here in 1779 (the front and spire were added in 1827). Note the pedimented portico which rests on Doric columns, the elliptical window in the pediment, and the elegant spire. The bell was cast (and later recast due to a crack) at Paul Revere's factory in Canton, Massachusetts. Several beautifully-preserved 18th-century buildings, including the parsonage, are clustered around the church.

(13) At the intersection, detour east (left) on Rte. 9 a short distance to 700-acre **Spofford Lake**, where there's a nice little public beach.

Side Trip

(14) Continue east on Rte. 9 for a few miles to Chesterfield Gorge, where a short footpath leads to a cascading brook coursing through a deep gorge carved into bedrock. A small museum exhibits local flora and fauna.
----

(15) Back on Rte. 63, continue south to the hilltop town of **Chesterfield.** For the next several miles, there are turnoffs leading to trails in **Pisgah State Park**, largest in New Hampshire's park system. The park is a largely undeveloped, 13,168-acre tract of rough forest terrain, ponds, mountain ridges, and wetlands, and is a popular destination for day hikers (overnight camping is not allowed).

Side Trip

----

(16) Detour west on Rte. 9 toward Vermont. Just before the Connecticut River, turn left onto Gulf Rd., bear left at the fork, and continue for another 2 1/2 miles to the red Society for the Protection of New Hampshire Forests (SPNHF) gate, marking the entrance to Madame Sherri Forest. The forest is named for the Parisian theatrical fashion designer who once had a home here. All that remains of her estate is a stone foundation; today, the 488-acre tract is home to beaver, moose, and deer. The forest abuts the eastern slope of 1,335-ft Wantastiquet Mountain, whose ledges provide great views of the Connecticut River, Berkshires, and Mt. Monadnock.

----

(17) **Hinsdale**, the last town before the Massachusetts border, was named for Ebenezer Hinsdale, who built a fort and gristmill here in 1742. He was attracted by the water power possibilities at the confluence of the Connecticut and Ashuelot rivers. The spot was also attractive to Indians, who called the junction Squakeag, "Place for spearing salmon."

At the junction of Rtes. 63 and 119, turn west (right) onto Rte. 119 and follow signs directing you past **Hinsdale Greyhound Park** and through Brattleboro, Vermont to I-91.

Information

Greater Lebanon Chamber of Commerce (448-1203), P.O. Box 97, On the Mall, Lebanon 03766; www.lebnanonchamber.com

Greater Claremont Chamber of Commerce (543-1296), Tremont Square, Claremont 03743.

Hanover Chamber of Commerce (643-3115), 37 S. Main St., Hanover 03755.

Society for the Protection of New Hampshire Forests (224-9945), 54 Portsmouth St., Concord 03301.

***

For a free, comprehensive guide to *Canoeing on the Connecticut River,* call **PG&E** at 653-9232.

Lodgings

(6) Chase House B&B (800-401-9455 or 675-5391), Rte. 12A, Cornish. Closed Nov. & Dec. All eight rooms in the handsomely restored inn and an 1810 house have antiques and reproductions; six have private baths. $$

(7) Goddard Mansion (800-736-0603 or 543-0603), 25 Hillstead Rd., Claremont 03743. 10 guest rooms in a 1905 summer mansion overlooking Mt. Ascutney. Many have river views; some have private baths. Kids welcome. $$

(8) Maple Hedge B&B (826-5237, 55 Main St., Charlestown 03603. www.maplehedge.com. Antiques-furnished guest home in the Historic District. $$

(9)(R) Walpole Inn (756-3320), RR1, Box 762, Main St., Walpole 03608. www.walpoleinn.com. Eight guest rooms with private bath, TV and phone; four with soaking tubs and three with gas fireplaces. Clay tennis court. Restaurant features traditional New England dishes and contemporary specialties. $$-$$$

(15) (R) Chesterfield Inn (800-365-5515 or 256-3211), Rte. 9, W. Chesterfield. One-time tavern which opened its doors in 1798 now has 13 rooms in main and guest house (some with fireplaces and/or jacuzzis); highly regarded dining room. $$-$$$

Not on Drive

Darby Brook Farm (835-6624), Alstead 03602. www.darbybrookfarm.com. Federal-style 1790s inn has two guest rooms with working fireplaces and shared bath on lovely grounds near the river. May-Oct. $

Restaurants

(2) (L) Home Hill Country Inn (675-6165), River Rd., Plainfield. Four-course prix fixe classic French cuisine in the formal dining room of a four-square mansion overlooking the river. The seven guest rooms have private bath; some have fireplaces. $$$

(7) Indian Shutters Restaurant (826-4366), Wheeler-Rand Rd., Claremont. Classic American favorites, including prime rib, baked stuffed shrimp, and a buffet with soup and salad bar. $-$$

(7) Todafrali's New York Style Deli (543-3520), 162 Washington St., Claremont. Subs, salads, pizza, desserts, and daily specials. $

(7) Tumble-Inn Diner (542-0074), Tremont Square, Claremont. Breakfast (from 5:30 a.m.) and lunch in a 1941 Worcester diner. $

(9) John Cooper's Ice Cream and Sandwich Shop, Walpole.

(17) Village Pantry (336-7570), 14 Main St. Hinsdale. Polish cooking; B, L, D Mon.-Sat.; B, L Sun. $

Attractions

(3) Saint-Gaudens National Historic Site (675-2175), Rte. 12A, Box 73, Cornish 03745. Memorial Day weekend through Oct.; Sun. concerts early July - mid-Aug. Grounds open until dusk. $

(7) Claremont Opera House (542-4433), Tremont Square, City Hall. Performances throughout the year.

(9) Old Academy Museum, Main St., Walpole; 603 756-3449. July and Aug., Sat. and Sun. 2-4.

(9) Walpole Historical Society (756-3308), Walpole. June-Sept., Wed. and Sat. 2-4 p.m.

(14) Chesterfield Gorge Natural Area, Rte. 9. Mid-May-Columbus Day. $

(15) Pisgah State Park (239-8153), P.O. Box 242, Winchester, NH 03470. Or: NH Division of Parks and Recreation (271-3556), 172 Pembroke Rd., P.O. Box 1856, Concord 03302

Not on Drive

American Precision Museum (802-674-5781), S. Main St., Windsor, VT. Cross the bridge to visit this museum dedicated to early machine tools and the locally-manufactured Enfield rifle; housed in an 1846 mill. Also, Maxwell Parrish exhibit. Late May-Oct. $.

Activities

(3) Northstar Canoe Livery (542-5802), Balloch's Crossing, Rte. 12A, Cornish. Canoe and shuttle service; half, full an overnight rentals.

(7) Claremont Speedway (543-3160), Thrasher Rd., Claremont. Stock and modified cars race Saturday nights at 7:30 from May-Sept.

(17) Hinsdale Greyhound Park (800-NH-TRACK or 336-5382), Rte. 119, Hinsdale. Year-round racing.

Not on Drive

Bascom's Sugar House (835-2230) between Alstead and Acworth off Rte. 123A.

Crafts and Galleries

(1) **AVA Gallery and Art Center** (448 3117), 11 Bank St., Lebanon. NH and VT artists.

(1) **Pearce Design and Ultimate Reflections** (800-371-4996), 41 Glen Rd., West Lebanon. Jewelry and crafts exhibited in studio-gallery. Closed Sun.

(3) **Cornish Colony Gallery and Museum** (675-6000), Rte. 12A, Cornish.

(15) **Stone House Antiques & Books** (363-4866), jct. Rtes. 9 and 63, Chesterfield. American, English and Continental furniture, paintings, prints, silver and porcelain.

(15) **Hemlock Hill Antiques** (256-3281), Cross Rd., W. Chesterfield. Country pine and Shaker furniture, pewter, quilts, crocks, and decoys. Closed Tues.

Not on Drive

Vermont State Craft Center (802-674-6729), Windsor House, Rt. 5, Windsor, VT. Open Mon.-Sat. year-round; Sunday June-Jan. Juried pieces from NH artists and craftspeople.

Shopping

(1) **Colonial Antiques Market** (298-8132 or 298-7712), Colonial Plaza, Rte. 12A, W. Lebanon. More than 100 booths piled with antiques, collectibles, and lots of fun stuff. Outdoor flea market Sun., weather permitting.

(1) **Power House Mall**, Ret. 10, W. Lebanon.

(7) **Pleasant Street Antique Center** (542-1006), 66 Pleasant St., Claremont. Three stories with wares of more than 100 dealers.

(7) North Country Smokehouse (800-258-4303 or 543-301), near airport, Claremont. Smoked meats, poultry, sausage.

(7) Pleasant Street Antique Center (542-1006), 66 Pleasant St., Claremont. 100+ dealers.

(7) Putnam Brothers Sugar House (826-5515), Rte. 12A south of Claremont. Maple syrup and products; weekend sugarhouse tours.

(9) Boggy Meadow Farm (756-3300), off Rte. 12, Walpole.

(9) The Bookchase (399-4989), and Lucienne Elshout Books, Prints and Antiques (399-4883), Major Leonard Keep House, Rte. 12, Westmoreland.

(9) Burdick Chocolates (800-229-2419 or 756-3701), Main St.,Walpole. Handmade chocolates from French Valrhona chocolate. The mouse with toasted almond ears is a house specialty; the seconds are a great deal. Cafe.

(11) Stuart and John's Sugarhouse and Pancake Restaurant (603 399-448), Rte. 63 at Rte. 12, Westmoreland. Sugarhouse and restaurant open third weekend in Feb.-April, and third weekend in Sept.- November, weekends 7 a.m.-3 p.m. Store open year round.

(15) Stone House Books (363-4866), Rtes. 9 and 63, Chesterfield. Closed Mon. except by appt.

Not on Drive

Bascom's Sugar House (835-2230), Rt. 123A, Alstead. One of New England's largest maple syrup manufacturers has a small gift shop.

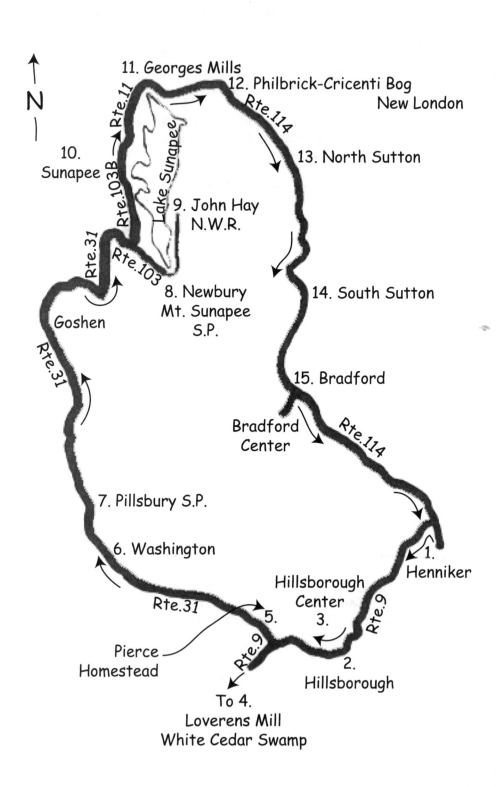

N

11. Georges Mills

12. Philbrick-Cricenti Bog
New London

Rte.11

Rte.114

10.
Sunapee

Rte.103B

Rte.11

Lake Sunapee

13. North Sutton

9. John Hay
N.W.R.

Rte.31

Rte.103

Rte.103

14. South Sutton

8. Newbury
Mt. Sunapee
S.P.

Goshen

15. Bradford

Rte.31

Bradford
Center

Rte.114

7. Pillsbury S.P.

6. Washington

1.
Henniker

Hillsborough
Center

Rte.31

5.

3.

Rte.9

Pierce
Homestead

Rte.9

2.
Hillsborough

To 4.
Loverens Mill
White Cedar Swamp

Drive 5

Along the Contoocook to the Lake Sunapee Range

65 miles

Lively college towns, serene villages, and the boyhood home of New Hampshire's only U.S. president are highlights of this drive through the hills and valleys of the state's west central region. The route follows the shores of lovely Lake Sunapee, and includes a wildlife refuge, a fascinating bog environment, and an 8,000-acre state park.

(1) Begin your tour in **Henniker** -- the "only Henniker on earth."   Native daughter Edna Dean Proctor, a noted poet, wrote of her town:

> "The vales of Henniker are spread
> their banks all set with golden grain,
> Oer stately trees whole vistas gleam
> -- A double forest -- in the stream ... "

The double-arched Edna Dean Proctor stone bridge which spans the Contoocook River in town is an excellent vantage point from which to see the remains of the paper, leather-board and wooden novelty mills which once thrived here.   Today the town's major industry is education: the buildings of **New England College** dominate downtown; the college has offices in an old mill as well as in the former, 1805 Henniker Inn.   Shops and restaurants, attracted by the school's 1,000+ students, line the small Main Street.   The **Henniker Pharmacy** on Main Street, a local institution since 1889, is a good place to find out what's going on around town. The **Henniker Historical Society** publishes "A Guide to Henniker's Historical Markers."

The Legend of Ocean Born Mary

In 1720, while en route with her husband from Londonderry, Ireland to Londonderry, New Hampshire, Elizabeth Wilson went into labor. Shortly after the baby's birth, pirates boarded the ship. Discovering the infant and mother below, the pirate captain, Pedro, offered safe passage for all if Elizabeth would name the baby Mary. When she agreed, he and his men left the passengers and booty behind. Before the pirates set sail, the captain returned with a wrapped parcel for the new mother. Inside was a bolt of grayish-green brocaded silk. "Let Mary make her wedding gown from this," he said, and went back to his ship.

On her 18th birthday "Ocean-Born Mary" was wed in a gown made from the silk. She settled in Henniker with her husband, and bore four sons. After she was widowed, Captain Pedro, ready to retire from pirating, moved to town, built a grand house, and invited Mary and her sons to move in. A few years later the captain journeyed to the coast and returned with a large, heavy chest, which he buried with the help of one of his men.

Mary died here in 1814 at the age of 94, and is buried in the Old Cemetery behind Town Hall. Efforts by treasure hunters to locate and unearth Captain Pedro's chest have proved futile.

Pat's Peak Ski Area, just to the south on Rte. 113, is a great place to hike off season, as are New England College's cross-country ski trails.

Baseball great Ted Williams knew what he was doing when he came to the Contoocook River, known locally as the "Tooky," to fish for trout: the restricted fishing area in the rapids above the dam between Henniker and Hillsborough has a reputation as one of the finest

spots around. Fishing is restricted to the use of artificial flies or lures, with no more than three hooks; and there is a limit of two trout, 12 in. minimum length. Follow Main St. (which turns into Western Ave. toward Hillsborough): the restricted area starts a few hundred yards above the dam.

----

(2) Head west on Rte. 9/202 (or follow the more scenic Western Avenue until it intersects with Rte. 9/202) to **Hillsborough**, named for Col. John Hill, who was granted land along the river in 1740. There are actually several villages here: Hillsborough Center, Hillsborough Upper Village, Hillsborough Lower Village, and Hillsborough proper. Like many of the river towns, Hillsborough was a thriving mill center well into the turn of the 20th century, and several of the now-deserted buildings still stand alongside the Contoocook. If you're passing through in mid-July, you may be in time for the Hillsborough Balloon Fest and Fair at Grimes Field. There's a fine riverfront trail here, with sign telling about the river and surrounding areas.

Side Trip

(3) Care for a quick trip 200 years back in time? In Hillsborough, turn right onto School St. (which turns into Center Rd.), continue past a Morgan horse farm and Fox State Forest (named for Caroline Fox, who donated the 1,445-acre parcel with more than 20 miles of hiking trails to the state in the early 1900s) to Hillsborough Center. A cluster of late-18th and early 19th-century buildings, a church, and a cemetery make up the original township, part of a grant to the first minister, Rev. Jonathan Barns. Note the double cross-panels on the front door of his 1774, two-story frame house at the northeast corner of the Common: they were believed to keep witches out. At the northern end of the Common -- the site of the first meeting house (1794) -- a path leads through the woods to a lookout.   Well-known

93

pewtersmith Raymond Gibson has his studio in one of the homes bordering the Common.

Back on Rte. 9/202, as you continue through town, watch for the Dutton Houses (also known as the Twin Houses). The two Greek Revival-style homes, built in 1860 by a wealthy merchant, are exactly alike in every detail. Today they house the **Dutton Club Restaurant**.

Side Trip

It's just a short hop from "downtown" Hillsborough to a place where you can take a dip, catch some trout, and see a fine bit of craftsmanship. Just out of town, turn right onto Beard Rd. and drive 6/10 mi. to Beard Brook, a local swimming hole, fishing spot, and picnic area. Continue for another two mi. to Gleason Falls, site of the area's first grist mill. Here stands one of the town's three mortarless stone arch bridges, built in the mid-1800s by Scottish and Irish stonemasons of locally-quarried granite.

Side Trip

(4) At the intersection of Rtes. 9 and 31, detour south on Rte. Rte. 9 to one of the region's rarest forms of wetland, the Loverens Mill Atlantic White Cedar Swamp.

New Hampshire has 30 White Cedar Swamps, defined as wetlands where cedars form more than 25% of the canopy. The oldest trees here have stood for about 130 years, but research shows that Atlantic white cedars have grown locally for 4,000 years. In its Winter, 1999 *Conservancy News*, the Nature Conservancy, custodian of the swamp, describes what it's like to enter the area:

"Walking into an Atlantic White Cedar Swamp is like entering a shadowy, prehistoric world. Dark green-

crowned Atlantic white cedars (*Chamaecyparis thyoides*) typically stand in tight gray ranks with wet feet covered in sphagnum mosses, but they may also be interspersed with brighter yellow birch (*Betula alleghaniensis*) or red maple (*Acer rubrum*). Blown down trees make walking a challenge, as can shrubs such as highbush blueberry (*Vaccinium corymbosum*) and sweet pepperbush (*Clethra alnifolia*).

----

(5) The Federal, two-story **Franklin Pierce Homestead National Historic Landmark** at the intersection of Rtes. 9/202 and Rte. 31 was built in 1804 by the fourteenth president's father, Gov. Benjamin Pierce, a hero of the Revolutionary War and two-time governor of New Hampshire. The future president -- one of eight children -- moved to the house when he was six weeks old, and spent his early years here. The home shows shows how an affluent family lived in small-town New England at the outset of the 19th century. Of particular interest are the ballroom; examples of hand-stenciling; French wallpaper with a scene of the Bay of Naples; and period furnishings.

(6) Head north on Rte. 31. **Washington**, perched on a hill at an altitude of 1,507 ft., is one of the loftiest towns in the state. In December of 1776, what was then Camden became the second town in the country to change its name to honor General George Washington. A cluster of handsome buildings clustered on the Common at the center of town include: the Washington Center School, in service from 1883 to 1993; the 1787 Congregational Church (the steeple was added later); and the 1790 Faxon House. A marker proclaims that Washington was the birthplace of the Seventh Day Adventist Church in 1842. To visit the site of the "first Christian society's" first building, take the second left opposite the Common onto Millen Pond Rd. and continue for 2 1/3 mi.

(7) Continue north on Rte. 31 to the lovely and secluded **Pillsbury State Park**, 8,000 acres of mostly undeveloped woods, marshes, ponds and bogs

teeming with birds and other wildlife. Bear, moose, and great blue heron sightings are common, and the laugh of the loon and the howl of coyotes are often heard. The park is at the northern terminus of the Monadnock-Sunapee Trail, a 47-mile footpath that begins at Mt. Monadnock to the south (*see Drive 3*). There are facilities for primitive camping, picnicking, swimming, paddling, and, of course, hiking.

Continue on Rte. 31 through Goshen Four Corners and Goshen. Goshen was the birthplace, in 1812, of John W. Gunnison, who after graduating from West Point in 1837, traveled west to the Great Salt Lake as a surveyor and mapmaker, and later published a history of the Mormons. In 1853 he was chosen to command an expedition from St. Louis through Colorado and Utah to survey and map land for a transcontinental railroad. He was killed that year by an Indian arrow. Gunnison, Colorado, and that state's Gunnison River and Black Canyon of the Gunnison National Monument are named for him.

(8) Turn east (right) onto Rte. 103 and follow the road as it winds along a ridge toward Sunapee and the Mt. Sunapee range. To the west, in the distance, is Vermont and Stratton ski resort. Continue east on Rte. 103 to **Newbury**, at the south end of Lake Sunapee, named for the Abenaki word "soo-Napi" -- "wild goose waters" or "place of clear waters." The state's sixth largest lake, in the shadow of 2,743 ft. Mt. Sunapee, is nine miles long and three miles wide. Formed about 10,000 years ago when glacial ice sheets retreated, it has only one island -- Great Island -- which divides the lake into two sections. The first inhabitants were Abenakis, attracted to the lake's shores by the abundant fish and wildlife.

The Sunapee region blossomed as a summer resort in 1849 when the railroad arrived. **Mount Sunapee Resort**, southern New Hampshire's largest ski area, is now a year-round destination. Activities include lift-served mountain biking (rentals are available at several businesses in the area, including **Bob**

Skinner's Ski & Sport Shop and **Outspokin' Bicycle & Sport**), and aerial sky rides to the summit lodge and observation tower on a high speed super quad chairlift. Each August the resort is the site of one of the premier craft shows in the state, the juried League of New Hampshire Craftsmen's Fair.

Sunapee State Park Beach has a 1,500 ft. sandy swimming area, bath house, boat rental, picnic area, and fishing. The lake -- home to a rare species of native golden trout -- is popular among anglers.

Side Trip

(9) Continue east on Rte. 103 to Rte. 103A and head north on Rte. 103A for 2 1/2 miles to the Fells Historic Site at the John Hay National Wildlife Refuge. Hay, who served as Secretary of State under Presidents McKinley and Roosevelt, purchased 800 acres of land and built a lakefront estate here in 1891 under the "New Hampshire Farms for Summer Homes" program, developed by the state to get people to buy abandoned farms. Hay named his estate "The Fells" after the highlands in his native Scotland, and three generations of Hays served as stewards of the land until, in 1960, 68 acres were donated to the state Forest Service. In 1987, 163 acres were given to the U.S. Fish and Wildlife Service, which made that portion into a wildlife refuge. Today's Fells is renowned for its superb gardens, wonderful lake views, and wooded hiking trails. Visitors can tour Hay's estate.

----

(10) Continue west on Rte. 103 to Rte. 103B, and head north along the lake's west shore to **Sunapee** and follow signs to **Sunapee Harbor**, alongside the Sugar River. The town has been a summer resort since the late 1800s; back then, guests would arrive by train and be met by steamships which would transport them to lodgings around the lake (one ship could accommodate 650 passengers). Sunapee might

97

have developed even sooner if not for the Civil War: the first steamboat, the 65-ft.-long side-wheeler *Surprise*, was launched July 4, 1859, but ended its run when the captain went off to war.

Lake Sunapee's golden age ended with the arrival of the automobile, the decline of the steamship trade, and the Depression. The last grand hotel burned to the ground in the 1960s. But there's still plenty of activity at the harbor for tourists today: 1 1/2 hr. narrated tours are given aboard the *M.V. Mt. Sunapee II*; and a hot buffet dinner is served nightly aboard the antique paddle wheeler *M.V. Kearsarge*. On summer weekends, musicians perform on a small stage next to the **Wild Goose Country Store**. There's entertainment Wednesday nights at the bandstand in front of **Harbor Falls Deli**. The Riverwalk, a landscaped park and demonstration garden along the Sugar River, begins at the harbor and ends at Coffin Park near the new Town Hall.

Folks in these parts have often shown an inventive streak. In 1869, after 14 years of tinkering, Sunapee resident Enos M. Clough built a horseless carriage featuring 5,463 pieces, two cylinders, three forward speeds, and three reverse speeds. He drove it as far as St. Johnsbury, Vermont, but it was banned in Sunapee because it frightened the horses. One year earlier, in 1868, Sunapee resident John B. Smith invented something more immediately practical: a clothespin machine that turned out 125 finished pins a minute.

----

(11) Continue north on Rte. 11 to **Georges Mills** at the northern end of the lake. **Sargent's Marina** at the public boat landing rents pontoon and ski boats, runabouts, and personal watercraft.

(12) Continue on Rte. 11 to the intersection of Rte. 114, and continue on Rte. 114 (Newport Rd.), under I-89 toward New London. Approximately 1 1/2 miles

past the underpass, watch for a wide shoulder. It's the trailhead for the **Philbrick-Cricenti Bog** (if you see Cricenti's Shopping Center you've gone too far -- backtrack 1/2 mi.). Don't get "bogged down" by the name -- this is a rare and fascinating, tundra-like environment: a wooden boardwalk floats on a mat of sphagnum moss, winding past mosses, ferns, bog laurel, and insect-eating pitcher plants. Pick up a trail guide at the beginning.

Continue into **New London**, the market town for the Mt. Sunapee/Mt. Kearsarge region (2,937-ft. Mt. Kearsarge and **Mt. Kearsarge State Forest** are to the east). The focal point of this pretty little town is the Village Green, bordered by the historic, 1792 **New London Inn**. The gazebo here is a venue for summer band concerts. You wouldn't be surprised to see Mr. Chips crossing the campus of the prototypical New England **Colby-Sawyer College**, which opened its doors in 1837 as the New London Academy for young women. The **Barn Playhouse**, in a restored, circa 1790 barn, is home to one of New England's original summer theaters. Off Sunapee Rd., in the oldest part of town, the **Historical Society** oversees Old New London Village -- eight buildings built between 1800 and 1830. Among them are the 1800 post-and-beam Griffin Barn and the town's first country store.

(13) Continue south on Rte. 114 to **North Sutton**, birthplace of flour magnates George A. and John S. Pillsbury, and home of 50-acre **Wadleigh State Park** on the southern shore of **Kezar Lake**. The beach, nestled under a stand of pines, is a welcome sight on a hot summer's day. The 1840 **Follansbee Inn**, overlooking the lake, offers fine accommodations. A three-mi. trail around the lake begins nearby.

Head up Harvey Rd. from the center of town to visit the **Matthew Harvey Homestead and Muster Field Farm Museum.** The homestead, built in 1784 by one of the town's first settlers, was used as a tavern for many years. A number of historic buildings, including an 1810 schoolhouse and blacksmith shop, were moved to the muster field and now give visitors a glimpse of days gone by. The field was the parade grounds for the 30th New Hampshire Regiment.

(14) In **South Sutton**, stop in at the **Nunsuch Dairy**, where Courtney Haase raises Toggenburg goats to make goat cheese and Smoked Friar's Cheese. The **Old Store Museum** displays a trove of antiques and an 1863 schoolhouse which is open for touring on Sunday afternoons in July and August.
(15) Continue south on Rte. 114 to **Bradford**, whose proximity to lakeside beaches, three state parks, and several ski areas has made it an upscale, year-round vacation community.

Side Trip

Just past the intersection of Rtes. 114 and 103 turn onto River Rd., through the 1854 Bement Bridge which spans the west branch of the Warner River, to Bradford Center, where several buildings--including an 1838 meetinghouse with a Gothic-style tower, and a schoolhouse-- are preserved and under the auspices of the Bradford Historic Society.

Continue on Rte. 114, past Lake Massasecum, back to Henniker.

Information

Hillsborough Chamber of Commerce (464-5858), P.O. Box 541, Hillsborough.

New London Chamber of Commerce (877-526-6575), P.O. Box 532, New London 03257. www.newlondonareanh.com.

Lake Sunapee Business Association (800-258-3530 or 763-2495), Sunapee 03782. www.sunapee.vacations.com.

Monadnock-Sunapee Greenway Trail (357-2115 or 225-7274), P.O. Box 164, Marlow, 03456.

The Nature Conservancy of New Hampshire (224-5853), 2 1/2 Beacon St. Concord 03301. www.tncnt.tnc.org.

New London Chamber of Commerce (526-2911), 270 County Rd., New London.

Lodging

(1)(R) Colby Hill Inn (800-531-0330 or 428-3281), The Oaks, P.O. Box 778, Henniker 03242 www.colbyhillinn.com. Historic inn has 16 antiques-filled rooms with private baths (some with fireplaces), a swimming pool, and air conditioning. Menu includes lamb, poultry and seafood dishes. $$-$$$

(1)(R) Meeting House Inn and Restaurant (428-3228), 35 Flanders Rd., Henniker. 200-year-old, air conditioned country inn near Pat's Peak has six rooms with private baths. Hot tub and sauna rental. Breakfast is delivered to the room; dinner is served in the restored barn next door. $$

(2) Inn at Maplewood Farm (800-NH-INN-95 or 464-4242), 447 Center Rd., P.O. Box 1478, Hillsborough 03244. 1790s farmhouse has four spacious suites with private baths and antique radios with tapes of classic radio shows. $-$$

(8) Lakeview Motor Lodge (800-882-8807 or 763-2701), 1349 Rte. 103, Newbury. www.sunapeelakeview.com. Two-story motel near State Park Beach and Mt. Sunapee has rooms with private baths, TV, VCR, refrigerators, coffee makers, and lake views. Outdoor picnic tables and grills. $$

(8) Mt. Sunapee Motel (763-5592), 1386 Rte. 103, Mt. Sunapee 03255. At the entrance to Sunapee State Park, standard units and two-room efficiencies. $-$$

(10) Georges Mills Cottages & Lodging (888-891-8567 or 763-2369), Rte. 11, Otter Pond, Sunapee 03782 . http://personalpages.tds.net/~cottages.
Comfortable, year-round lakefront cottage colony also has air-conditioned, housekeeping suites and apartments. Swimming, sailing, fishing, skating. $-$$

(10) The Burkehaven (763-2788), 179 Burkehaven Hill Rd., Sunapee Harbor 03782.
www.burkehavenatsunapee.com. Motel overlooking Sunapee Harbor has 10 spacious rooms with double beds, showers, TV; outdoor pool. Pets welcome. $-$$

(10) Dexter's Inn & Tennis Club (800-232-5571 or 763-5571), Stagecoach Rd., Sunapee 03782. 17 rooms with private baths and one cottage on an estate with great views, gardens, tennis courts, a pool, and lake access. MAP.

(11) Coggswell's Cottages on Sunapee (763-5835), 770 Jobs Creek Rd., Georges Mills 03751. Five lake-front or lake view 2-bedroom cottages with porches and barbecue grills. Docks; boat slips and rentals, small beach. $-$$

(12) Hide-Away Inn (526-4861 or 800-457-0589), Twin Lake Villa Rd., New London 03257. www.hideawayinn.net. Seven guest rooms with private baths in a country farmhouse with a fieldstone fireplace. Dinner available. $$$

(12) Maple Hill Farm (800-231-8637 or 526-2248), 200 Newport Rd., New London 03257. Unpretentious, 19th-century farmhouse bordering Little Sunapee Lake, ideal for families. Outdoor spa, indoor basket-ball court/dance floor, farm animals, boats. $-$$

(12) (R) New London Inn (800-526-2791 or 526-2791), 140 Main St., New London 03257. www.newlondoninn.com. Classic 1792 country inn on the green has 28 rooms with private baths and a highly-regarded restaurant. Full breakfast. $$-$$$

(12) Twin Lake Village (526-6460), 21 Twin Lake Villa Rd., New London. Villa and Victorian houses at an unpretentious, 100-year-old resort on Little Lake Sunapee. Private beach, boats, nine-hole golf course. Late June-Labor Day. MAP.

(13) Follansbee Inn on Kezar Lake (800-626-4221 or 927-4221), North Sutton 03260. www.follansbeeinn.com. 23 antiques-furnished rooms (11 with private bath) in a rambling 1840 inn overlooks Kezar Lake. Private waterfront and boats. $$

(15) Candlelite Inn B&B (888-812-5571 or 938-55871), 5 Greenhouse Lane, Bradford 03221. www.virtualcities.com/nh/candleliteinn.htm. 1897 country Victorian on three acres has ix lovely rooms with private baths and views. Breakfast (with dessert) overlooking the pond. $$

(15) Mountain Lake Inn (938-5622 or 800-662-6005), 2871 Rt. 114, Bradford. www.mountainlakeinn.com. 18th-century inn on 168 acres overlooking Lake Massasecum and mountains has nine rooms with private baths in the original inn an a 1930s addition, a four-room cabin, and lakefront beach. $$

(15) Rosewood Country Inn (938-5253), Pleasant View Rd., Bradford 03221. www.bbonline.com/nh/rosewood. Romantic inn on 12 landscaped, hilltop acres has rooms with private baths and canopy or four-poster beds; some suites with fireplaces and two-person jacuzzis. Fireplaced dining room and "candlelight and crystal" breakfast.

Restaurants

(1) Que Pasa Mexican Restaurant (428-8226), Main St., Henniker. Tex-Mex, vegetarian, and "gringo" dishes. $-$$

(2) Caron's Restaurant, Henniker St., Rte. 9, Hillsborough. Good, solid fare in an authentic Kullman Diner. Homemade desserts and soups. $

(2) Diamond Acres Seafood (478-3121), 737 W. Main St., Hillsborough. Great fresh fish, good portions. $

(2) Dutton Club Restaurant (464-4001). Beef, chicken and fish buffet style with a salad and dessert bar. No credit cards. BYOB. L, D Thurs. - Sun. $-$$

(8) Murphy's Grille (763 3113), 1407 Rte. 103, Newbury. Family favorites including burgers and pasta and fresh, fried fish. $

(10) The Anchorage Restaurant (763-3334), Sunapee Harbor. Contemporary fare overlooking the lake. Outdoor deck; entertainment and dancing on weekends. $-$$

(12) (L) Colonial Farms Inn (800 805 8504 or 526 6121, Rt. 11, New London. Elegant, candlelight dining in an 1836 inn with five air-conditioned guest rooms ($$) with private baths. $$-$$$

(12) (L) Inn at Pleasant Lake (800-626-4907 or 526 6271), 125 Pleasant St., P.O. Box 1030, New London 03257. One of the region's most acclaimed restaurants, overlooking Pleasant Lake and Mt. Kearsarge, serves a five-course, candlelit dinner ($42/person). 12 guest rooms ($$-$$$) with views and private baths. D, closed Tues. $$$

(12) MacKenna's Restaurant (526-9511), New London Shopping Center, New London. Strawberry pancakes, Texas Style French toast, fried clams, and homemade strawberry rhubarb pie are just a few house specialties at this popular spot. $

(12) Wildberry Bagel Co. (526-2244), 178 Main St., New London. Fresh baked goods, biscotti, baklava, spanokopita; sandwiches, soups, and espresso bar. 6 a.m.- 3 p.m. (2.00 p.m. Sun.) $

(15) Bradford Junction Restaurant and Bakery (938-2424), Rt. 114, Bradford. Housed in a former train depot, this popular spot serves delicious homemade breads, soups, and Yankee fare. B, L. $

Attractions

(1) Henniker Historical Society (428-6267), Academy Hall, 5A Maple St., Henniker.

(l) Pat's Peak Ski Area (428-3245), Henniker.

(3) Fox State Forest (464-3453), Center Rd., Hillsborough.

(5) Franklin Pierce Homestead (478-3165 or 464-5858), Rtes. 9 and 31, Hillsborough Lower Village. Memorial Day-Columbus Day, Sat. and Sun.; July and Aug., Mon.-Sat. 10-4, Sun. 1-4. $

(7) Pillsbury State Park (863 2860), Rte. 31, Washington. $

(8) Mount Sunapee Resort (763-2356; 800-258-3530 for lodging), Rte. 103, Newbury.

(8) Stony Brook Wildlife Sanctuary, Chalk Pond Rd., off Rte. 103, Newbury. 360 acres of marsh and forest with marked trails. For information: NH Audubon Society (224-9909).

(8) Sunapee State Park Beach (271-3254), Rte. 103, Newbury. $

(9) The Fells Historic Site at the John Hay National Wildlife Refuge (763-4789), Rte. 103A between Newbury and Blodgett Landing. Grounds open daily dawn-dusk; house tours weekends and holidays Memorial Day-Columbus Day. Garden tours daily in summer. $

(10) Sunapee Historical Society Museum, Sunapee Harbor. Memorial Day-early July and Sept.-Columbus

105

Day, Sat. and Sun. 1-4; July and Aug., Sun., Tues., Thurs.-Sat. 1-4; Wed. 7 pm-9 pm.

(12) New London Historical Society (526-6564), Little Sunapee Rd., New London.
(12) Colby-Sawyer College (526-2010), New London.

(13) Matthew Harvey Homestead and Muster Field Farm Museum (927-4276), Harvey Rd., N. Sutton. Sundays, July and Aug.

(13) Wadleigh State Park (927-4724), Rte. 14, Kezar Lake, N. Sutton. Picnic area, bathhouse, swimming beach. $

(14) Old Store Museum (927-4183), Rte. 114, South Sutton.

Off the Drive

Mount Kearsarge State Forest/Winslow State Park (526-6168), Rte. 11. A curving roads ascends the NW slope of Mt. Kearsarge to a picnic area overlooking the White and Green mountains. Trail to summit. $

Rollins State Park (456 3808), off Rte. 103. A road goes part way up the mountain; trails to summit. $

Activities

(2) Bellanger's (464-3262) and Ed Lappis (478-5666), Hillsborough. Hot air balloon rides.

(2) Hillsborough Trout Farm (464 3026), 154 Old Henniker Rd., Hillsborough. Fish without a license in three stocked ponds; Wed.-Sun.

(2) Mahanan Park, Rte. 9, Hillsborough. Picnic tables, sandy beach with a lifeguard, nature walk, boat ramp, and dock. $

(2) Sleeper Hill Farm (478-1100), 20 Severance Rd., Hillsborough Upper Village. Trail rides weekends and holidays.

(8) LaPorte's Skindiving (763-5353), Rte. 103, Newbury. Rentals.

(8) Outspokin' Bicycle & Sport (763-9500), Rte. 103, Newbury Harbor. Bicycle rentals.

(10) Bob Skinner's Ski & Sports (763-2303), Sunapee Harbor. Rental center for bicycles, in-line skates, and water sports equipment (including wake boards, tubes, and water skis).

(10) Dewey Beach, Lake Sunapee, off Rte. 11 and Garnet St. from Sunapee Harbor. Rafts, restrooms, children's play area, lifeguard. $

(10) Lake Sunapee Fishing Tours (863-9087), 14 Depot St., Sunapee.

(10) M/V Mt. Sunapee II and M/V Kearsarge (763-4030), Sunapee Harbor. Reservations recommended for M/V Kearsarge. Mid-May-Oct., call for hrs.

(10) Sunapee Welcome Center (763-4030), Sunapee Harbor. Kayak, canoe and hydro bike rentals.
(11) Sargents Marine (763-5032), Lake Sunapee, Georges Mills. Canoe, boat and motor rental.

(12) Barn Playhouse (800-633 2276 in NH; or 526-4631), Main St., New London. The state's oldest consecutively-operated theater presents plays and musicals in a renovated barn late June-early Sept.

(12) Custom Fly Shop (526-6682), 123 Main St., New London. Tube rentals and fly fishing equipment.

(12) Hogan Sports Center (526-3600), 100 Main St., New London. Colby-Sawyer College's sports facility has an indoor track, swimming pool, racquetball courts, and indoor and outdoor tennis courts.

(12) Norsk X-Country Ski Center (800-42-NORSK or 526-4685), Rte. 11, New London. Canoe, kayak, and windsurfer rentals, and tours on the Blackwater River.

(12) Spring Ledge Farm (526-6253), 220 Main St., New London. Pick your own strawberries; display gardens, and self-guided tours.

(12) Summer Music Associates (526-8750), P.O. Box 603, New London. Varied series of fine music at venues in Lake Sunapee-Kearsarge Region.

(12) Village Sports (526-4948), 140 Main St., New London. Mountain and road bike and snorkel equipment rentals.

(15) Mini Meadow Llamas (938-5268), Bradford. Half- and full-day treks.

Art/Crafts/Antiques

(1) The Fiber Studio (428-7830), 9 Foster Hill Rd., Henniker. Old barn filled with natural fiber yarns, ethnic beads, looms, spinning wheels, buttons, jewelry, knit and woven items, and other sundry stuff. Closed Mon. and some Sun.

(1) New England College, NEC Art Gallery (603-428-2211), Henniker. Exhibits throughout the academic year.

(3) Gibson Pewter (464-341), 18 E. Washington Rd., Hillsborough Center. Closed Mon.

(11) Prospect Hill Antiques (763-9676) Georges Mill. 8,000 sq. ft. barn houses one of New England's largest inventories of antique oak, walnut and country pine furniture.

(12) Artisan's Workshop (800-457-7242 or 526-4227), 186 Main St., New London. Local crafts.

(12) Marian Graves Mugar Art Gallery (526-3662), Colby-Sawyer College, 100 Main St., New London.
Shopping

(1) German John's (464-5079), Rt. 114, Henniker. Sourdough breads, crusty rolls, kuchen, and soft pretzels.

(1) Henniker Pharmacy (428-3456), downtown Henniker. Coffee, wines, groceries, and toys.

(2) Morse Sporting Goods (464-3444), 85 Contoocook Falls Rd., Hillsborough. Fishing equipment, hatch reports, hand-tied flies, canoes, boat regulations, and licenses.

(3) Richard Withington (464-3232), 590 Center Rd., Hillsborough Center. Auctions Thurs. at 10 a.m. April -Columbus Day.

(10) Wild Goose Country Store (763-5516), Sunapee Harbor. Old-fashioned country store: collectibles, gifts, penny candy, and more.

(12) Kearsarge Bookshelf/Bradford's Hallmark (526-6535), 107 The Gallery, 46 Newport Rd., New London. Local authors, topo maps, balloons, greeting cards.

(12) Morgan Hill Bookstore (526-5850), 170 Main St., New London. Books, music, stationery, cards, and puzzles.

(14) Nunsuch Dairy (927-4176), Rte. 14, S. Sutton.

Off the Drive
The Dorr Mill Store (800 846 3677 or 863-1197, Hale St., Guild. National center for rug hooking, braiding, home sewing and quilting with wool has natural and hand dyed woolens, patterns, books, accessories, and sportswear. The Woolen Mill Store (863-6377) here sells locally made products including pottery, blanket jackets, prints, and porcelain bags; Christmas items.

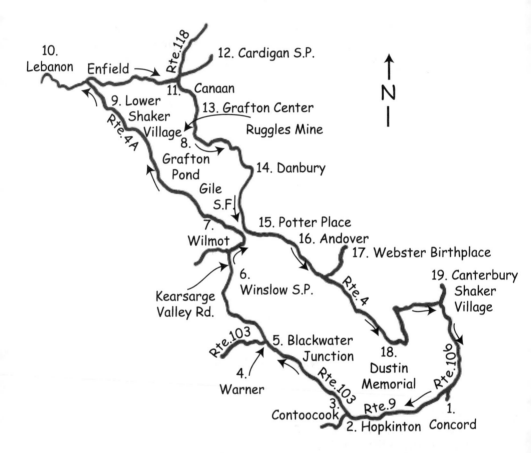

10. Lebanon

Enfield

Rte.118

12. Cardigan S.P.

11. Canaan

9. Lower Shaker Village

13. Grafton Center

Ruggles Mine

Rte.4A

8. Grafton Pond

Gile S.F.

14. Danbury

7. Wilmot

15. Potter Place

16. Andover

17. Webster Birthplace

Kearsarge Valley Rd.

6. Winslow S.P.

Rte.4

19. Canterbury Shaker Village

Rte.103

5. Blackwater Junction

18. Dustin Memorial

Rte.106

4. Warner

Rte.103

3. Contoocook

Rte.9

1.

2. Hopkinton

Concord

N

Drive 6

The Capital and
Two Shaker Villages

140 miles

Begin this drive without driving -- Concord, New Hampshire's capital, is a pleasantly walkable city. Once on the road, explore the rolling countryside around Mt. Kearsarge, and visit a Shaker Village with an inn where you can spend the night. Look for minerals at an old mine, learn about the humble origins of "the godlike Daniel," and finish with an authentic Shaker meal at another of the sect's preserved villages.

(1) With a population of just above 38,000, **Concord** is a study in the small city as state capital. The southern New Hampshire high-tech boom is pressing against its borders and spreading out into the suburbs, but central Concord, the town that has collected along State and Main streets on the west side of the Merrimack River, comes across to the visitor as little more than an upcountry village big enough to sprout brick buildings ... and one big granite one with a proud golden dome.

One of the earlier inland settlements of colonial New Hampshire, Concord was founded in 1659 as the Plantation of Pennycook -- "Pennycook" being an Indian word meaning "crooked place," after the twisting course the Merrimack follows here. But due to political shenanigans, it would be almost 200 years before Main Street was laid out. By the beginning of the 19th century, Concord had grown into a prosperous market town, and center of a fledgling granite quarrying industry that was to make the town's name famous wherever American public buildings were erected during the expansive era that was to follow.

The early years of the new century saw two developments that did more than anything else to boost Concord's importance: in 1808, an act of the state legislature moved New Hampshire's capital from Portsmouth to Concord, strategically located in the center of the state. And just seven years later, the Middlesex Canal was completed, affording the town a direct, fully navigable water route to Boston. With the rapids at Amoskeag (*See Drive 2*) circumvented by the canal's locks, only one day was required to take laden barges downstream from Concord to Boston, and five days to bring them back. Suddenly, seacoast granite from Rockport and Quincy, Massachusetts had competition from the interior.

Concord is a town easily mastered by a visitor on foot. Pick up a free *Walking Tour Brochure* at the **Chamber of Commerce** or at the kiosk (seasonal) in front of the State House; or a copy of *Concord On Foot*, sold at the Chamber, Museum of New Hampshire History, and bookstores. Highlights include the gold-domed **State House**, built of Concord granite hewn by state prison inmates and dedicated in 1819. This is the country's oldest state capitol in which a legislature still meets in its original chambers. Out front are statues of New Hampshire's most famous sons -- Revolutionary General John Stark; Franklin Pierce, the Granite State's only president; anti-slavery champion John Parker Hale; and Daniel Webster, born in Franklin (*see #17 below*) and trained at Exeter and Dartmouth. Across Main St., the 1852 Eagle Hotel (now rehabbed as **Eagle Square Marketplace**) was once a popular gathering spot for state legislators, and lodged dignitaries as diverse as Jefferson Davis, Eleanor Roosevelt, and Charles Lindbergh.

The state-of-the-art **Christa McAuliffe Planetarium,** with a 40-ft. domed theater, honors the Concord High School teacher who died in the explosion of the space shuttle *Challenger* in 1986.

"She helped people. She laughed. She loved and is loved. She appreciated the world's beauty. She was curious and sought to learn who we are and what the universe is about. She relied on her judgment and moral courage to do right. She cared about the suffering of her fellow man. She tried to protect our spaceship earth. She taught her children to do the same."

Christa McAuliffe's husband, Steven, wrote the inscription on her tombstone at Calvary Cemetery on North State St. To visit, enter at the third gate, bear right, then take the first left and go to the back of the cemetery. Look for the large, black granite stone.

The permanent collections of the **New Hampshire Historical Society**, formerly housed in the Society's 1911 headquarters on Park St., are now located on Eagle Square at the Society's **Museum of New Hampshire History** at the Hamel Center, a restored 19th-century stone warehouse (the headquarters building now contains a library and changing exhibits). A perennial favorite among the museum's exhibits is a conveyance that played a major part in the city's history: a Concord Coach, one of many manufactured by the Abbot-Downing Company, founded here in 1813 as a wagon-building concern and destined to become the General Motors of the era of horse-powered travel. A unique suspension system employed "throughbraces" instead of a traditional spring-type suspension, which gave the vehicles a swinging motion, not the up-and-down jolting of conventional springs. The ornately-painted, yellow and red coaches with polished metal and wood paneling were used throughout the world -- notably in the American west, and at Africa's diamond mines.

Before you leave town, drive out North Main Street to visit the **Pierce Homestead**, home of 14th president Franklin Pierce, who was in nearby Hillsbororough in

1804. He lived with his wife, Jane, in this 1838 Greek Revival home (moved from its original location in 1971) after serving in the U.S. Senate, and before becoming president.

Turn off Main St. onto Pleasant St. (which becomes Rte. 9) and head west, past the state office complex and the prestigious college preparatory **St. Paul's School**, whose art collection includes several mobiles by Alexander Calder. As it enters the Contoocook Valley, the road quickly narrows to two lanes, passing by the northern tip of Little Turkey Pond, **Mill Brook Gallery & Sculpture Garden**, and several well-tended farms.

(2) The town hall at **Hopkinton**, an attractive village whose early growth was impeded because of frequent Indian attacks, once served as the state capitol. For an overview of state history, visit **The New Hampshire Antiquarian Society**, headquartered in a red brick, Palladian-windowed building built in 1890 and now listed on the National Register of Historic Places. Be sure to see the stained glass windows at St. Andrew's Episcopal Church in the center of town; the one with the cross-and-lilies design is the work of Louis Comfort Tiffany. As you head west out of town on Rte. 103, watch for the First Congregational Church and Meeting House at the intersection. It was built in 1789, and has a bell cast at the Massachusetts foundry of Paul Revere.

(3) Along the way to **Contoocook**, watch for signs for **Gould Orchards** on Gould Hill Road. This 230-year-old old family farm, overlooking the White Mountains, grows more than 80 varieties of apples; the adjacent store sells home-baked goodies, maple syrup, apple cider, and local crafts. As you enter the town, watch for the Contoocook Village Cemetery, which contains a number of 18th-century stones. At Fountain Square, the unusual covered railroad bridge (closed to traffic) spanning the Contoocook River was built in 1849-50 when the Concord and Claremont Railroad laid its first 33 miles of track from Concord to Bradford. It was

washed off its abutments several times during floods in the 1930s, but was hauled back into place each time, and eventually restored.

(4) Continue west on Rte. 103. The Hopkinton Fair is held each September at the fairgrounds just west of town. Head through Davisville and Warner Lower Village, whose beautifully-preserved, 18th-century homes look jarringly out of place in the shadow of I-89. The highway's proximity explains why **Warner,** which during its heyday in the mid-1800s had seven railroad stations and 24 schools, is today a sleepy little village. On the way into town, watch on the left for the Warner-Dalton Covered Bridge, which spans the Warner River. Built circa 1853 and rebuilt in 1963, it's said to be one of the oldest in the state. The 1840s Warner-Waterloo Bridge, a Town lattice truss design rebuilt in 1972, is just west of Warner on Rte. 103.

At **Mt. Kearsarge Indian Museum,** the state's only museum with a Native American focus, curator/founder Bud Thompson uses documents and an extensive collection of artifacts to vividly recount the history of the peoples who dwelled for more than 15,000 years in the Eastern Woodlands, Plains, and Southwest. There's a traditional Indian garden, Medicine Woods living museum, and replicas of Indian dwellings. Guided tours are given on the hour, and special events throughout the year include a July Pow Wow.

Just past the museum, the auto road at **Rollins State Park** climbs part way up the southern slope of Mt. Kearsarge to a parking area, picnic sites, and hiking trails. The easy-to-moderate 1.2 mile Rollins Trail winds through a red spruce forest to a tower on the 2,937 ft., glacially-scoured summit.

(5) A mile out of Warner, turn right off of Rte. 103 onto North Road and continue straight as it follows alongside I-89 for eight miles. Turn right and follow Kearsarge Valley Road until it intersects with Rte. 11. Turn east (right) onto Rte. 11 and continue to the junction of Rte. 4A in Blackwater Junction (the

Blackwater Junction Restaurant has great sandwiches and lunch specials). Turn north onto Rte. 4A.

The 53-ft., 1887 Town lattice truss Cilleyville Bridge at Blackwater Junction is one of the most photographed on this drive. Does it look like it's leaning to one side? According to Thedia Cox Kenyon, in her book *New Hampshire's Covered Bridges*, a local carpenter in charge of construction hired two assistants to help him. Part way through the job they became vexed with the carpenter and decided to "play a lasting joke on him, one that others could share in for a long time to come. They proceeded to cut certain important timbers just a bit short--not so much that it would be noticed immediately, but enough to let time get in its work effectively."

Side Trip

(6) For another view of Mt. Kearsarge, turn off Kearsarge Valley Rd. onto Kearsarge Mountain Road to Winslow State Park, on the northwest slope of the mountain. The park was named for Admiral John Angnum Winslow, who was in command of the *U.S.S. Kearsarge* when it sank the *Alabama* in the English Channel on June 19, 1864. An auto road goes to a parking lot at the beginning of the well-worn, moderately difficult 2.2-mi. Winslow Trail, which climbs through a coniferous forest to a summit fire tower. A cellar hole here is all that remains of a grand 19th-century resort hotel.

---

(7) Rte. 4A passes through **Wilmot**, home to the fine restaurant **La Meridiana**; past a wildlife viewing area at Gardner Memorial Wayside Park in Gile State Forest, and through miles of scrub land reminiscent of the interior of Maine.

(8) About six miles past the wayside park, watch on the right for Grafton Pond Road. It leads to the Society for the Protection of New Hampshire Forests' Grafton Pond Reservation and secluded Grafton Pond, home to smallmouth bass, horned pout, and pickerel. There's a boat launch here.
----

(9) Just ahead, the Lower Shaker Village and its "Great Stone Dwelling" hove into view. This structure stands on the grounds of **The Enfield Shaker Museum,** and is the largest main dwelling ever built by a Shaker community. At the time of its construction in 1840, the massive, four-story building fashioned of stones quarried at nearby Canaan was the most expensive in the state except for the State House. It was built to house adult disciples of the communal sect, which flourished in New England and New York State during the early 1800s. Today the Great Stone Dwelling serves as **The Shaker Inn**, and each of the simple guest rooms is furnished with historically correct Shaker-style furniture. Even the inn's dining room maintains the simple Shaker motif. The top floors house Shaker artifacts.

The Shakers' village at what they called their "Chosen Vale" on the southern shore of Lake Mascoma was founded in 1793 and survived until 1923. Because the Shakers would take in any child who needed shelter, by the 1850s 350 adults and 100 children lived and worked here. They built more than 200 buildings, farmed 3,000 acres of land, raised Merino sheep to make woolen products, and sold seeds, herbs, and brooms. Today a non-profit charitable organization, founded in 1986 to preserve the legacy of the Enfield Shakers, owns 28 acres of land and eight Shaker buildings, including the 1854 Cow barn -- the only remaining wooden Shaker cattle barn. There's a museum, gift shop, and gardens; and artisans are on hand to demonstrate Shaker crafts. The Shaker

Sacred Feast Ground is part of a state-owned 2,500-acre nature preserve.

When declining membership forced the Shakers to put their village up for sale in 1923, it was purchased by the LaSalette Order of Catholic priests. In 1927, a Hartford, Connecticut woman named Mary Keane accompanied the LaSalette fathers -- her spiritual mentors -- to Enfield, and gave them money to build a chapel next to the Stone Dwelling. The priests began construction in 1930, but had to shave several feet off of the plans when Ms. Keane lost her fortune in the Depression. She died penniless in 1932.

With its bronze doors, Italian marble floors and altar, stained glass windows, and pipe organ designed and built by the French Canadian firm Casavant Fréres, the chapel is representative of a different kind of spirituality that that of the Shakers, but is every bit as beautiful in its own way. The Order sold and deconsecrated the chapel in 1985, but kept ownership of the windows, and maintains a shrine across the way. Mary Keane (the chapel is now named for her) is the only lay person buried in the shrine's cemetery.

Organ recitals on the three-manual, 26-rank pipe organ are held at the chapel Sundays at 4:30 p.m. in July and August.

Side Trip

(10) To visit Lebanon, a thriving mill town until the 1940s, continue straight on Rte. 4A to Rte. 4W. Ammi Burnham Young, architect of the Shakers' Great Stone Dwelling, was born here in 1798. The oldest of nine children, he appears to have received no formal education -- yet he rates among the preeminent architects of New England's Greek Revival "Granite Age" of the early to mid-19th century. Young designed Lebanon's 1828 First Congregational Church, overlooking the rectangular town green in the

downtown **Colburn Historic District**. He was also responsible for the **Vermont State House** in **Montpelier**; **Boston's Custom House**; and other buildings throughout the U.S.

From the Shaker village, turn right and continue on Rte. 4A along Mascoma Lake, long a favorite spot for fishermen (brown and rainbow trout, large and smallmouth bass, and white perch), and turn right over Shaker Bridge (the original was washed out in the hurricane of 1938) onto Main St. Continue past the Shaker Bridge Motel, through Enfield Village (if you have time, poke through Danford and Sons Plumbing, Hardware, and Antiques), and turn east (right) onto Rte. 4.

(11) Continue past **Enfield Granite Company** into **Canaan**. At the historic marker in the center of town, turn left onto **Canaan Street** to the state's first historic district, settled by folks from Norwich, Connecticut and incorporated in 1761. The mile-long stretch of road is lined with 18th- and 19th-century Federal and Greek Revival buildings, including the 1793 National Register of Historic Places **Old Meeting House** with its original bell clock; the 1794 Grand View Hotel (closed); and the 1828 Gothic Revival Old North Church. The area, with pretty little Canaan Street Lake and a commanding views of several mountains, was a popular summer resort in the late 1800s and early 1900s. The **Inn on Canaan Street**, a favorite of parents who come to visit their boys at the nearby Cardigan Mountain School, has spacious second-floor guest rooms and serves a bountiful breakfast buffet.

The Canaan Historical Museum building is a replica of Noyes Academy, incorporated in 1834 to provide equal education for all children. Some local people didn't believe that "equal" should apply to black children, however. The *New Hampshire* volume in the 1930s *American Guide Series* relates: "Opposition

arose between the abolitionists and their opponents ... This eventually led to rioting in the summer of 1835 when the abolitionists armed themselves with iron bars and axes and with a string of 50 yoke of oxen marched toward the school. The fence around the building was first destroyed, then a team of 95 cattle were attached to the building and it was hauled near the south church. Peace eventually came to the little community and the building was repaired but the school never attained any large success. It was destroyed by fire in 1839."

Return to Rte. 4A and continue east.

(12) Turn off Rte. 4 onto Rte. 118 and follows signs to 5,000-acre **Cardigan State Park**, on the western slope of 3,121-ft. Mt. Cardigan. Several hiking trails, including the moderately difficult, three-mi. West Ridge Trail beginning in the parking area, lead to a fire tower at the treeless, granite summit of "Old Baldy" (a fire in 1855 left the top barren). The Appalachian Mountain Club maintains **Cardigan Mountain Lodge** on the mountain's eastern flank.

(13) Continue east on Rte. 4; watch on the right for Tewksbury Pond, a popular spot for trout fishing. That's 1,785-ft. Isinglass Mountain to the west. In **Grafton Center**, look for the turnoff for **Ruggles Mine** just across from the 1798 Congregational Christian Church .

In 1803 Sam Ruggles discovered mica on his property on the side of Isinglass Mountain. Knowing that the semi-transparent mineral was used in the manufacture of lamp chimneys and stove windows, he set his family to mining and hauling it by teams of oxen to Portsmouth for shipment to relatives in England, who sold it. For many years the family worked only at night, fearful that the mine's location would be discovered.

After the Ruggles family, several corporations, including General Electric and Bon Ami, worked the mine and removed feldspar and huge "books" of mica up to three and four feet across. Today, Ruggles Mine is open to the public. Although it's primarily an open pit mine, there are also giant rooms and tunnels with arched ceilings to explore, and visitors can drive up an access road to the summit of Isinglass Mountain for views of the surrounding mountains and countryside. Mineral collection is permitted, and more than 150 kinds, including beryl, rose, and smoky quartz, have been harvested (blasting operations in 2000 exposed many new veins). It's estimated that about $30 million in valuable minerals have been taken from the mine since Sam Ruggles discovered it.

(14) Continue east on Rte. 4, alongside the Smith River, through Grafton to **D a n b u r y**, called Cockermouth until 1788 when local folk requested the name be changed. The trails at **Ragged Mountain Ski Area** are great for off-season hiking.

(15) Continue on Rte. 4. At **Potter Place** an historic marker remembers Richard Potter, a 19th-century magician and ventriloquist who is buried nearby on a small plot of his once-extensive estate.

It's difficult for a roadside marker to do justice to the rich legend of Richard Potter. G. Dana Taylor, in a letter to the editor of the December, 1906 issue of Houdini's *Conjurers' Monthly Magazine*, does a better job:

"He was born in 1783 and lived 52 years. He was part Hindoo and was married ... Potter was a hypnotist and a celebrated ventriloquist. Here are a few wonders he performed. Before a score of people and in the open air, free from trees, houses or mechanisms, he threw up a ball of yarn and he and his wife climbed up on it and vanished in the air. A person coming up the road was asked what the people were gazing at, and being told, he said he met them [the Potters] going down

the road. Potter also crawled through a solid log. One day he happened to be passing a farm, where several men were trying to start a load of hay, which was to be pulled up the hill into a barn. Potter laughed at them and unhitching the horses, he produced a rooster from his pocket and hitching him on with a string he pulled the load up into the barn. The next morning when they went to pitch off the hay, they found it at the foot of the hill ... Potter Place, N.H. is named after him and in his door yard is erected a small gravestone inscribed 'In Memory of Richard Potter, the Celebrated Ventriloquist, Aged 52 years. Died Sept. 20, 1835.' Beside him lies his wife, who died at 45 years of age ..."

Potter was actually the son of MAssachusetts colonial official Sir Charles Henry Frankland, an English baronet born in India, and Dinah, one of his Black servants.

Just past the Potter marker is the sign for Covered Bridge #15, the 1882 Town lattice truss Keniston Bridge which spans the Blackwater River. Note how the overhangs at each end are supported by heavy slanting timbers, giving, as Ms. Kenyon says in *New Hampshire's Covered Bridges*, "an impression of forward thrust not unlike that of the raked prow of a ship cutting through water." Beyond the bridge is the Old Center Cemetery.

The Andover Historical Society Museum exhibits its collection in an 1874 Victorian-style railroad station in Potter Place.

(16) In 1848 the four-year college preparatory Proctor Academy opened in a Unitarian church in **Andover.** Except for a short period in the late 1800s, when it relocated to Wolfeboro, the school has dominated the small rural town since it opened, and today its 250-acre campus lines both sides of Rte. 4.

(17) Continue east to **Salisbury**, on the western bank of the Merrimack and Pemigewasset Rivers. At the intersection, turn north (left) onto Rte. 127 to North Rd. to the **Daniel Webster Birthplace**. The brilliant orator and statesman was born in this two-story frame house (moved from its original, nearby location and later restored) in 1782, and spent his early years here. It's filled with period furnishings and Webster memorabilia.

(18) Back on Rte. 4, continue through **Boscawen** to the **Hannah Dustin Memorial State Historic Site**, on an island at the confluence of the Merrimack and Contoocook Rivers. The 35-ft.-high statue commemorates Mrs. Dustin who, in March 1697, a week after giving birth in Haverhill, Massachusetts, was taken prisoner in an Indian raid and forced to march with her child, "Captive," toward Canada. One night while the Indians slept, Hannah grabbed a hatchet and, with help from some of the other captives, killed and scalped her captors. She was rewarded with a bounty when she returned to Haverhill with 10 scalps.

(19) Continue on Rte. 4, along the Canterbury Scenic and Cultural Byway and underneath I-93, and turn north (left) onto Rte. 132. Take a right turn onto Center Road into **Canterbury Center**, with its fine country store, 1736 Town Hall, and historic cemetery.

From here, follow signs to **Canterbury Shaker Village**. Founded in the 1780s, it was the sixth in an eventual string of 19 Shaker communities that stretched from Maine to Kentucky. At its peak in 1860, about 300 people lived here in 100 buildings on 4,000 acres, and, like their brothers and sisters in Enfield, farmed, sold seeds and herbs, manufactured medicines, and crafted useful articles.

This village, however, is preserved far better than Enfield. The last Canterbury Shaker, Sister Ethel Hudson, died in 1992 at the age of 96, and the village remained in Shaker hands since its inception. Twenty-four of the original buildings stretch over 694 acres,

123

and approximately half are included in the 90-minute tour designed to bring the Shaker legacy to life. Artisans demonstrate traditional Shaker crafts, and offer classes throughout the season. The **Creamery Restaurant** serves lunch, and four-course, family-style candlelight dinners by reservation from May through October on Fridays and Saturdays; and on Saturdays in April, November and December. There's also a gift shop.

Follow signs to Rte. 106 and head south (right) back to Concord.

Information

Greater Concord Chamber of Commerce (224-2508), 40 Commercial St., Concord 03301. www.concordnhchamber.com. Information kiosk on State House Plaza Memorial Day-Columbus Day.

Greater Lebanon Chamber of Commerce (448-1203), P.O. Box 97, on the Mall, Lebanon 03766. www.lebanonchamber.com.

Lodging

(1) Centennial Inn (225-7102). 96 Pleasant St., Concord 03301. www.someplacesdifferent.com. 32 rooms and suites, dining room, and a lounge in Victorian brick building. $$-$$$

(1) Comfort Inn (226-4100), 71 Hall St., Concord 03301. Chain motel with indoor pool, hot tub and sauna. $$

(1) Courtyard Marriott (225-0303), 70 Constitution Ave., Concord 03301. 90 rooms, suites, indoor pool, jacuzzi, and exercise room, restaurant, and conference center. $$-$$$

(1) A Touch of Europe B & B (888-228-9131 or 225-5741), 85 Centre St., Concord 03301. www.atouchofeurope.com. Three guest rooms with private baths in historic home near downtown. $-$$

(4) Turtle Pond Farm B & B Cottages (877-861-8623 or 456-2738), 4 Bean Rd., Warner 03278. www.turtlepondfarm.com. Gracious lodging on 16 acres surrounded by the Mink Hills. Pool and spa in season, tennis, and hiking trails. $$

(7) Inn at Ragged Edge Farm (735-6484), New Canada Rd., Wilmot 03287. www. raggededgefarm.com. C. 1790 country estate with 17 guest rooms, suites and family lodgings, tavern, indoor pool, tennis, sauna, sundeck. $$-$$$

(7) Riverview Farms Inn (800-392-9627 or 526-4482), 1 Village Rd., Wilmot Flat 03287. Restored inn has junior and master suites with antiques and kitchenettes; one with fireplace. $$-$$$

(9) Mary Keane House (888 239 2153 or 632 4241), Lower Shaker Village. www.tneorg.com/marykeane. Gracious Victorian on grounds of Shaker Village has rooms and suites with private baths, and a private beach. $$

(9) Shaker Farm B & B (800-613-7664 or 632-7664), Rte. 4A, Enfield. www.shakerfarm.com. New England's oldest Shaker B&B, built in 1794, has six guest rooms (three with private baths), a lovely common room, and spacious grounds. $-$$

(9) (R) The Shaker Inn at the Great Stone Dwelling (888-707-4257 or 632-7810), 447 Rte. 4A, Enfield 03748. www.theshakerinn.com. All rooms have private baths, and Shaker reproduction furniture with some original detailing. $$-$$$

(11) The Inn on Canaan Street (523-7310), 92 Canaan St., Canaan 03741. Spacious guest rooms, bountiful breakfast buffets, and 14 acres of gardens, fields, and meadows. $$

(12) Cardigan Mountain Lodge (744-8011), R.F.D. 1, Bristol 03222. www.outdoors.org. Appalachian Mountain Club property offers a variety of lodging options, including platform tents, campsites, and two- to five-bunk rooms; family-style meals. Mid-June to Labor Day and weekends until Columbus Day. $

(14) Inn at Danbury (768-3318), P.O. Box 137, Rte. 104, Danbury 03230. www.innatdanbury.com. Thirteen nicely appointed guest rooms (some with fireplaces) in a c. 1870 farmhouse and addition. Outdoor heated pool, patio, adult hot tub, and English gardens. Saturday dinner by reservation. $$

(14) Schoolhouse Corner B & B (768-3467), 61 Eastern District Rd., Danbury 03230. Family-friendly, rambling inn overlooking Ragged Mountain has three guest rooms and a suite (two with private bath), a guest kitchen, TV room, and lots of porches to enjoy the views. $-$$

(16) Highland Lake Inn (735-6426), Maple St., E. Andover. www.highlandlakeinn.com. 10 spacious rooms with private baths in graciously restored, 1767 B&B. Beach access. $$

(17) Horse Haven B& B (648-2101), 462 Raccoon Hill Rd., Salisbury 03268. Comfortable rooms with shared bath in 1805 farmhouse on working horse farm. $

Restaurants

(1) Durgin Lane Deli (228-2000), 2 Capital Plaza, Concord. Middle-Eastern treats include stuffed grape leaves and falafel. B, L, D. Closed Sun. BYOB. $

(1) **Endicott Grill** (224-0582), 6 Pleasant St., Extension, Concord. Sophisticated fare at one of the city's "in spots" includes fresh seafood, Angus beef, and home baked flatbreads. $-$$

(1) **Hermanos Cocina Mexicana** (224-5669), 11 Hills Ave., Concord. Authentic cuisine, a tequila bar, and live music on weekends.$

(1) **Tio Juan's** (224-2821), 1 Bicentennial Sq., Concord. Mexican fare and cocktails served in the cells of the former police station. $

(5) **Blackwater Junction Restaurant**, Blackwater Jct. B, L, D. $

(7) **La Meridiana** (526 2033), Rte. 11, Wilmot. Northern Italian fare including calamari, *osso buco*, veal served by candlelight; homemade deserts such as cannoli and *zuppa inglese*. Extensive wine list. D $$

(9)(L) **Shaker Inn at the Old Stone Dwelling** (632-7810), Rte. 4A, Shaker Village, Enfield. Specialties in this restored Shaker-style restaurant include gourmet herb lunches, soups, salads, pan seared Atlantic salmon, and roasted duckling. B, L (in season), D, Sun. brunch (closed Mon.). $$

(15) (L) **Potter Place Inn & Restaurant** (735-5141), 88 Depot St., Andover. Contemporary American cuisine featuring fresh fish, poultry, beef, pork and veal. Save room for homemade desserts. D (closed Mon. in winter). $$

(19) **The Creamery Restaurant** (783-9511), 277 Shaker Rd., Canterbury. $-$$

Attractions

(1) **Christa McAuliffe Planetarium** (271-7827), 3 Institute Dr., Concord. Reservations rec. Tues.-Sun. $

(1) Eagle Square Marketplace, N. Main St., Concord.

(1) First Church of Christ, Scientist, N. State and School Sts., Concord. Mary Baker Eddy contributed money to build Concord's highest building.

(1) Kimball-Jenkins Estate (225-3932), 276 N. Main St., Concord. Costumed docents greet visitors to this 1882 Victorian brick and granite mansion, with many of its original furnishings.

(1) Merrimack River Outdoor Education Area and Conservation Center (224-9945), 54 Portsmouth St., Concord. 75 acres of woods and riverfront; solar-heated headquarters of the Society for the Protection of New Hampshire Forests.

(1) Museum of New Hampshire History (226-3189), The Hamel Center, 6 Eagle Sq., Concord. Two floors of exhibits in a 19th-century stone warehouse. Tues.-Sat., 9:30-5; Thurs. and Fri. until 8:30; Mon. 9:30-5 in Dec. and July-Oct. 15. $

(1) New Hampshire Historical Society (225-3381), 30 Park St., Concord. Mon.-Fri. 9-4:30; Sat. and Sun. noon-4:30.

(1) New Hampshire State House and State House Plaza (271-2154), 107 N. Main St., Concord. Self-guided tours weekdays.

(1) The Pierce Manse (224-9620), 14 Penacook St., Concord. Mid- June-Labor Day, Mon.-Fri. or by appt. $

(1) Silk Farm Audubon Center (224-9909), 3 Silk Farm Rd., Concord. 20 acres, Society HQ. Nature store.

(1) St. Paul's School (225-3341), 325 Pleasant St., Concord. The Hargate Art Center exhibits works by well- and less-known artists.

(1) Upham-Walker House, 18 Park St., Concord. 1831 Federal-style home of Nathaniel Upham is decorated with period furnishings.

(2) NH Antiquarian Society (746-3825), 300 Main St., Hopkinton. Thurs & Fri. 10-5; Sat. 10-2.

(4) Mt. Kearsarge Indian Museum (456-2600), Kearsarge Mountain Rd. Warner. May-Oct., Mon.-Sat. 10-5; Sun. 1-5. $

(4) Rollins State Park (456-3808), Rte.103, Warner. Seasonal. $

(6) Winslow State Park (526-6168), off Rte. 11, Wilmot. Seasonal. $

(9) Enfield Shaker Museum (632-4346), 24 Caleb Dyer Lane, Rte. 4A, Lower Shaker Village, Enfield. Memorial Day-Halloween, Mon.-Sat. 10-5; Sun. 12-5; after Halloween-Memorial Day, Sat. 10-4 and Sun. noon-4. $

(9) La Salette Shrine & Center (632-7087), Lower Shaker Village, Rte. 4 A, Enfield.

(12) Cardigan State Park (548-3373), off Rtes. 4 and 118, Orange. Picnic area, hiking trails. Seasonal. Seasonal. $

(13) Ruggles Mine (523-4275), Rte. 4, Grafton. Mid-May-mid-Oct., daily 9-5 (until 6 in July and August); last ticket sold an hour before closing. $

(14) Ragged Mountain Ski Area (768-3475), off Rte. 4, Danbury.

(17) Daniel Webster Birthplace (934-5057), Flaghole Rd., Franklin. Mid June-Labor Day, weekends 10-5. $

(19) Canterbury Shaker Village (783-9511), 288 Shaker Rd., Canterbury. May-Oct., 10-5 daily; April, Nov., and Dec., weekends. $

Activities

(1) Capitol Center for the Arts (225-1111), 44 S. Main St. Big name entertainment to classic movies.

(1) Contoocook River Canoe Company LLC (753-9804), Concord. Canoe and kayak sales and rentals; shuttle service.

(1) Hannah's Paddles Canoe Livery (753-6695), Concord. Canoe and kayak rentals on the Merrimack River.

(19) Tamarack Farm (783-9226), 125 Ashby Rd., Canterbury. Sugarhouse tours, hay and sleigh rides, syrup and cream.

Off the Drive

New Hampshire International Speedway (783-4931), Rte. 106 N., Loudon. NASCAR and motorcycle racing at the New England home for the Winston Cup and Loudon Motorcycle Classic.

Tight Lines Fishing Services (800-526-6550 or 526-9299), Elkins Business Loop, Elkins. Fishing guide service and fishing equipment.

Art Galleries/Crafts

(1) Capital Craftsman Romance Jewelers (224-6166), 16 N. Main St., Concord. Handcrafted gifts and jewelry, pottery, porcelain, and other media.

(1) Gondwana Imports (228-1101), 86 N. Main St., Concord. One-of-a-kind global artifacts including African sculpture, natural fiber clothing, and jewelry.

(1)Heart & Soul (225-4155), 34 Pleasant St., Concord. Pottery, rugs, and woodenware from the art studio at Riverbend Mental Health Center; clothing, jewelry, and musical instruments from around the world.

(1) League of NH Craftsmen (228-8171), 36 N. Main St., Concord. Juried handcrafted gifts and furnishings by regional craftspeople.

(1) Mill Brook Gallery & Sculpture Garden (226-2046), 236 Hopkinton Rd. (Rte. 202/9), Concord. Sculpture gardens with fountains and birdbaths, and an art gallery. April - Dec.

(3) The Artisan's Barn (746-2899), 849 Main St., Contoocook. Eclectic mix of NH handcrafts includes pottery, baskets, jewelry, and furniture. Closed Mon.

(3) Covered Bridge Frame Shop & Gallery (746-4996), Fountain Square, Contoocook. Works by NH artists; special exhibits.

(9) Dana Robes Wood Craftsmen, Inc. (800-722 5038 or 632-5385), P.O. Box 708, Lower Shaker Village, Enfield. Craftsmen build Shaker-design pieces, from lumber selection to final assembly. Also, wooden giftwear.

(16) Ragged Mountain Woodworks (735-6100), 7 Pleasant Rd., Andover. Hardwood furniture inspired by Shaker and early American traditions. Weekdays; weekends by appt.

(18) New Hampshire Art Association (799-6414), 150 King St., Boscawen. Paintings, original etchings, photography and sculpture. Tues.-Thurs., 10-4.

Shopping

(1) Borders Books, Music, Video,and Cafe (224-1255), 76 Fort Eddy Rd., Concord.

(1) Executive Sweets (226-1022), 2 Capital Plaza, Concord. Truffles, Swiss fudge, gourmet white hot chocolate, and other goodies.

(2) Beech Hill Farmstand (224-7655), 107 Beech Hill Rd., Hopkinton. Homemade baked goods, local products, make-your-own sundaes,and farm animals. May-Oct.

(2) The Fragrance Shop (746-4431), College Hill Rd. Hopkinton. 18th-century barn with more than 250 varieties of field grown plants; display garden; herb wreaths, dried flowers, and crafts. Mid April-Dec., Tues.-Sat.

(2) Gould Hill Orchards (746-3811), 656 Gould Hill Rd., Contoocook. Aug.- Thanksgiving.

(7) Farm Mt. Wool Co. & Elk Farm (526-9665), N. Wilmot Rd., Wilmot. Pastures of grazing elk; store features NH woolen comforters, homespun and mill spun yards, washable sheepskins, maple syrup, elk products. Sat. and by chance.

(7) Kearsarge Lodge Antiques (927-4594), Kearsarge Valley Rd., Wilmot. Americana, primitives, folk art, decoys, painted items, and more. Daily in season; Tues.-Sun. winter.

(11) Enfield Granite Company (523-8204), Rte. 4, Canaan. Granite gifts of all sorts. Closed Sun.

(19) Heritage Herbs and Baskets (753-9005), Hannah Dustin Rd., Canterbury. Herb garden, and a barn packed with handmade baskets, books, herbs, and other handicrafts. May-Oct.

(19) Old House Smoke House (800-339-4409 or 783-4405), off Shaker Rd., Canterbury. Wood-smoked meats including bacon, turkey, ham, duck, salmon and trout; and cheeses, wine, and jams. Also, antique radio museum. Labor Day-New Year's, daily; closed Mon. rest of year.

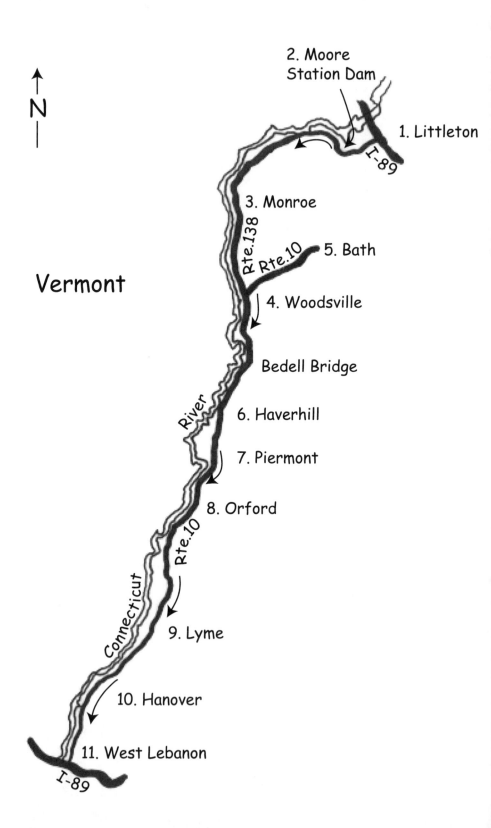

N

2. Moore Station Dam

1. Littleton

I-89

Vermont

3. Monroe

Rte.138

Rte.10

5. Bath

4. Woodsville

Bedell Bridge

6. Haverhill

River

7. Piermont

8. Orford

Rte.10

Connecticut

9. Lyme

10. Hanover

11. West Lebanon

I-89

Drive 7

The Northern Connecticut River Valley

62 miles

This drive along the northern reaches of the Connecticut River, since colonial times the border between new Hampshire and Vermont, begins at the enterprising town of Littleton and winds through lovely, sparsely-settled dairy country. Gracious old towns such as Orford and Lyme seem little changed since the earliest steamboats plied the river, well over 150 years ago. At the drive's southern end, one of America's most renowned colleges surrounds a picturesque village green.

(1) In the late 1800s, a single factory in **Littleton** turned out 20,000 axes and scythes in a year. Sheep farms in surrounding rural communities supplied wool to the town's mills, which worked overtime during the Civil War to weave cloth for uniforms. And a man named Ben Kilburn, who had a talent for photographing mountain scenery, founded a company that by the turn of the century was the largest producer of stereopticon images in the world.

The swift-flowing Ammonoosuc River which supplied the water power for these factories (the river drops a total of 235 ft. through a series of rapids as it passes through town) continues to flow, and Littleton still makes things like shoes and abrasives, and a black fly bite treatment appropriate to these climes come late spring.

But today, tourism keeps the town's economic wheels turning. Littleton's once-workaday Main Street is no longer given over solely to necessities -- although the buildings that house today's cafés and boutiques retain their 19th-century character, especially above ground-floor level. The best way to explore is on foot. Stop in at the **Chamber of Commerce** for a copy of the brochure, "Walking Tour of Main Street." Among the highlights along the route are the Community Center, housed in an 1884 Queen Anne-style mansion representative of the grand homes that once lined Main Street; and the 1880s Tilton Opera Block, Littleton's largest brick building, in which Henry L. Tilton planned to house a sumptuous performance space for grand opera. Much to his dismay, the town's Musical Society voted to attach an opera house to the 1895 Town Building (the structure with the four-story octagonal tower), and the wide double doors on the first and second floors of Tilton's building -- meant to serve as an entrance to the hall -- go nowhere to this day. Plays and musical performances are still presented in the Opera House in the National Historic Register Town Building.

The Georgian Revival movie theater in the Salomon Block (now Jax Jr. Cinemas 1 & II) was Littleton's first "picture show," and the venue for the 1941 world premiere of "The Great Lie," starring Littleton-area summer resident Bette Davis. The star drew the largest crowd in the town's history when she arrived for the premiere.

The white-columned Greek-Revival **Thayers Inn**, one of the state's oldest, has been in continuous operation since it was built between 1848 and 1850 to accommodate tourists brought here by the railroad. The public rooms are impeccably Victorian, and the accommodations range from simple but tidy to quite plush. Even if you're not staying here, climb up to the cupola, five stories above the street, for a wonderful view of the town and the hills beyond. Then check out the one guest room kept just for show, and preserved as it looked when the hostelry opened. A few doors up is the venerable **Littleton Diner**, cosmetically remodeled on the outside but every bit the 1940s beanery inside. The food is o.k.; the ambiance is classic.

The 1880s Tannery Building at 111 Saranac St. housed the Saranac Buck Glove Company, founded in 1869 by Ira Parker, who revolutionized the industry with a unique tanning process. By the early 1900s the firm was using more than 350,000 skins to produce 82,000 pairs of gloves and mittens each year. It supplied gloves to every governor of the state of New Hampshire, to the U.S. Military during WW II, and to Admiral Richard Byrd, who wore Saranac's gloves on expeditions to the North and South Poles.

Side Trip

From Main St., head east out of town a few blocks on Rte. 302 and turn right, by the hospital, onto Mt. Eustice Rd. to visit one of the area's most poignant sights, the Wallace Horse Cemetery. The word "cemetery" might be a bit grandiose for this small, fenced-in wooded plot that holds the remains and tack of several beloved Morgan horses who belonged to the Wallace family from 1889 until 1919. We doubt that the horses were Jewish, but in that religion's time-honored tradition of placing a stone on the grave of a loved one, horse lovers leave behind mementos of their visits.

Head west out of town on Rtes. 18/135 toward the Connecticut River and Vermont. For a bird's eye view of Littleton, and a great view of the Presidential Range to the east, park at **Kilburn Crags Park** and follow the trail for about a mile to the scenic lookout.

(2) Continue west to the State of New Hampshire Welcome Center overlooking **Moore Station Dam**, New England's largest conventional hydroelectric station. Moore is part of the Fifteen-Mile-Falls Development, a three-station hydroelectric project that has been

producing electricity from the power of the river's steep falls since 1926. About 100 years ago this stretch was the most dreaded section for workers driving logs to mills downriver. The concrete and earth dam here is 2,920 ft. long and 178 ft. high, and, with 3,490 acres of storage, the reservoir is one of the North Country's larger bodies of water. The facility generates enough electricity to power a city the size of Providence, R.I. The reservoirs and tailraces created by the dams attract wildlife such as muskrats, beaver, otters, ducks, geese, osprey, and bald eagles. There's a boat launch, and a picnic area.

When New York Governor DeWitt Clinton, father of the Erie Canal, was visiting Fifteen Miles Falls, he was asked if a canal could be built to connect the Connecticut and St. Lawrence rivers. He said that the task would be impossible, but predicted that the power of the falls would later be put to use.

Turn south on Rte. 135 onto one of the state's "Scenic and Cultural Byways" for your first glimpse of the Connecticut River Valley. Much of the land here is devoted to small dairy farms which, like their counterparts across the river in Vermont, are steadily diminishing in number due to the grim equation of rising production costs and flat or decreasing milk prices.

Comerford Station, at one of the narrowest spots on the river, is home to a second hydroelectric station, capable of generating enough power to supply electricity to 17 cities approximately the size of Littleton. The dam is more than 2,200 ft. long and reaches 17 ft. at its highest point. There's a boat launch, and a small sandy beach.

(3) Watch for bald eagles near the third and smallest facility at McIndoe Falls Dam, just north of **Monroe**.

(4) The 1829 **Haverhill-Bath covered bridge** which spans the Ammonoosuc River as you come into **Woodsville** is the oldest bridge entirely located within New Hampshire. It's a Town lattice design (see Drive 3) with a sidewalk on one side, giving it a saltbox effect. In its early days, the bridge was a meeting place for salmon fishermen who would salt their catch down and ship it all over the country.

With its brick buildings and old-fashioned storefronts, Woodsville, a one-time railroad center at the junction of the Ammonoosuc and Connecticut Rivers, has an early 20th-century, small-town America movie set feel. The town wasn't named for its location, or for its principal product -- prior to the coming of the railroad in 1854, a sawmill was the main industry -- but for John L. Woods, who bought the mill in 1829 and helped to develop the town.

Side Trip

(5) In Woodsville, turn east on Rte. 302 to Bath, home of the state's longest covered bridge, the 400-ft.-long Bath Village bridge. Built in 1832 and restored in 1988, the Burr truss bridge is nicknamed the "Kissing Bridge" (so are a lot of others in New England; covered bridges offered temporary privacy in small towns where everybody had their eyes on everybody else). The circa 1790 National Register of Historic Places Brick Store claims to be America's oldest continuously-operated general store. In the time-honored tradition of country stores, it sells everything from homemade fudge and baked beans to weathervanes and natural soaps. As you head back toward Woodsville on Rte. 302, detour east (left) on Rte. 112 a short distance to the 1810 Swiftwater covered bridge, one of New England's most scenic spots. "Big Eddy" -- the swimming hole under the bridge--is a wonderful place to take a dip.

Why were bridges covered in the first place? There are almost as many answers as there are country sages to offer them -- including the suggestion that horses were less likely to become skittish in mid-crossing if they couldn't look down at the water. The real reason, however, is that the builders simply wanted to protect the framework and roadbeds from the elements.

When Rte. 135 ends just outside Woodsville, continue south on Rte. 10. Watch on the right for a state historic marker which tells the story of Robert Rogers and his famed "Rogers' Rangers," who were supposed to rendezvous with a supply party sent north from Fort No. 4 (*see Drive 4*) after destroying an Indian village in St. Francis, Quebec on October 4, 1759. When the men arrived, near exhaustion and out of supplies, they discovered that their relief party had already come and gone. Many subsequently died of starvation and exposure. As the marker grimly puts it: "early settlers found their bones along these intervales."

The intervales lying among the hills between Woodsville and Hanover to the south are among the prettiest parts of the Connecticut Valley and the state. The landscape alternates between snug little towns and empty valleys, once farmed but now grown back to forest, that seem like the loneliest places in New England outside the great Maine woods. But the next town always comes along quickly enough, just when you crest a hill and expect another stretch of forest.

If you're in North Haverhill (pronounced HAY-v'ril) at the end of July, you're in time for the classic North Haverhill fair. The fairgrounds are just to the south of town.

Just past the junction of Rtes. 25 and 10, turn right and follow the narrow dirt road to **Beddel Bridge Historic Site**, where the last of five covered bridges to span the river at this location (the first was erected in

1866) was washed away in a storm on Sept. 14, 1979 -- just after it had been restored. There's a grassy picnic area overlooking the river.

(6) The surprise in **Haverhill --** perched high above the river -- is the elegant Historic District with its large, neat Common bordered by a fine collection of Federal-era and Greek Revival homes and handsome public buildings, including the 1816 Haverhill Academy (founded in 1794). Had Eleazar Wheelock accepted the town's offer of 50 acres in 1770, a much larger institution would have surrounded the Haverhill Common today. But Wheelock turned Haverhill down, and instead built his Dartmouth College farther south in Hanover. Haverhill was left to be remembered as the home of Colonel Charles Johnston, a hero of the Battle of Bennington (his circa 1770 house, the first frame house in town, is near the Common), and as the site, in 1868, of the last public hanging in New Hampshire. Turn left onto Court St. to see Alumni Hall, the town library, and several antique shops.

While trying to steal $3,000 his employer, George Maxwell, had earned from the sale of his farm, laborer Samuel Mills killed Maxwell with an axe. After rooting through Maxwell's effects, Mills found the proceeds: $30 in cash and the balance in IOUs. Mills then stole Maxwell's horse and buggy, rode to Gorham, and hopped a train west. A persistent Boston detective tracked him to a copper mine in Illinois and brought him back for trial. More than 3,000 people came to Haverhill on May 6, 1868 to see him hung. Marching to the gallows, he addressed the crowd: "I'm guilty. I hope to be forgiven. I bid farewell to this world and hope we shall meet in heaven. Tell the people that Samuel Mills died like a man." (*Yankee* magazine, May 1968).

One day in the late 1700s Jonathan Arnold, the founder of St. Johnsbury, Vermont, stopped with his bride at the Haverhill home of his friend, Samuel

141

Ladd. As the couple was leaving the next day, Mr. Ladd picked up a willow switch Mrs. Arnold had dropped by the doorway and stuck it into the dirt nearby. He told the young woman that there was a saying that if this was done, the woman who dropped the switch would marry someone in that house. Several years late the widow Arnold and Mr. Ladd were wed. The switch grew into a bush.

Near Haverhill, the Connecticut River cradles a wide stretch of fertile land called the Great Oxbow, known by the Indians as *Ump-Ammonoosuc* ("a fair fishing place"). In 1770 provincial officers John Hazen and Jacob Bayley petitioned the colonial government for a road to run through the untamed wilderness from the seacoast to the new town of Haverhill. Province Road, as it was called, ended at the meadows of the nearby Little Oxbow.

(7) The hills near tiny **Piermont**, on a plateau overlooking the Connecticut Valley, were once quarried for stone to make whetstones. Today the major industry is **Gould's Country Smokehouse**, which has been smoking meat and poultry since 1921.

(8) **Orford** is regarded by many as the loveliest of all the Upper Valley towns. Washington Irving said, "In all my travels in this country and Europe I have never seen any village more beautiful than this. It is a charming place; nature has done her utmost here." The town's outstanding architectural feature is the string of seven white mansions, built between 1773 and 1839, that line "The Ridge" above Rte. 10 and the river. One, the circa 1815 General John B. Wheeler House at the southern end of the row, was designed by Asher Benjamin during his association with Charles Bulfinch. The oldest house belonged to inventor Samuel Morey.

In 1793 Orford resident Samuel Morey (brought here by his father in an ox cart when he was four years old) made history when he launched the nation's first steam-powered paddlewheel boat on the Connecticut River. The story goes that he was so incensed when Robert Fulton was later given credit for the invention, that he scuttled his craft in nearby Lake Morey.

Just south of town, detour a short distance on Rte. 25A to **Mt. Cube Farm,** owned by the family of the late Meldrim Thompson, a former New Hampshire governor and newspaper publisher. On Saturday mornings from July to October, the proprietors serve up pancakes with syrup made at the farm.

(9) Continuing south, Rte. 10 winds along the east bank of the Connecticut to **Lyme**, chartered in 1761 and once the sheep-raising capital of New England. The village is clustered around a big, grassy Common whose centerpiece is the elegantly-spired, 1812 Lyme Congregational Church. The bell, cast by Paul Revere, rings on the hour. Behind the church is an old cemetery, worth a brief stroll. Next to the church is the longest line of contiguous horse sheds in New England. Built in 1810 by the son of the church's builder, they once numbered 50: 27 remain.

During the 19th century, Lyme was a stop for stagecoach passengers traveling between Boston and Montreal, and between Littleton and Concord; at one time there were 13 inns to accommodate them. Today, the 1809 **Alden Country Inn**, built by a descendent of John Alden of Pilgrim fame, is the town's chief hostelry. **Lyme Country Store** is a fun spot to poke around, and stock up on picnic supplies.

(10) "It is a small college," Daniel Webster once said in a landmark court case regarding the charter of **Dartmouth College**, his alma mater, "but yet there are those who love it." Indeed there are -- many more so

143

now than in 1818, when he spoke. But beloved though Dartmouth still may be, it is "small" only by the standards of the giant institutions with which it makes up the Ivy League. For a small New England town like **Hanover**, Dartmouth is big enough, and old enough, long since to have obscured any distinction between the campus and the community. To outsiders, Dartmouth is Hanover, and Hanover Dartmouth.

The town does predate the school, although not by very many years. In 1761 Governor Benning Wentworth, that prolific creator of colonial New Hampshire towns (generally to his own benefit, as he was in the habit of keeping the choicest acreage for himself) issued a charter for a tract of 22,400 acres on the east bank of the Connecticut River where Hanover now stands. The parcel was a township in name only for nearly four years, until in the spring of 1765 Colonel Edmund Freeman and his family traveled upriver to carve a farm out of what still was wilderness. It was Freeman, by most accounts, who gave the town the name of the ruling English House of Hanover.

Meanwhile, far to the south, in Lebanon, Connecticut, Reverend Eleazar Wheelock was contemplating a move of his own, one that would forever change the fledgling village of Hanover. Wheelock ran a Christian school for young Indians, and had been busy raising funds with which to relocate and expand his mission. He sent one of his former pupils, a Mohegan preacher named Samson Occom, on a speaking tour of England to solicit contributions for this venture. Occom must have been an impressive character -- quite apart from the proof he offered of the efficacy of the King James Bible and a Latin grammar when applied to a New England native -- because he came back with a pledged endowment of £11,000 sterling and the patronage of the Earl of Dartmouth.

Thus fortified, Rev. Wheelock began to entertain invitations from a number of communities that wanted the new school within their borders. Hanover won, through successful use of the same tactic a modern town might use to lure a corporate headquarters to its new office park: it offered land (3,000 acres), money, lumber, and the manpower of its citizens. What the yeomen hoped for in return were prestige and improved real estate values. Little did they suspect they were in for a medical school, a ski jump, a winter carnival, an art museum, the **Hanover Inn**, and one of the great libraries of North America.

King George III granted Rev. Wheelock the charter for Dartmouth in 1769, and the following year he arrived in Hanover with his books. The later-adopted motto of Dartmouth College -- *Vox Clamantis in Deserto*, "A Voice Crying in the Wilderness" -- is a quite accurate suggestion of what those earliest years must have been like, with Rev. Wheelock holding classes in a log cabin. Wilderness though it may have been, however, the picture didn't include many Indians. They simply never showed up, and before long Dartmouth was a white man's college. It graduated four students at its first commencement exercise in 1771 (Gov. John Wentworth, Benning's nephew and successor, arrived via a 75-mi. road he had built for the occasion from his summer residence in Wolfeboro (*see Drive 8*).

Today the college has highly respected liberal arts and mathematics departments, and counts among its graduate facilities the renowned Amos Tuck School of Administration and Finance. The Dartmouth Medical School is affiliated with several hospitals and a string of community clinics.

A tour of the campus need not stray from the Green, as most of the buildings of architectural or historic interests to outsiders border it almost directly. Be sure to visit **Baker Memorial Library**, the college's central library, on the northern side of the green. Its holdings include: 150 volumes of *incunabula* (books printed before 1501); the Hickmott Shakespeare Collection, including copies of all four folios, nearly 40 quarto volumes, all known pre-1700 editions of *Macbeth*, and more than 200 volumes representing the finest achievements of the bookbinder's art; all first and limited editions of Stephen Crane; a comprehensive Melville collection; and the first three volumes of the enormous "elephant folio" edition of John James Audubon's *Birds of America* in the original copies owned by Daniel Webster (speculation is that Webster didn't own Volume Four because he didn't pay Audubon for the first three). In the basement reading room, Mexican artist Jose Clemente Orozco painted a series of murals illustrating his critical view of the triumph of Western civilization in the New World; the murals were executed while Orozco was teaching in the art department between 1932 and 1934.

The other not-to-be-missed attraction at Dartmouth is the **Hood Museum of Art**. Among the collections are American 18th-century portraits, works by Italian masters, an abstract by Dartmouth grad Frank Stella, and Picasso's *Guitar on the Table*. In front of Parkhurst Hall on North Main St. is the school's landmark 94-ft. Parkhurst Elm.

Before leaving Hanover, stop in at the local **League of New Hampshire Craftsmen**. Established in 1932 to preserve traditional hand craftsmanship (*see Drive 8*), the League represents hundreds of craftspeople whose works are juried and on display for sale at locations throughout the state (others are in Concord, North Conway, Exeter, Meredith, Wolfeboro Falls, and Center Sandwich (the last is also known as Sandwich Home Industries).

(11) In **West Lebanon**, turn right onto Rte. 12A at the Dunkin Donuts and drive the next few miles past a sprawl of big box stores, fast food restaurants, and malls. I-89 is just ahead.

Information

Greater Lebanon Chamber of Commerce (448-1203), P.O. Box 97, On the Mall, Lebanon 03766. www.lebnanonchamber.com.

Hanover Area Chamber of Commerce (643-3115), 216 Nuggett Building, Main St. PO Box 5105, Hanover 03755. www.hanoverchamber.org.

Littleton Area Chamber of Commerce (444-6561), 120 Main St., P.O. Box 105, Littleton. www.littletonareachamber.com

***

For a free, comprehensive guide to *Canoeing on the Connecticut River,* call PG&E at 653-9232.

Lodging

(1)(R) Adair, A Country Inn (444-2600), 80 Guider Lane, Bethlehem 03574. www.adairinn.com. Elegant lodging features beautifully-decorated guest rooms with period antiques; suites and cottages also available. The landscaped grounds were designed by the Olmsted Brothers. Tim-Bir Alley (see "Restaurants" below) has an excellent reputation. $$$-$$$$

(1)(R) The Beal House Inn and Flying Moose Cafe (888-616-BEAL or 444-2661), 2 W. Main St., Littleton 03561. www.BealHouseInn.com. Restored, 1833 inn close to town has eight pleasant rooms and suites with private baths, four-poster beds and down comforters; some fireplaces. The restaurant specializes in wood-grilled cuisine, homebaked breads, and super desserts. $$

(1) Littleton Motel (444-5780), 166 Main St., Littleton. The state's oldest motel is right in town. Outdoor pool; discount at Bethlehem Country Club. Non-smoking. $$

147

(1) **The Mulburn Inn** (800-457-9440), 2370 Main St., Bethlehem 03574. www.mulburninn.com. Cary Grant and Barbara Hutton spent their honeymoon in the Adams Room, one of seven in this handsome turn-of-the-century Victorian estate built for the F.W. Woolworth family. $$

(1) **Thayers Inn** (444-6469), 111 Main St., Littleton 03561. www.thayersinn.com. 40 rooms and suites with private baths, TV, AC, and phones. $-$$

(6) **The Gibson House** (989-3125), RR l, Box 193, On the Green, Haverhill 03765. www.gibsonhousebb.com. The 1850 National Register home, studio and gallery of artist Keita Colton has four luxury guest rooms with private baths, great views, and fabulous gardens. $$$

(7) **Piermont Inn** (272-4820), One Old Church St., Piermont 03779. Late-1700s stagecoach stop has two spacious, antiques-filled rooms in the original inn and four in an adjacent carriage house; all have private baths. Dinner by advance reservation. $-$$

(8) **White Goose Inn** (800-358-4267 or 353-4812), Rte. 10, P.O. Box 17, Orford 03777. 1766 brick house has 10 guest rooms in the main house and four in the newer Gosling House next door. $$

(9)(R) **Alden Country Inn** (800-794-2296 or 795-2222), On the Common, Lyme 03768. www.aldencountryinn.com. Restored inn has 15 updated rooms with private baths, phones, and AC. The Tavern & Grille serves dinner nightly, breakfast weekends, and a fine Sun. brunch. $$-$$$

(9) **Breakfast on the Connecticut** (888-353-4440 or 353-4444), 651 River Rd., Lyme 03768. Riverfront estate has 15 rooms with private bath (some with whirlpools and gas fireplaces), TV, VCR, and phones in main house and a round barn. Dock, kayaks, and canoes. $$-$$$

(9) Loch Lyme Lodge (800-423-2141 or 795-2141), 70 Orford Rd., Rte. 10, Lyme 03768. Year-round 1784 main lodge with four rooms, and 26 cabins open Memorial-Labor Day. Private beach, rowboats, canoes, windsurfer, tennis courts. Seasonal restaurant. No credit cards. $-$$

(10) Chieftain Motor Inn (800-845-3557 or 643-2550), 84 Lyme Rd., Hanover 03755. www.chieftaininn.com. Pleasant motel accommodations on the river two miles north of town. $-$$

(10)(R) Hanover Inn (800 443-7024 or 603-643-4300), On the Green, Hanover 03755. www.HanoverInn.com. Dartmouth's elegant, 4-story, 92-room inn overlooking the campus is *the* local gathering place. Restaurants a wine bistro and the formal Daniel Webster Room (see below). $$$

Restaurants

(1) Bishop's Homemade Ice Cream Shoppe (603-444-6039), 183 Cottage St., Littleton. Seasonal. $

(1) Littleton Diner (444-3994), 145 Main St., Littleton. B, L, D. $

(1) The Miller's Fare (444-214), 16 Mill St., Grist Mill, Littleton. Riverside deck, fresh baked goods, coffee bar, sandwiches, deli salads, wine and beer. L. $

(1) Tim-Bir Alley (444-6142), Adair Country Inn, Old Littleton Rd., Bethlehem. One of the North Country' finest restaurants serves new American cuisine with Southeast Asian and southwest American overtones. Reservations. D Wed. - Sun. in season. $$-$$$

(1) Topic of the Town, Main St., Littleton. Old-fashioned, family restaurant with solid, American fare. B, L, D. $

(4) Chalet Schaefer (747-2071), 85 Central St., Woodsville. German cuisine and, in foliage season, game dishes including wild boar and bison. L Mon.; L, D Tues.-Fri.; D Sat. $$ *check this*

(4) Central West Restaurant (747-8249), 23 Central St., Woodsville. Salads, sandwiches, and heartier American fare served in casual surroundings. L, D. $

(4) Wells River Diner. Classic diner cooking. B, L, D. $

(7) Colatina Exit (802-222-9008), Main St., Bradford, VT. Cross the river for good, reasonably-priced Italian food served by candlelight. $-$$

(10) Daniel Webster Room (643-4300 or 800-443-7024), Hanover Inn, Hanover. Fine continental cuisine served in the formal dining room; terrace overlooking the Green open in warmer months. $$-$$$

(10) La Poule á Dents (802-649-2922), Main St., Norwich, VT. Cross the river for gourmet French specialties such as seafood risotto with shrimp, lobster and salmon, with truffle infused olive oil; the desserts are homemade. $$-$$$

(11) Shorty's Mexican Roadhouse, Rte. 12A, (near Kentucky Chicken), W.Lebanon. Southern New Hampshire chain serves up large portions of well prepared South of the Border fare. $-$$

(11) A Taste of Africa's Karibe Tulé (863-1275), Briggs Opera House, 2 Main St., White River Jct., Vt. Genuine African cuisine, with dishes such as curried goat and peanut chicken stew. D Wed.-Sun. $-$$

Attractions

(1) Littleton Historical Museum (444-6586). Exhibit of Kilburn stereoscopic viewers, local art and historical memorabilia. Wed. 1:30-4:30 or by appt.

(2) Moore Station Dam, Fifteen Mile Falls Development, N. Monroe 03771. Visitor Center Memorial Day-Columbus Day weekend. Grounds open daily.

(5) Bedell Bridge Historic Site (323-7350), off Rte.10, N. Haverhill.

(10) Dartmouth College. Hood Museum of Art (646-2808), Dartmouth Green, Hanover. Tues.-Sat., 10-5; Sun. noon-5.

(10) Montshire Museum of Science (802-649-2200), Norwich, VT. Cross the bridge from downtown Hanover to this first-rate, hands-on museum on 100 acres. $

(10) Webster Cottage (646-3371), N. Main St., Hanover. 1780 home of the daughter of Dartmouth College's founder; Daniel Webster lived here during his senior year (1801). Seasonal; call for hrs.

Activities

(8) Boland Balloons (802-333-9254), Post Mills Airport, W. Fairlee, VT. Hot air balloon rides.

(8) Mt. Cube Farm (353-4814), Rte. 25A, Orford.

(8) Fairlee Marine (802-333-9745), Rte. 5, Fairlee, Vermont. Rents 17 ft. aluminum canoes, 14 ft. rowboats with 2 hp motor and trailer; and party barge with 15 hp motors. June 1-Sept. 1.

(10) Dartmouth Outdoor Rentals (445-2371), On the Green, Hanover. Bicycle rental.

(10) Dartmouth Riding Center at Morton Farm (646-3508), Hanover. Trail rides.

(10) Hanover Hot Tubs (643-6003), 11 Lebanon St., Hanover. Personal hot tub rentals; 1/2 hour or longer.

(10) Hopkins Center (642-2422), Dartmouth Green, Hanover. Live theater and film.

(10) Ledyard Canoe Club (643-6709), Hanover. On the river, north of Ledyard Bridge. Canoe and kayak rental.

(10) Storrs Pond Recreation Area (643-2134), off Rt. 10, Reservoir Rd., Hanover. Swimming in 15-acre pond with sandy beach or in Olympic-sized pool. Picnicking, nature trails. $

Antiques, Crafts and Galleries

(1) Tannery Marketplace (444-1200), 111 Saranac St., Littleton. Architectural antiques, collectibles, and artisans' studios and galleries in the historic Saranac Tannery building.

(10) League of New Hampshire Craftsmen (643-5050), 13 Lebanon St., Hanover. Open Mon.-Sat.

(12) Colonial Antiques Market (298-8132 or 298-7712), Colonial Plaza, Rte. 12A, W. Lebanon. 100+ antiques and collectibles booths; outdoor flea market Sun. in season, weather permitting.

Shopping

(1) Chutter's General Store (444-5787), Main St., Littleton. Proclaimed by the Guinness Book of World Records to have the largest candy counter of earth, the 112 ft., three-tiered counter holds more that 600 jars of candy.

(1) Littleton Grist Mill (444-7478 or 888-284-7478), 22 Mill St., Littleton. Renovated mill houses shops, a restaurant, and gallery.

(7) Gould's Country Smokehouse (272-5856), Rte. 10, Piermont.

(8) Mt. Cube Farm (353-4709 or 353-4814), Rte. 25, Orford.

(9) Lyme Country Store (795-2213), On the Common, Lyme.

(10) Dartmouth Bookstore (800-462-9009 outside NH; 800-624-8800 in state). One of the state's largest bookstores -- with more than 130,000 titles-- has been family owned since 1884.

(10) Hanover Park, 40 S. Main St., Hanover. Stores include Kaleidoscope, which sells wood products from around the world, and Pompanoosuc Mills, which manufactures high-end wood furniture.

(12) Power House Mall, Rte. 10, W. Lebanon.

Not on Drive

Ammonoosuc River Trading Company & Marketplace (444-1136), 3247 Rte. 302, Lisbon. Large collection of antiques, reproductions, folk art, weathervanes and gifts housed in a 200-year-old barn.

N

W. Rattlesnake Mtn.
Natural Area

12. Center Sandwich

11. Rte.113   Rte.109

10.
Squam
Lake   13. Moultonborough(Old Country Store)

Holderness   Rte.171 14. Loon Center

Rte.3   8.
Center   15. Castle in the Clouds
Harbor
9.   Rte.109 16. Abenaki Tower

Chamberlain-
Reynolds Forest

7.   Rte.100
Meredith   Lake
Winnipesaukee   17. Libby Museum

Weirs Beach 5. Rte.11B   1. Wolfeboro

Rte.3   4.
Ellacoya
6.   State Beach
Laconia   3.   Rte.28
Mount Major

2.
Alton Bay

Drive 8

Around Lake Winnipesaukee

78 miles

Lake Winnipesaukee, 28 miles long and with 283 miles of shoreline, is the largest freshwater lake contained entirely within one state in the U.S. It has 274 wooded islands, and is surrounded by three mountain ranges: the White Mountains, and the Ossipee and the Belknap Ranges. This drive circles the lake, and takes in places as diverse as a center for New Hampshire craftsmanship, a neighboring lake famous for its movie role, and an industrialist's dream castle.

Lake Winnipesaukee takes its name from an Indian word roughly translated as "smile of the Great Spirit." The story goes that centuries ago Ellacoya, daughter of Chief Ahanton of the Penacook Tribe which lived along the northern shores of the lake, was courted by Kona, the chief of a hostile tribe to the south. Ahanton was at first enraged to find Ellacoya in love with his sworn enemy, but Ellacoya prevailed on her father not to kill Kona. Impressed as much by Kona's bravery as by his daughter's Pocahontas-style entreaties, Ahanton gave the couple his blessing. After the wedding feast, Kona and Ellacoya set out under starry skies for Kona's village, and at the moment their canoe reached the middle of the lake the clouds parted and the sun emerged to sparkle on the waters.

Legend aside, recent archaeological excavations have documented that Native Americans camped on Winnipesaukee's shores as early as 8000 BC. The Penacook encampment, Aquadochtan, along the once-narrow stream that connects Paugus Bay to the lake proper, is believed to have been one of the largest seasonal Indian communities in New England. Discoveries of arrowheads, stone knives, household artifacts, and even gravesites, verify the site's importance.

Modern-day anglers are drawn to the big lake for much the same reason as those early inhabitants: Winnipesaukee continues to offer some of New Hampshire's best salmon and trout fishing.

(1) **Wolfeboro**, the largest town on the lake (we're not counting Laconia, which has frontage only on Paugus Bay), calls itself "America's oldest summer resort" because of its popularity with a single discriminating vacationer. It was here, on a smaller nearby lake later named after him, that Colonial Governor John Wentworth created his 6,000-acre country estate in 1769 (*see Drive 9*).

Today, Wolfeboro, on Wolfeboro Bay, is a bustling resort town. Main Street is lined with boutiques and restaurants. Private yachts and sightseeing boats (including the **M/S Mount Washington**; see below) bustle in and out of the harbor, jockeying for space with windsurfers and water skiers. A good way to sightsee (particularly in summer, when traffic can be extremely frustrating) is aboard **Molly the Trolley**. Among Wolfeboro's places of interest are **Hampshire Pewter Company**, where you can watch craftsmen create fine "Queen's Metal" pewter pieces; Brewster Free Academy (52 S. Main St.), built to educate students "of good moral character;" the Romanesque Municipal Building, with its handsome clock tower; **Wolfeboro Historical Society's** museum complex, which includes a 19th-century schoolhouse, a replica of an early firehouse, and an 18th-century farmhouse; the natural history **Libby Museum** (see p. 166); and the **Wright Museum**, showcasing the enterprising spirit of Home Front America during WW II with a huge collection of memorabilia, vehicles, films and artifacts.

The **New Hampshire Antique & Classic Boat Museum** traces the history of pleasure boating in the Lakes Region

(2) Head south out of town on Rte. 28 along the eastern shore of the lake to **Alton Bay**. The first M/S *Mt. Washington* was built here in 1872, and the town is now a port of call for its 230-ft. predecessor.

That huge building overlooking the bay is **Bay View Pavilion**. It first opened for business in 1921 as a roller skating rink and dance hall, but soon provided a venue for big name entertainers including Louis Armstrong, The Dorsey Brothers, and Harry James. The original building burnt in 1928, but was quickly rebuilt and now hosts a variety of entertainment, Fourth of July fireworks, and music festivals. Free summer concerts are presented at the town's bandstand.

One day in March, 1996 a privately-owned dam on nearby Meadow Pond gave way, flooding the streets of Alton Bay with 92 million gallons of water, and opening a 30-ft.-deep, 600-yd.-long sinkhole on Rte. 140. The ensuing damage, a result of design flaws and construction errors, cost $5 million to repair.

----

(3) Head west out of town on Rte. 11 along the shores of Alton Bay. After approximately 4 1/2 mi., watch for signs for **Mount Major**. The 3-mi. hike to the summit follows an old logging road for some distance before getting steeper and traversing several ledges. At the 1,780-ft. summit there's a stone shelter built in 1925 and terrific views.

(4) As you continue along the southwest shore, the Ossipee and Sandwich Mountains loom across the lake. **Ellacoya State Beach**, the only state swimming area on the lake, has a 600-ft. sandy beach,

bathhouse, refreshment stand, and picnic area.

(5) Turn off Rte. 11 onto Rte. 11B to **Weirs Beach**. Native Americans used a basket-woven trap called a "weir" to catch shad passing through the Weirs Channel as the fish migrated from from Lake Winnipesaukee to the Merrimack River.

The town in whose name the old Indian weir survives is easily the gaudiest -- and in summer, the busiest -- of Lake Winnipesaukee's shoreside communities. It's been a major tourist destination since the second half of the 19th century when the Boston, Concord, and Montreal Railroad first pulled into town; by 1900, four express trains arrived daily from Boston. Weirs Beach is a little bit of Wildwood, New Jersey in New Hampshire, with video arcades, bowling alleys (which use the diminutive "candlepins"), water slides, and even an annual Miss Winnipesaukee pageant. It's also the mid-point for the **Winnipesaukee Railroad**, and home port of the M/S *Mount Washington.*

When the old M/S *Mt. Washington* burned, owner Captain Leander Lavalee had two options: he could buy a new boat at a cost upwards of $250,000, or he could shop for a used vessel. Opting for the latter, Capt. Lavallee purchased the 203 ft. iron-hulled steamship *Chateaugay*, an 1888 Lake Champlain passenger ship that had been converted to an automobile ferry in 1925. He paid $20,000, then had the superstructure removed and the hull cut into 20 sections for rail shipment from Burlington, Vermont to Lakeport, on Paugus Bay. Once reassembled, the hull was fitted with a new superstructure and two triple-expansion steam engines. Rechristened *Mt. Washington II*, the boat was launched on Winnipesaukee in August 1940. Capt. Lavalee's company went bankrupt and, after the war, new owners refitted the old steamship with twin diesel engines. She emerged as the *M/S Mount Washington*. This is the vessel which sails out of Weirs Beach today.

In 1652, Governor John Endicott of the Massachusetts Bay Colony sent an expedition up the Merrimack River. Members discovered Lake Winnipesaukee, and carved their initials on the appropriately-named Endicott Rock to mark the colony's northern boundary. Today the rock is a State Historic Site, and stands -- with the initials still visible -- in **Endicott Rock Park** in the center of town. There's a swimming beach here ($10 parking fee in season).

Although it's primarily a family resort, the atmosphere at Weirs Beach changes for a weekend every June during the Loudon Classic Motorcycle Weekend (*see below*).

Side Trip

Consider renting a boat and heading to Stonedam Island Wildlife Preserve for a delightful day on the largest undeveloped island in the lake. There's a self-guided nature tour, and occasional nature programs organized by the Lakes Region Conservation Trust, which administers the island.

Side Trip

(6) Head south on Rte. 3 and bear right onto Business Rte. 3 into Laconia. Throughout its history as an industrial center, the city has been home to companies manufacturing everything from nails to knitting machines to railroad cars. The oldest original brick textile mill in America, Belknap Mill, now houses a textile museum and arts center. But most people associate the town with New Hampshire International Speedway's annual Loudon Classic (also known as "The Nationals"), a June event that draws more than 100,000 motorcyclists and racing fans. Although the track is actually 10 miles away, Laconia is the major service area for the throngs.

----

(7) Head north out of Weirs Beach on Rte. 3, past a raft of antique stores, restaurants, the **Funspot**, and motels, to **Meredith**, the self-proclaimed "latchkey to the White Mountains" (note: coming into town, you'll pass a **League of New Hampshire Craftsmen** store. It's an offshoot of the main store that we'll be visiting in Center Sandwich (*see #12 below*). Before I-93 was built through the Pemigewasset Valley to the west of here, the latchkey metaphor meant a good deal more, but in any event, Meredith is still a good staging ground for further exploration of the shores of Winnipesaukee and smaller nearby lakes.

At the intersection of Rtes. 3 and 25, a portion of **The Inns and Marketplace at Mills Falls** is housed in a turn-of-the-century linen mill straddling water running from an underground canal connecting Lake Waukewan in the hills above to Winnipesaukee below. The **Waterfall Café** at the top of the waterfalls is a delightful spot for breakfast or a light lunch. Turn left here to go into downtown Meredith.

Side Trip

(8) Turn east (right) onto Rte. 25 and head into to the village of Center Harbor. Once clustered with small summer hotels, today this is a quiet community of private homes -- and two fine inns. The old-fashioned Red Hill Inn, a 35-room lakefront mansion, was built in 1904 by Leonard Tufts, whose father invented the ice cream soda fountain. The building was very nearly burned down for fire department practice before its 1985 salvation by the present innkeepers. The Tudor-style Kona Mansion, built in 1900 by one of the partners in Boston's Jordan Marsh department store, is on 100 acres, and has a 9-hole, par-3 golf course, tennis courts, private beach, and a boat dock.

(9) Take Rte. 25B west from Center Harbor back toward Rte. 25 for a few miles. Turn right onto

College Road to the Chamberlain-Reynolds Memorial Forest and take the 3.4 mile hike up Red Hill for spectacular views of Winnipesaukee and Squam Lake (*see below*). There's also a boardwalk through the wetlands habitat, where a sharp eye can spot great blue herons, ducks, belted kingfishers and nesting loons. In late August and September, watch for migrating warblers. The property is administered by the Squam Lakes Association (SLA). There's also a swimming beach here.

----

(10) Continue north on Rte. 3 (If you've taken the side trips immediately above, continue to the intersection of Rte. 3 and turn north) to **Squam Lake**, the second largest of New Hampshire's more than 1,300 glacially-shaped lakes and ponds. Along with Katharine Hepburn and Henry Fonda, Squam starred in the 1981 movie *On Golden Pond* -- but you'd never know the lake had been discovered by Hollywood when you drive into its main village, sleepy **Holderness**. This is primarily because, with the exception of one stretch of back road that connects Center Sandwich with Center Harbor, hardly any of the routes that circle the lake come anywhere near its shores.

Development is tightly controlled by the **Squam Lakes Association**, and it's not hard to imagine that, 20 years later, Norman Thayer of *Golden Pond* fame would still be entirely at home in one of the lake's tasteful cottages, set well back from the shore. Turn right onto Rte. 113 to reach the **Science Center of New Hampshire**, a 200-acre nature center with native wildlife in a woodland setting, nature trails, interactive exhibits, and animal programs. Hop aboard one of the center's 28-ft. pontoon boats for a loon cruise, or take their Golden Pond Tour, and then visit the three-acre, low-maintenance Kirkwood Gardens.

When the production crew for *On Golden Pond* were

161

ready to shoot the loon scenes, they had a problem: there were no loons on Squam Lake. They contacted Herb Cilley, a retired University of New Hampshire maintenance man and self-taught ornithologist who lives at Bow Lake, to the south. Mr. Cilley brought some loons up from his lake so they could get their shot. In 1991 he was presented with the North American Loon Foundation's "Outstanding Friend of the Loon" award.

Ready to enjoy a secluded picnic or take a dip? Rent a canoe, kayak, three-person sailboat or 14-ft. electric boat at the Squam Lakes Association and head to Moon or Bowman Island. Both allow primitive camping with advance reservations.

Rte. 113 winds through some of the state's prettiest countryside, past horse farms, lakes, and old cemeteries (there's a particularly interesting one just after you enter Sandwich).

Side Trip: West Rattlesnake Mountain Natural Area

(11) If you're up for a short, somewhat steep, but extremely rewarding hike, turn right onto Pinehurst Rd. about 4 9/10 mi. past the Science Center, and continue for 9/10 mi. (bear left at the fork). Park just before the gate at the "Pinehurst" sign, and follow signs to the Pasture Trail -- it begins on the left by an old sugarhouse. The trail leads to the peak of 1,260- ft. West Rattlesnake Mountain, where there are views of the lakes, islands, and surrounding mountains. Just before the summit, look for the clump of gnarled red pine trees. If you're feeling ambitious, you can cross the Ridge Trail to 1,289 ft. East Rattlesnake.

---

(12) At the intersection of Rtes. 113 and 109 is the lovely village of **Center Sandwich,** surrounded by the

Ossipee Mountains, Red Hill, and the Squam and Sandwich ranges. The village is famous as the place where the **League of New Hampshire Craftsmen** got its start. Its predecessor, Sandwich Home Industries, was the 1926 creation of Mrs. J. Randolph Coolidge, a wealthy Massachusetts native who encouraged the preservation, practice and teaching of traditional home artisanry, and helped set up a shop where New Hampshire natives could sell their handicrafts. In 1931 the state government got behind the idea, and the League of Arts and Crafts -- later the League of New Hampshire Craftsmen -- began to establish stores throughout the state. The descendant of the original shop is still here, selling everything from pottery to handcrafted toys to homemade jams. Across the street is the **Corner House Inn**, a fine place for lunch or dinner: be sure to poke through the inn's antiques and country gift shop.

The **Sandwich Historical Society Museum** operates the 1850 Elisha Marston House, a handsome, antiques-filled Cape Cod structure with subtle Greek Revival decoration. The Methodist Meetinghouse, with its unusual free-standing brick chimney, is one of the most photographed buildings in the state. Sandwich Fairgrounds on the outskirts of town comes to life in early October with the Sandwich Fair, a traditional country fair held since the 1880s (for information, call 274-7062).

Take Rte. 109 south out of town toward Sandwich.

Side Trip

Since 1987 the people of Sandwich and Tamworth have been working to protect more than 3,000 acres of undeveloped land in the Bearcamp Valley, home to the pristine Bearcamp River immortalized by John Greenleaf Whittier (who summered in Tamworth) in his poem *"Sunset on the Bearcamp."* Today, the Bearcamp River Trail crosses six parks, preserves and public conservation properties, 10 privately-managed

tree farms, six unpaved town roads, and a dozen historic sites.   It offers several hiking options, including a one- to two-mi. walk, or a 12-mi. hike from Sandwich Notch in the White Mountain National Forest to Hell's Gate, a rocky gorge in South Tamworth. For a brochure, send a self-addressed stamped envelope and a request for a *Bearcamp River Trail Guide* to the Sandwich Land Trust, Sandwich Town Hall, Center Sandwich 03227.

----

(13) The **Old Country Store** at the intersection of Rtes. 25 and 109 in **Moultonborough** was built as a stagecoach stop in 1781, and is one of the oldest continually-operating stores in America.   Among the exhibits in the upstairs museum is the Concord Coach which passed through town in the mid-1800s.   The store is a trove of New Hampshire-made products, groceries, and gifts.

Turn left onto Rte. 25, which coincides with Rte. 109 for a short distance. On your left, at the intersection of Rtes. 25 and 109, the experts at the **Winnipesaukee Skydiving Center** at Moultonborough Airport take just a half-hour to teach you to jump from more than 10,000 ft. Of course, you'll be securely attached to a professionally certified Tandem instructor, so your 45-second free fall will be closely monitored. The entire experience takes 5-7 minutes, and you'll be able to view the lake from a unique perspective, indeed. If you'd rather something a bit tamer, sightseeing flights are also offered.

(14) Turn south (right) and continue on Rte. 109. At Moultonborough Central School, turn right onto Blake Rd. and follow signs to the 193-acre **Loon Center and Markus Audubon Wildlife Sanctuary,** headquarters for the Loon Preservation Committee. Remember those loons in *On Golden Pond* ? Some were really decoys, one of which is on exhibit in the center, which is devoted to loon education and preservation. You can press a button to hear the harrowing cry and idiot laugh of the bird whose population is decreasing in

New England as humans intrude upon their breeding grounds. Trails pass through woodlands, upland forests, marshes, streams, and a mile of Lake Winnipesaukee shoreline, where, if you're lucky, you'll hear the real McCoy.

Side Trip

(15) Back on Rte. 109, bear left off Rte. 109 onto Rte. 171 for the short drive to the not-to-be-missed Castle in the Clouds, the wonderfully eccentric centerpiece of a 6,300-acre estate that shoe industrialist Thomas G. Plant designed as a retirement home for himself in 1913. The mansion, built of granite quarried on site and overlooking the Ossipee Mountains, is filled with household conveniences that Mr. Plant created, including a centralized intercom system, a central vacuuming system with its own incinerator, and a self-cleaning oven. Mr. Plant's favorite room, the library, had a secret private reading room that only he had access to.

Mr. Plant moved here in 1914 with his bride, Olive, who was 24 years younger and a foot taller than him. The couple lived here until Mr. Plant died -- destitute -- in 1941. A combination of factors contributed to his bankruptcy, including a devastating fire at his Boston shoe plant (said to be the largest single fire in Boston's history); and investment in Russian bonds just before the October Revolution, and in sugar just before its collapse after World War I. But when offered money in return for permission to harvest his land, Mr. Plant refused: he didn't want to damage his property. At the time of his death he was in debt for approximately $500,000. His friends took up a collection for his burial.

In addition to touring the estate, visitors can rent horses at the stable for a one-hour guided trail ride, and take a tram to tour the Castlesprings water bottling facility and Lucknow microbrewery.

165

----

(16) Backtrack to Rte. 109 and continue south through Melvin Village, on Tuftonborough Bay. Just past the village, watch on the left for **Abenaki Tower.** A 6/10 mi. trail goes to the tower, whose steep ascent offers rewarding views of Lake Winnipesaukee and the Ossipee Mountains.

(17) On the outskirts of **Wolfeboro**, overlooking Winter Harbor, dentist Henry Libby built the **Libby Museum** in 1912 to house his extensive collection of mounted specimens and local artifacts. Among the objects displayed are Abenaki maps and drawings, artifacts from the site of Gov. John Wentworth's summer home, and a 350-year-old dugout canoe. A plaque next to the museum commemorates the 67-mi. road that Gov. Wentworth built to travel to Dartmouth College for the 1771 commencement.

Information

Alton/Alton Bay Chamber of Commerce (875-5777) P.O. Box 550, Alton 03809. Information at the bandstand and pavilion in the center of town.

Greater Laconia/Weirs Beach Chamber of Commerce (524-5531), 11 Veterans Square, Laconia 03246. www.laconia-weirs.org.

Lakes Region Association Information Center (800-60-LAKES for brochure; or 744-8664), P.O. Box 430, New Hampton 03256. www.lakesregion.org.

Lakes Region Conservation Trust (279-3246), P.O. Box 1097, Meredith 03253. www.lrct.org.

Meredith Area Chamber of Commerce (877-279-6121 or 279-6121), P.O. Box 732, Meredith 03253. www.meredithcc.org.

Squam Lakes Area Chamber of Commerce (968-4494), 3 Thompson St., Ashland 03217.

www.SquamLakesChamber.com.
Squam Lakes Association (968-7336), U.S. Rte. 3,
P.O. Box 204, Holderness 03245.
www.squamlakes.org.

Squam Lakes Conservation Society (279-1309), P.O.
Box 796, Meredith 03253.

WWW.WEIRSBEACH.COM. On-line vacation planning
guidebook.

Wolfeboro Chamber of Commerce (800-516-5324 or
569-2200), P.O. Box 547, Wolfeboro 03894.
www.wolfeborochamber.com

Lodging

(1) The Heritage on Lake Winnipesaukee (formerly
Pick Point Lodge) (800-282-1533, 569-1533 days;
569-5233 evenings), P.O. Box 1200, Wolfeboro Falls
03896. www.ivacation.com. Private waterfront,
fireplaced cottages (up to four bedrooms with three
baths), two private sandy beaches, and boats. May-
Oct. $$$

(6) Shalimar (800-742-5462 or 524-1984), Rte. 3,
Winnisquam 03289. www.shalimar-resort.com. Lake
resort has singles, double, and king accommodations;
a full-service restaurant; private beach; paddle and
row boats and canoes; indoor heated pool; jacuzzi;
whirlpool; and sauna. $$-$$$

(1) Pow Wow Lodges & Motel (569-2198 May-mid-Oct;
225-2968 mid-Oct-May), Mirror Lake, Wolfeboro
03894. Lakefront housekeeping cottages with
individual docks and small private beaches for each
unit; motel with two-room housekeeping units and
single rooms. $$-$$$

(1)(R) The Wolfeboro Inn (800-451-2389 or 569-
3016), 90 N. Main St., Wolfeboro.
www.wolfeboroinn.com. Deluxe accommodations in a

167

restored, 1812 inn with a modern addition overlooking the bay. Each of the 44 individually-decorated guest rooms and suites have baths, TV, and AC; some have water views and decks. Private beach and boat cruises. New England cuisine and Italian fare in the 1812 dining room; lighter fare in the tavern. $$$

(5) Naswa Resort (888-556-2792 or 366-4341), 1086 Weirs Blvd., Laconia 03246. www.naswaresort.com. Lakefront cottages, motel and efficiencies. Beach, docks, and watercraft and Sea-Doo rentals. Dining room with entertainment. $$-$$$

(7) Inns at Mill Falls (800-622-6455 or 279-7006), Rtes. 3 & 25, Meredith. www.millfalls.com. Three year-round, lake-front inns with in-room fireplaces, indoor pool, restaurants, and saunas. $$-$$$

(7) The Nutmeg Inn (279-8811), 80 Pease Rd., Meredith. 1763 inn has eight guest rooms with private baths, original floor boards, secret passages, and some fireplace. Outdoor pool. $$

(8)(R) Kona Mansion (253-4900) P.O. Box 458, Center Harbor 03226. 10 guest rooms; four one- and two-bedroom housekeeping cottages, and two three-bedroom chalets. Breakfast and dinner in the ornate, Victorian dining room. MAP available. $$-$$$

(8)(R) Red Hill Inn (800-5-RED HILL or 279-7001), Rte. 25B, Center Harbor 03226. www.redhillinn.com. 23 guest rooms--many with fireplaces, private balconies and great views, in the inn, 1850 Farmhouse, and adjacent cottages. $$-$$$

(10)(R) The Manor on Golden Pond (800-545-2141 or 968-3348), Rte. 3, Holderness. Turn-of-the century estate overlooking Squam Lake has 17 well-appointed guest rooms and 6 suites, and cottages. Most have wood burning fireplaces and views, some have two-person whirlpools. The restaurant has a fine reputation and an outstanding wine list. $$-$$$ www.manorongoldenpond.com.

(13) Olde Orchard Inn (800-598-5845 or 476-5004), Rte. 109, Lees Mill Rd., Moultonborough 03254. www.oldeorchardinn.com. 1790 Federal on 12 acres has nine guest rooms with private baths. $$

On Lake Winnipesaukee

Three Mile Island (466-2727), AMC property with 47 cabins on a 43-acre wooded island. June-Sept. by reservation. Education programs, sailing, swimming.

Restaurants

(1) (L) Lakeview Inn (569-1335), 120 N. Main St., Wolfeboro. American and continental specialties, and home baked breads and pastries; lighter fare in the lounge. Rooms ($$) with private bath in the inn and adjacent motel. D $$-$$$

(1) Bittersweet (569-3636), Wolfeboro. International menu with German and Italian specialties. $-$$

(2) Shibley's (875-3636), Rte. 11, Alton Bay. Popular drive-in serves up seafood, burgers, ice cream. L, D $

(4) Victorian House (293-8155), Rte. 11, Gilford. 1821 Victorian-style stagecoach stop specializes in regionally-raised meats and produce. D $-$$

(5) J T's Bar-B-Q and Seafood (366-7322), Rte. 3, Weirs Beach. Family-friendly spot serves up popular favorites including including ribs, chicken, lobster pie, and prime rib. $

(5) Kellerhaus (888-KLR-HAUS), Rte. 3, Weirs Beach. Home of the "Build Your own Sundae"; candy store, waffle breakfast. $

(7) Hart's Turkey Farm Restaurant (279-6212), Rtes. 3/104, Meredith. Since 1954, featuring turkey, prime rib, seafood, and pasta. Homemade pastries and ice

cream. $-$$

(7) The Boathouse (279-2253), Inn at Bay Point, Meredith. Part of the Common Man chain, the restaurant on the bay turns out creative dishes in upscale surroundings. $$-$$$

(7) Café Lafayette (800-699-3501), S. Main St., Meredith. Hop aboard a restored, 1924 Pullman railcar for a five-course gourmet meal as the train makes a 2 1/2 hour tour of the lake. Sat.-Wed., end of May-Labor Day. $$$

(10) Squam Lakeside Farm, Rte. 3, Holderness. Three home cooked meals daily, including lobster rolls; homemade ice cream. $

(12) Corner House Inn (284-6219), Center Sandwich. Dinner at this 150-year-old former inn features lobster and mushroom bisque, and entrées such as double thick lamb chops and shellfish sauté. Dinner nightly; lunch June-Oct., and Sun. the rest of the year. $$-$$$

(13) Maurice Restaurant Francais and Bistro (476-268), Rtes. 25/ Old Rte. 109, Moultonborough. French specialties elegantly served; the downstairs bistro serves casual fare. L Mon-Fri., D. $$-$$$

(13) The Woodshed (476-2311), Rte. 109, Lees Mill Rd., Moultonborough. Popular for more than 20 years, the restaurant, in an authentic 1860s barn and farmhouse, serves American fare including prime rib, seafood, and steaks; raw bar. $-$$

Attractions

(1) Libby Museum (see #17), Rte. 109N, Wolfeboro.

(1) Wright Museum (569-1212), Rte. 28, 77 Center St., Wolfeboro.

(1) New Hampshire Antique & Classic Boat Museum

(569-4554), Rte. 28, 397 Center St., Wolfeboro.
(1) Wolfeboro Historical Society complex (569-4997 or 569-3667), South Main St., Wolfeboro. July and August; closed Mon. $

(1) Wentworth State Beach (569-3699), Rte.109, Wolfeboro. Swimming, picnicking, bathhouse. $ (*see Drive#9*)

(4) Ellacoya State Beach (293-7821), Rte. 11, Gilford. $.

(5) Stonedam Island Wildlife Preserve (279-3246), Lakes Region Conservation Trust, Box 1097, Meredith 03253 (*see "Information" above*).

(6) Belknap Mill Society (524-8813), 25 Beacon St., East, The Mill Plaza, Laconia. Lakes Region's oldest cultural center hosts art exhibits, concerts, and industrial exhibits.

(10) Maxfield Parrish Family Trust Exhibition & Museum Store (968-7348), Rte. 3, Curry Place, Holderness. Museum/gift shop.

(10) Science Center of New Hampshire (968-7194), Rte. 113, Holderness. May 1-Oct. $.

(12) Sandwich Historical Society Museums (284-6269), Maple St., Center Sandwich. Early June-Sept., Tues.-Sat.

(14) The Loon Center and Markus Wildlife Sanctuary (476-LOON), off Lees Mills Rd., Moultonborough. Center open 9-5; gift shop 10-4; grounds dawn-dusk. Free.

(15) Castle in the Clouds/Castle Springs (800-729-2468 or 476-2352), Rte. 171, Moultonborough. Mid-May-mid-October daily; weekends in May. $

(17) Libby Museum (569-1035), Rte. 109, Wolfeboro. Late May-Labor Day. $

Not on Drive

New Hampshire International Speedway (783-4931), 1122 Rte. 106N, Loudon.

Activities

(1) Lake Winnipesaukee Music Festival (800-505-2612 or 569-1440), Moody Mountain Farm, Pork Hill Rd., Wolfeboro. Performances by world-class musicians.

(1) Dive Winnipesaukee (569-8080), 4 N. Main St., Wolfeboro. Certified divers can visit wrecks aboard the dive vessel "Lady-Go-Diva". Rental gear. Shop also rents windsurfers, canoes, sailboats, rowboats, and paddle boats.

(1) Gadabout Golder Guide Service (569-6426), 79 Middleton Rd., Wolfeboro. Fishing guide service.

(1) Millie B (800-339-5257 in NH; 569-5257), Wolfeboro Town Dock, Wolfeboro. Half-hour antique speedboat rides include a pass by the former Chiang Kai-shek Estate. Daily in summer, weekend spring and fall.

(1) Molly the Trolley (800-339-5257 in NH; 569-5257). Wolfeboro, Alton, Gilford. Narrated tours on turn-of-the-century trolley; optional stop for dinner and an evening of theater at Lakes Region Summer Theatre (800-643-9993 in NH; 279-9933), Rte. 25, Meredith.

(1) Nordic Skier Sports (569-3151), Main St., Wolfeboro. Bicycle, board, and skate rentals.

(1) Piche's Ski Shop (569-8234), Lehner St., Wolfeboro (also in Gilford). Rentals of just about everything for the outdoors, including mountain bikes, rollerblades, tents, tennis, golf, watersports, skis and snowboards, and car racks.

(1) Wet Wolfe Rentals (569-1503), Back Bay Marina, Wolfeboro. SeaDoos, paddle boats, fishing and pleasure boats.

(1) The Winnipesaukee Belle (800-451-2389 or 569-3016), 90 N. Main St., Wolfeboro. 150-passenger side paddlewheeler cruises the lake.

(1) Winnipesaukee Kayak Co. (569-9926), 1 Bay St., Wolfeboro. Kayak rentals; river, lake and ocean excursions, including midnight tours.

(1) Wolfeboro Airport (569-1310), Forest Rd., Wolfeboro. Airplane and seaplane rides.

(2) Bay View Pavilion (875-3033), Alton Bay.

(2) Parker Marine and Sons (875-2600), Alton Bay. Boat rental.

(4) Gunstock (800-GUNSTOCK), Rte. 11A, Gilford. Spring-fall activities at the downhill ski area include mountain biking (rentals) and guided horseback trail rides.

(4) New Hampshire Music Festival (524-1000), 88 Belknap Mountain Rd., Gilford. Six week festival of classical music.

(5) Anchor Marine Corporation (800-366-8119 or 366-4311), Winnipesaukee Pier, Weirs Beach. Ski and deck boat, and pontoon rentals.

(5) Mount Washington Cruises (888-843-6686 or 366-531), Weirs Beach. Leaves from Weirs Beach, Wolfeboro, Alton Bay & Center Harbor. Daytime and evening dinner/dance cruises. May-Oct.

(5) Queen of Winnipesaukee (366-5005), Weirs Blvd., Weirs Beach. 46-ft. sailing yacht offers 1 1/2 and 2 hr. trips.

(5) Seaplane Services (524-0446), Rte. 3, Weirs Beach. Sightseeing rides.

(5) Surf Coaster (366-4991), Weirs Beach. Waterslides and wave pool.

(5) Thurston's Marina (800-834-4812 or 366-4811), Rte. 3, Weirs Beach. Ski and pontoon boat, and Tigershark watercraft rentals.

(5) Weirs Beach Water Slide (366-5161), Rte. 3, Weirs Beach. Slide from 2 hrs. to all day.

(5) Winnipesaukee Pier (366-5188), Weirs Beach. SeaDoo and boat rentals, arcade, and miniature golf.

(5) Winnipesaukee Scenic Railroad (745-2135), Meredith and Weirs Beach. Cruises alongside the lake weekends Memorial Day-June; daily July-Labor Day, weekends in fall.

(5) Winnipesaukee Railroad (279-5253), Weirs Beach. Turn-of-the-century coaches tour the countryside. Dinner tour (BYOB). Early May-Columbus Day.

(6) Winni's Sailboarder's School & Outlet (528-4110), Laconia. Sailboards, kayaks, sailboats and PedalBoat rentals; river trips.

(7) Meredith Marina (279-7921), 2 Bayshore Drive, Meredith. Rentals of cruising, fishing, and ski boats, canoes, boogie boards and tubes.

(7) Sports & Marine Parafunalia (279-8077), Rte. 25, Meredith Shopping Center and (293-8998), Rte. 11B, Gilford. Water ski and wakeboard rentals at both locations; kayak rentals at Gilford store.

(10) Squam Lake Tours (968-7577), P.O. Box 185, Holderness 03245. Guided tour includes a motor past Thayer Cottage immortalized in the movie *On Golden Pond*.

(10) Squam Boat Livery (968-7721), Rte. 3 at the Bridge, Holderness. Canoe, kayak, sunfish rentals.

(10) Golden Pond Tour (968-7194), Rte. 3 at the Holderness Bridge, Holderness. Squam Lake tour.

(13) Wild Meadow Canoes & Kayaks (800-427-7536 or 253-7536), Rte. 25 Moultonborough/Center Harbor Town Line. Canoe, kayak and small boat rental.

(8) Riveredge Marina (800-675-4435 or 968-4411), 81 River St., Ashland. Boat, fishing, and pontoon rentals on Squam Lake.

(10) Winnipesaukee Skydiving Center (476-JUMP), Moultonborough Airport, Moultonborough. Must be 18 years of age or older. Open Wed.-Sun. daily, by appointment Mon. and Tues.

Crafts, Galleries and Antiques

(1) Hampshire Pewter (800-639-7704 or 569-4944), 43 Mill St., P.O. Box 1570, Wolfeboro. Craftsmen use colonial techniques to create handcast Queen's Metal TM pewter. Factory tours Mon.-Fri.

(1) Kokopelli (569-4416), Rte. 28N, Center St., Wolfeboro Falls. Museum-quality Native American jewelry, hand-carved fetishes, and hand-turned wooden vases.

(6) Almost All Antiques (527-0043), 100 New Salem St., Laconia. 60+ dealers.

(6) Laconia Pottery Gallery (528-4997), 45 Court St., Laconia. New England potters make and showcase their work here.

(7) Oglethorpe (279-9909), Rte. 3, Mill Falls Marketplace, Meredith. American handicrafts include jewelry,wooden items, ironware, fibreware and

175

pottery.

(7) Old Print Barn (279-6479), 1008 Winona Rd., P.O. Box 978, Meredith. Antique and modern prints, oil paintings, watercolors and photographs.

(7) Burlwood Antique Center (279-6387), 194 Daniel Webster Highway, Rte. 3, Meredith. 175+ antique dealers in a three-story mall.

(7) Antiques at Ivy House (279-4604), Waukewan Rd., Meredith. 18th-century barn filled with American primitive, French and English County furniture, accessories, and collectibles. Also antique quilts and linens. Weekends Memorial Day-Labor Day or by appt.

(7) Annalee Doll Gift Shop and Museum (800-433-6557 or 279-3333), 44 Reservoir Rd., Meredith. Home base and headquarters for the dolls created by Annalee Thorndike. Museum has more than 500 doll and animal creations spanning over 60 years of doll making.

(12) Ayottes' Designery (284-6915), Rte. 113, Center Sandwich. Handwoven home accessories, clothing and rugs, hand-dyed yarn, and handcrafted wood and pottery. Closed Sun. and Mon.

(12) Sandwich Home Industries, League of NH Craftsmen (284- 6831), Main St., Center Sandwich. Mid-May-mid-Oct. Also, Rte. 3, Meredith (279-7920); and 64 Center St., Wolfeboro (569-3309).

Shopping

(1) Camelot Bookstore (569-1771), 16 N. Main St., Wolfeboro. Books and gifts.

(4) Pepi Herman Crystal Studio (528-1020 or 800-HANDCUT), Lily Pond Rd., Gilford. Museum, studio and gallery of hand-cut crystal.

(5) Basket World (800-528-3304 or 366-5595), Weirs Beach. Handmade baskets, furniture, and accessories.

(5-6) Old Burlwood Country Store (279-3021), Rte. 3 between Weirs Beach and Meredith. Old-fashioned country store with turn-of-the century items, penny candy, specialty foods, toys, and gifts.

(7) The Christmas Loft (279-5711), Rte. 3, Meredith. More than 10,000 ornaments, trees, and lights galore. Collectible dolls.

(7) Fermentation Station (279-4028), 72 Main St., Meredith. Home brewing supplies, cigars, and a walk-in humidor.

(7) Innisfree Bookshop (279- 3905), Meredith. General bookstore, music, toys, cards and gifts.

(7) Bayswater Book Co. (253-8858), Center Harbor. Full-service bookstore with coffeehouse ambience.

(8) Keepsake Quilting (253-4026), Senter's Marketplace, Rte. 25B, Center Harbor. "America's largest quilt shop" has more than 8,000 bolts of cotton fabric and quilts for sale.

(10) The Loon's Nest Gift Shop (968-7348), Rte. 3, Holderness. Antiques and collectibles, local maple syrup, candies, and jams, used books, and loon items.

(13) Old Country Store (476-5750), Rtes. 25/109, Moultonborough.

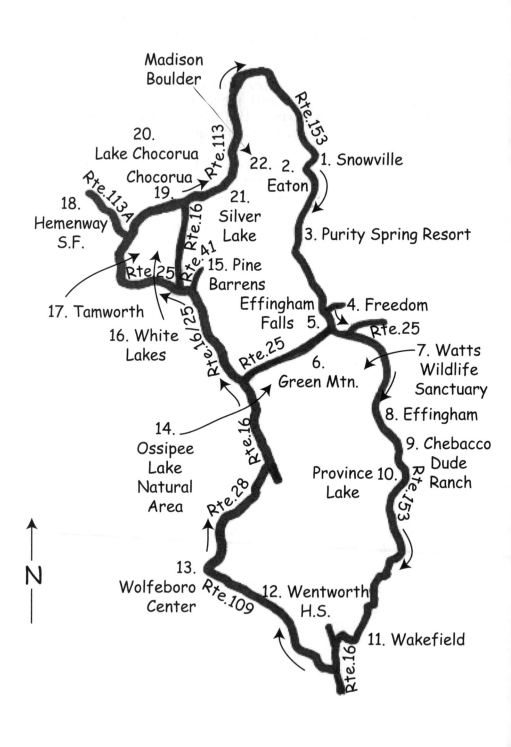

Madison
Boulder

20.
Lake Chocorua

Chocorua

18.
Hemenway
S.F.

Rte.113A

19.

Rte.113

22. 2.
Eaton

21.
Silver
Lake

15. Pine
Barrens

Effingham
Falls 5.

Rte.16

Rte.41

Rte.25

1. Snowville

Rte.153

3. Purity Spring Resort

4. Freedom

Rte.25

17. Tamworth

16. White
Lakes

Rte.16/25

Rte.25

6.
Green Mtn.

7. Watts
Wildlife
Sanctuary

8. Effingham

9. Chebacco
Dude
10. Ranch

14.
Ossipee
Lake
Natural
Area

Rte.16

Rte.28

Province 10.
Lake

Rte.153

13.
Wolfeboro
Center

Rte.109

12. Wentworth
H.S.

11. Wakefield

Rte.16

N

Drive 9

The Eastern Border Lakes

80 miles

This drive meanders along the Maine border, threading together a skein of tidy small towns set amidst rolling countryside and amply supplied with comfortable inns and resorts. The route loops around lovely lake Ossipee, then skirts the eastern slopes of Mt. Chocorua, a scenic southern outrider of the White Mountains.

(1) Head south out of Conway on Rte. 153, following the Saco River Valley to Crystal Lake, and turn left on Brownfield Rd. to reach **Snowville**, a tiny village settled in the early 1800s by Joseph Snow. He left his Maine home at age 24 to find a suitable homestead, and ended his search at the base of Foss Mountain. Here he found a brook that provided water power for his Snow Brothers Sleigh Factory. Homes built by Snow and his relatives still stand along Brownfield Road.

Even if you don't stay overnight at the elegant **Snowvillage Inn**, on the flank of Foss Mountain, do try to dine here: candlelit dinners include entrées such as roast rack of lamb and filet of beef tenderloin. Continue past the inn to the summit for spectacular views of Mt. Washington and the Presidential Range.

Helen Keller often stayed at the nearby summer home of her editor, Nella Henney. Mrs. Henney tied a rope from her front door to a tree so the blind woman could enjoy walking alone. "Sunshine bewitches the weariness out of us ... rains give me the fairy thrill of

dripping like the wildflowers at my feet. This is a nest of peace, twice blessed", she wrote.

----

(2) Back on Rte. 153, continue along the western side of Crystal Lake to tiny **Eaton Center** and its 1884, Greek Revival **Inn at Crystal Lake**. Just past the inn, the much-photographed, 1879 **Little White Church** on the lake shore is a popular spot for weddings.

(3) Just ahead on Purity Lake is 1,000-acre **Purity Spring Resort**, which has been catering to families for more than 100 years. Among the resort's offerings are boating, canoeing, fishing, water skiing, an indoor pool and fitness complex, and tennis courts. King Pine Ski Area is affiliated.

Just past the resort, turn left onto Horseleg Hill Rd. to the New Hampshire Audubon Society's 140-acre **Hoyt Wildlife Sanctuary**, a hardwood forest with a kettle-hole bog, frequented by great blue heron, pileated woodpeckers, black-throated blue warblers, and beaver. Look for pitcher plants and delicate rose pogonias in the lower bog, and white pine and rattlesnake plantain orchids on the highest eskers (elongated hills made up of gravel and other material left behind by a receding glacier).

Side Trip

(4) To visit Freedom, turn left off Rte. 153 onto Freedom Village Rd. This quintessential New England village with handsome homes, a white clapboard town hall, and an 1867 First Congregational Church got its name when it split away from Effingham. Victorian period rooms in the Freedom Historical Society and Museum depict middle class life of 150 years ago.

----

(5) Rte. 153 intersects with Rte. 25 at **Effingham Falls**. The first of the Effinghams -- on the Ossipee River-- grew to be a thriving mill town about 1820 when

Joseph Huckins harnessed the water from the falls to power saw and gristmills. In later years, bedsteads and woolen goods were manufactured here. Today the tidy homes in the Effinghams are testament to the booming, 19th-century economy.

Side Trip: Green Mountain

(6) The views of the Presidential Range and -- on a clear day -- the Atlantic Ocean from the top of the 50-ft.-high fire tower at the summit of 1,907 ft. Green Mountain are well worth the moderately steep 2.8 mile hike. At the intersection of Rtes. 153 and 25, turn west (right) onto Rte. 25; drive 2/10 mi., then turn left at a church onto Green Mountain Rd. Turn left onto High Watch Rd., then left again after 2/10 mile, at the T junction. The trailhead is 1 2/10 mile farther on the right, just past High Watch Learning Center.
----

(7) Continue south on Rte. 153, which follows the same course as Rte. 25 for a short distance before Rte. 25 veers into Maine. Approximately a mile after the road splits (bear right and stay on Rte. 153) watch on the left for the Audubon Society's 380-acre **Charles Henry & Mabel Lamborn Watts Wildlife Sanctuary**, where a trail wanders through forest and swamp alongside the Ossipee River. Watch for otter and waterfowl. There are maps in the mailbox.

(8) A roadside plaque in **Effingham** tells of Effingham Union Academy, the state's first state teachers' college, once located on the second floor of the Effingham Union Academy Building on the hill. The privately-owned, three-story Squire Lord's Mansion, with its second floor Palladian window and octagonal domed cupola, was built by Isaac Lord in 1822. The 1798 Effingham Meetinghouse was used for village gatherings for almost a century.

(9) A dude ranch in New Hampshire? There's not much range to ride at **Chebacco Dude Ranch** in **South**

Effingham, but the state's only dude ranch is a real working western-style operation, and there are plenty of them thar hills to explore. There are also comfortable accommodations and good food, including "chuck wagon" meals and barbecues.

(10) Several large stone hearths on the western shore of **Province Lake** are proof that Native Americans camped here long ago. Today's visitors are just as likely to find golf balls -- evidence of the 18-hole **Province Lake Golf Club** (open to the public), which is actually in Maine.

(11) Continue south to **Wakefield**, the "center of New England." More than 200 years ago this was the intersection of two stagecoach routes, and the village that grew up around it has changed little over the years. Twenty-six of the 18th- and 19th-century buildings in Wakefield Corner National Historic Area are listed in the National Register of Historic Places. **The Wakefield Inn**, built as a private residence in 1803 and then renovated and opened as a stagecoach stop in 1890, still retains many of its original features, including windows with Indian shutters and a three-sided fireplace in the common room.

Even if you're not traveling with kids, be sure to visit the **Museum of Childhood,** packed with thousands of dolls from around the world, doll houses, and music boxes. There's also an 1890s school room.

(12) Continue on Rtes. 153/16 a short distance and turn north (right) onto Rte. 109. Ahead is the turn-off for the **Governor John Wentworth State Historic Site**. A stone foundation is all that remains of the grand retreat the colonial governor built on his 6,000-acre estate overlooking Lake Wentworth in 1768.

The two-story mansion, set amidst stables, barns, and coach houses, was 100 ft. long, 40 ft. wide, and had six-ft.-high windows. Furnishings were hauled by horse-drawn wagons from Portsmouth to Lake Winnipesaukee, and then transported to a landing on

Lake Wentworth. No public official or private citizen had ever selected a summer home site so far out in the wilderness at that early date, and the logistics of the manor's construction and supply made it all the more impressive.

The governor had a 45-mi. road constructed to link Portsmouth with his retreat. His wife, Lady Frances, described her travels in a letter she wrote on October 4, 1780: "You may easily think I dread the journey, from the roughness of the carriage, as the roads are so bad and I, as great a coward as ever existed. ... The Governor would attempt, and effect if possible, to ride over the tops of the trees on Moose Mountain, while I even tremble at passing through a road cut at the foot of it. ...The roads are so precarious in the winter that it is impossible. ... I hope the roads will be better next year."

Governor Wentworth and his wife didn't have many years in which to enjoy their back-country Versailles. In 1775, before construction was completed, they were forced into exile by the onset of the American Revolution. Wentworth was later appointed governor of Nova Scotia; he built the magnificent Province House in Halifax, which still serves as the official residence of the lieutenant governor. His New Hampshire retreat burnt to the ground in 1820, the year of his death.

Just past the site is **Wentworth State Beach,** on the six-mi.-long lake.

(13) In **Wolfeboro Center**, at the intersection of Rtes. 109 and 28, turn north (right) onto Rte. 28. **Duncan Lake** in **Ossipee**, at the junction of Rtes. 28 and 16, was a favorite fishing spot of President Grover Cleveland. He named his fishing camp Acorn Lodge, and hauled in many a fine bass. Today the lake is stocked with rainbow and brook trout.

(14) Continue north on Rte. 16 to Center Ossipee and the intersection with Rtes. 25. Turn east (right) onto Rte. 25 to reach **Ossipee Lake Natural Area** and

Heath Pond Bog, whose acidic environment supports classic bog vegetation including magnificent bog orchids. There's a short loop trail here.

Although there's no public beach on oval-shaped, six-mile-long **Lake Ossipee**, it's a fine spot to fish for brook and rainbow trout. There's a boat launch at Deer Cove, on the western shore of the lake.

In the January, 1962 issue of *Yankee* Magazine, W. A. Swanburg related a curious incident that took place in 1914 on the south shore of Lake Ossipee, where a man named Frederick J. Small had moved with his wife. Mr. Swanburg described him: "gray haired, fiftyish, undersized, he walked with a limp and looked mean enough to bite." A self-described inventor who tinkered with electrical energy, Mr. Small insured his wife for $20,000, then proceed to rig a device that would burn down the house with her in it and leave behind no evidence. The house burned, but Mrs. Small didn't. She fell into lake water that had flooded the basement, where the sheriff found her "bludgeoned, strangled, and shot." The sheriff credited Lake Ossipee with the arrest of Mr. Small, who was hung in Concord Prison on January 15, 1918.

Backtrack west on Rte. 25 and turn right to continue north on Rtes. 16/25. As you approach West Ossipee, Rte. 25 branches off to the west. Bear left here to follow Rte. 25.

Side Trip

(15) Instead of bearing left to follow Rte. 25 as it breaks off from Rte. 16 at West Ossipee, continue into town on Rte. 16 and bear right at Rte. 41 north. Continue past Lily Pond. Turn right at a dirt road opposite the Carved in Bark shop to reach the Nature Conservancy's West Branch Pine Barrens (pine

barrens are woodlands that depend upon wildfires to hinder growth and maintain status quo). When a massive wildfire swept across eastern New Hampshire in 1947, the Ossipee Pine Barrens, a 3,000 acre wilderness of extremely rare pitch pine/scrub oak barrens, thrived. Today the state's last intact pine barrens, one of North America's finest "northern variant" pitch pine/scrub oak barrens, is home to a wide variety of birds and insects, including common nighthawks, rufous-sided towhees, brown thrashers, and 12 species of rare moths and butterflies (five are found nowhere else in the state). A network of trails threads through this rare ecosystem.

Side Trip: White Lake State Park

(16) At W.Ossipee, head north a few miles on Rte. 16 to White Lake State Park, on the shores of pristine White Lake at the edge of the White Mountain National Forest. A two-mile footpath loops through the Black Spruce Ponds preserve to a 72-acre stand of mature, native pitch pines designated a National Natural Landmark. There are views of the Sandwich Range, including Mt. Chocorua, from the sandy beach.

Just after bearing west onto Rte. 25 from Rte. 16/25, look on the right for the 132 ft. 7 in. Paddleford truss Whittier covered bridge, built in the 1870s across the Bearcamp River. The arch and steel telltales were added later.

(17) Continue west on Rte. 25 to Whittier, named for poet John Greenleaf Whittier, who spent many summers here. Just to the south is Mount Whittier, at the northern end of the Ossipee Range.

At the intersection of Rtes. 16 and 113, turn right onto Rte. 113. Continue past several "pick your own apple" farms into **Tamworth,** where President Grover Cleveland spent many summers. The **Barnstormers**

185

Summer Playhouse was founded by his son, Francis, in a converted feed store in 1931, and is now the oldest professional summer theater in the country. Dinner-theater packages are available with the 1833 Victorian **Tamworth Inn**, on the banks of the Swift River. The river flows from the Sandwich Range in Wonalancet, through Tamworth Village, then south to join the Bearcamp River which flows into Lake Ossipee.

Other Tamworth highlights include **Remick's Grocery Market**, a town institution since 1865; the 1792 church, and the cemetery, where many of the town founders are interred.

Two generations of Remicks served as physicians here from 1894 to 1993. Dr. Edwin C. Remick has preserved a slice of history at **The Remick Country Doctor Museum and Farm.** Exhibits include the family's home, with antique period furnishings and a turn-of-the-century doctor's office, and displays interpreting early farm life. Visitors to this living history museum are invited to participate in a variety of hands-on activities, and kids will enjoy learning about farm life a century ago.

Side Trip

(18) Detour north out of Tamworth on Rte. 113A to the Hemenway State Forest, where there's a short, self-guided nature trail as well as a trail to the Great Hill fire tower, which offers views of the Mt. Chocorua Scenic Area and White Mountain National Forest just to the north. There are maps on site. Several trails, including the Big Rock Cave Trail to a boulder cave, begin a bit farther north on Rte. 113A.

----

(19) Head east out of town on Rte. 113 to the junction of Rte. 16 and the village of **Chocorua**, in the shadow of Mt. Chocorua.

Rugged, 3,475-ft.-high Mt. Chocorua, at the eastern end of the Sandwich Range, is extremely popular with hikers. Trails start at various points in the area and merge just below the treeless summit (the Piper and Brook Trails go to the top). Consult the *AMC White Mountain Guide* for a description of the trails and locations of the trailheads, or write to the Chocorua Mountain Club, Chocorua NH 03817.

Side Trip

(20) Detour north of Chocorua Village, past the Riverbend Country Inn, to lovely -- and mostly undeveloped -- Lake Chocorua, on the southern side of Mt. Chocorua. There's a pleasant beach and boat launch on the northern edge of the lake.

The Legend of Mt. Chocorua

After many years of hostilities between the Indians and the early English settlers, Chocorua, chief of the Pequawket Indians, a "silent haughty warrior with brooding passion in his eyes," befriended a man named Cornelius Campbell, leader of a group of Englishmen who had settled in the Conway region. One day when Chocorua left his son in the care of Campbell and his wife, the boy ate some maple syrup laced with fox poison and died. Chocorua didn't believe that the incident was an accident and, when Campbell was away, slaughtered the Englishman's family.

As Ernest Poole relates the story in *The Great White Hills of New Hampshire*, "Campbell tracked the chief at sunrise up the mountain which bears his name and, when he reached the pinnacle, shouted to him to throw himself down. To that the Indian replied: 'The Great Spirit gave life to Chocorua and Chocorua will not throw it away at the command of a white man!'

187

'Then hear the Great Spirit speak in White Man's Thunder!' Campbell roared. He fired his musket. Chocorua fell, then raised himself on one arm and made the famous curtain speech, repeated later in thousands of cabins:

'A curse upon you white men! May the Great Spirit curse you when he speaks in the clouds and his words are fire! Lightning blast your crops! Wind and fire destroy your homes! The Evil One breathe death on your cattle! Panthers howl and wolves fatten on your bones.'

The curse long rested on the spot. Often raided by wolves and bears and their cattle dying of plagues, the settlers left the valley. And even though later the cattle plague was proved to be due to muriate of lime in the water which they drank, the story was still widely told."

----

(21) Continue east of Chocorua on Deer Hill Rd., past several apple orchards, to **Silver Lake**, in **Madison**. There's a boat launch to the south on Rte. 41, and there's good fishing for rainbow, lake and brook trout, large and smallmouth bass, and pickerel.

(22) At the intersection with Rte. 113, turn north and watch on the left for the turn-off to **Madison Boulder**. During the Ice Age, more than 25,000 years ago, the glacier retreated from this area, leaving behind the largest known glacial erratic (boulder) in North America, and one of the largest in the world. The National Natural Landmark measures 87 ft. long by 37 ft. high by 23 ft.wide, and is estimated to weigh 4,662 tons. Although it has become a target for spray-painted graffiti, this boulder in the middle of a forest in the middle of nowhere is still an awesome sight.

Continue north on Rte. 113 to return to Conway.

Information

Greater Ossipee Area Chamber of Commerce (800-382-2371 or 539-6201), Rte. 28, Ossipee 03864. www.ossipeevalley.org.

Greater Wakefield Chamber of Commerce (522-6106), P.O. Box 111, Wakefield 03872.

Mount Washington Valley Chamber of Commerce (800-367-3364 or 356-5701), Main St., North Conway 03860. www.mtwashingtonvalley.org.

New Hampshire Lakes Region Association (800-605-2537 or 744-8664).

Lodging

(1)(R) Snowvillage Inn (800-447-2818 or 447-2818), Snowville 03849. www.snowvillageinn.com. 18 rooms with private bath in three buildings. Hiking, x-c skiing, and snowshoeing. MAP available (*see "Restaurants" below*). $$-$$$

(2) The Inn at Crystal Lake (800-343-7336 or 447-2120), Rte.153, Eaton Center 03832. www.nettx.com/innatcrystallake. 11 rooms with private baths. $$

(3) Purity Spring Resort (800-373-3754 or 367-8896), Rte. 153, E. Madison 03849. www.purityspring.com. A variety of accommodations including rooms in the early 1800s Millbrook Lodge, hillside cottages, and a renovated farmhouse. Full American Plan. $$-$$$

(10) Chebacco Dude Ranch (522-3211), Rte. 153, Box 11, South Effingham 03882. www.chebaccoduderanch.com. $-$$

(11) Wakefield Inn B & B (800-245-0841 or 522-8272), 2723 Wakefield Rd., Wakefield 03872. www.wakefieldinn.com. Seven rooms with bath. Full

breakfast. Dinner served to guests by advance reservation. $-$$

(14) Mount Whittier Motel (539-4951), 1695 Rte. 16, Ctr. Ossipee 03814. www.mountwhittiermotel.com. Clean and pleasant family-friendly motel. Pool. $-$$
(14) Wabanaki Lodge (888-237-8642 or in NH, 323-8536), Box 118G, West Ossipee 03890. www.chocoruacamping.com. Rustic cottages on the secluded shore of Moore's Pond. Private sandy beach, recreation hall, boats, trails. $

(17)(R) Tamworth Inn (800-642-7352 or 323-7721), Main St., Tamworth 03886. www.tamworth.com. 16 rooms and suites with private bath. MAP avail. $$

(19)(R) Stafford's-in-the-Field (800-833-9509 or 323-7766), Box 270, Chocorua 03817. C. 1778 New England farmhouse in the forest has 11 guest rooms with private or shared bath, and four cottages in the shadow of Mt. Chocorua. The lantern-lit, seasonal dining room has an excellent reputation. $-$$

(19) Riverbend Country Inn (800 628-6944 or 323-7440), Rte.16, P.O. Box 288, Chocorua 03817. www.riverbendinn.com. Secluded romantic retreat has 10 lovely guest rooms, sitting rooms with fireplaces, a library, decks, and patio. Optional weekend dinner. $-$$

(19) Mt. Chocorua View B & B (888-323-8350 or 323-8350), Rte. 16, Chocorua. www.mtchocorua.com. Handsomely restored 1845 inn has six guest rooms (some with shared bath) and a two-room suite. Snowshoes and day packs available. $-$$

(21) Lakeview Cottage B & B (800-982-0418 or 367-9182), P.O. Box 1, Silver Lake 03875. 1876 lakefront Victorian inn has three guest rooms, swimming, boating, and hiking. $$

(21) Madison Carriage House B&B (367-4605), Rte. 113, Madison 03849. Five guest rooms with shared

bath in a village farmhouse. Kids (and pets, with prior approval) welcome. $-$$

(21) Maple Grove House (877-367-8208 or 367-8208), 21 Maple Grove Rd., Madison 03849. Recently renovated late 1800s Victorian farmhouse on 216 acres has four large, comfortable guest rooms with private bath and a spacious, two room suite. $$ www.virtualcities.com/ons/nh/t.

Off the Drive
Strathaven (287-7785), Rte. 113, N. Sandwich 03259. Four nicely decorated, antiques-filled guest rooms (two with private bath) in a beautifully-landscaped home near Sandwich Notch. $-$$

Restaurants

(1) Snowvillage Inn (800-447-2818 or 447-2818), Snowville. Four-course, gourmet candlelit dinners. $$

(14) The Yankee Smokehouse (539-RIBS), Rtes. 16/25, W. Ossipee. Authentic open pit barbecue. House specials include baby back pork ribs, smokehouse fries, baked beans, and corn chowder. Save room for the fabulous desserts. $

(14) Whittier House Restaurant & Tavern (539-4513), Rte. 16, W. Ossipee. Comprehensive menu includes everything from burgers to Greek salads to Schnitzel and seafood linguine. $$

Attractions

(3) Hoyt Wildlife Sanctuary (224-9909), Rte. 153, E. Madison.

(4) Freedom Historical Society and Museum (367-4626), Maple St., Freedom.

(8) Effingham Historical Society, Drakes Store, Effingham.

(11) Museum of Childhood (523-8073), Wakefield. Memorial Day week - mid-Oct., Wed.--Mon. $

(12) Wentworth State Beach (569-3699), Rte. 109, Wolfeboro. Beach, picnic area, bathhouse, grills. Seasonal. $

(16) West Branch Pine Barrens (224-5853), The Nature Conservancy, 2 1/2 Bacon St., Suite 6, Concord.

(17) Remick Country Doctor Museum and Farm (800-686-6117), 58 Cleveland Hill Rd., Tamworth. Mon.--Fri.,Year-round; July through October, Mon.--Sat.

(17) Tamworth Historical Society (323-8214 or 323-8639), 26 Gregs Way, Tamworth.

(17) White Lake State Park (323-7350), Rte. 16, Tamworth. Swimming, camping, hiking. Seasonal. $

(21) Madison Historical Society Museum (367-4687), Rte. 113 and East Madison Rd., Madison. Local artifacts, a peddler's wagon, 1900s kitchen. Tues. and Sun. 2-4 Memorial Day-Labor Day.

(22) Madison Boulder Natural Area (323-2087), off Rte 133, Madison.

Activities

(4) Fairfield Llama Farm (539-2865), P.O. Box 96, Freedom. Day-long llama treks with gourmet lunches.

(10) Province Lake Golf Club (800-325-4434 or 207-793-4040), Rte. 153, Parsonsfield, Me

(14) Canoe King(539-4799), Rte. 16, West Ossipee. Canoe and kayak rentals; shuttle service for Bearcamp River.

(14) Summer Brook Fish Farm (539-7232), Rte. 16, West Ossipee. Fly fishing, catch and release, or keep your catch.

(17) Barnstormers Summer Playhouse (323-8500) Plays and musicals.

(17) Concerts by the River; Other Store (next to the general store), Tamworth. Folk, bluegrass, children's shows, and whatever. Sunday afternoons in season. Donation.

Shopping

(4) Freedom Book Shop and Gallery (539-7265), Maple St., Freedom.

(11) Dutch Boutique, Wakefield. Imported Dutch giftware and locally- made products, including paintings and photographs by the owners.

(9) Taylor City Store, Rte. 153, S. Effingham.

(11) Wakefield Marketplace, Main St./ Rte. 16, Wakefield. Farmers' and crafts market Saturdays 9-4 in season.

(14) Lakewood Station Antiques (539-7414), Rte. 16, Ossipee. 50+ dealers.

(14) Tramway Artisans (539-5700), Rtes. 16/ 25, W. Ossipee. Two floors of handcrafts, jewelry, antique reproductions, pottery, etc.

(17) Remick's Grocery Market, Tamworth.

(19) Chocorua Village Country Store, Chocorua.

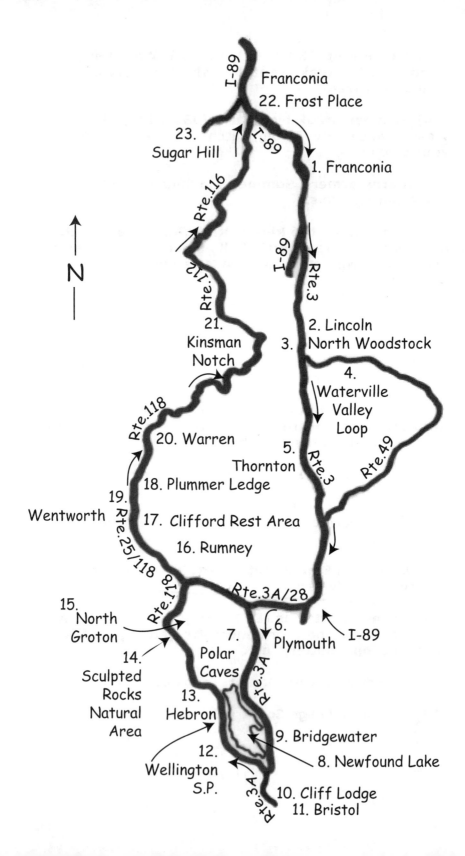

N

I-89
Franconia
22. Frost Place

23. Sugar Hill

I-89

1. Franconia

Rte.116

Rte.112

I-89

Rte.3

21. Kinsman Notch

2. Lincoln
3. North Woodstock

4. Waterville Valley Loop

Rte.118

20. Warren

5. Thornton

18. Plummer Ledge

Rte.3

Rte.49

19. Wentworth

Rte.25/118

17. Clifford Rest Area

16. Rumney

Rte.118

Rte.3A/28

15. North Groton

7. Polar Caves

6. Plymouth

I-89

14. Sculpted Rocks Natural Area

Rte.3A

13. Hebron

12. Wellington S.P.

9. Bridgewater

8. Newfound Lake

10. Cliff Lodge

11. Bristol

Rte.3A

Drive 10

Franconia Notch and the Western White Mountains

112 miles

A drive through the westernmost of the White Mountains' great north-south notches begins with a look at New Hampshire's most famous natural icon, then continues south through a popular resort region to serene Newfound Lake. Turning back to the north, the route takes in rugged Kinsman Notch at the western gateway to the White Mountains, and ends with a visit to one of Robert Frost's rural homesteads.

(1) Begin this drive at Exit #3 off I-93/Rte. 3, the gateway to the **White Mountain National Forest**. **Franconia Notch State Park** -- enveloping what is possibly the most spectacular stretch of interstate highway in the nation -- winds for eight miles between the peaks of the Kinsman and Franconia mountain ranges. From north to south, here are some of the highlights of Franconia Notch and environs:

-- Echo Lake, with a sandy beach, fishing, and boating facilities.

-- **Cannon Mountain Aerial Tramway**, first lift of its type in North America, which has carried almost seven million passengers to the top of the mountain since it made its maiden run in 1938. It's a five-minute ride to the 4,200 ft. summit, where there are walking trails and an observation tower. The **New England Ski Museum** and park headquarters/information booth are at the mountain's base.

-- The Old Man of the Mountain, a natural rock formation that towers 1,200 ft. above Profile Lake, also called the "Old Man's Washbowl." Daniel Webster said of the the Great Stone Profile: "Men hang out their signs indicative of their respective trades: shoemakers hang out a gigantic shoe; jewelers, a monster watch ... but up in the mountains of New Hampshire, God Almighty has hung out a sign to show that there He makes men." Five separate, horizontal granite ledges form the profile of the structure, which measures about 40 ft. from the chin to the forehead. Down below, Profile Lake attracts anglers who come to fly fish for brook trout.

-- At the southern entrance to the notch, the **Flume** is an 800-ft.-deep gorge formed over the course of countless millennia by Flume Brook. The rock here is granite, riven by intrusions of molten lava hardened into basalt dikes. By constantly wearing away at the dike over which it flows on its way to the Pemigewasset River, Flume Brook carved this deep chasm between 70-ft. granite walls. There's a walkway beside the stream, within the walls of the flume. A bus at the Visitor Center takes visitors to the gorge entrance.

In between Echo Lake and the Flume, there's a nine-mile, paved recreational trail for biking, several covered bridges (Sentinel Pine Bridge at The Pool, and Flume Bridge), rocks to climb, birds to spot (look for peregrine falcons on Cannon's cliffs), moose for drivers to watch out for, and some of the most spectacular views in the state. And there are fine hiking trails. In addition to the Appalachian Trail (the trailhead is near the Flume Parking area), some of the most popular include a 1 1/2 mi. loop to Bald Mountain and Artists Bluff (trail begins in the parking area on Rte. 18 across from Peabody Base Lodge); the three-mile round-trip hike to Lonesome Lake, which begins at Lafayette Place; and the hike to Kinsman Falls, less than one mi. round trip, which begins at the Basin. The information centers has detailed maps and guides, including the **Appalachian Mountain Club**'s excellent *AMC White Mountain Guide*

The section of I-93 that winds through Franconia Notch represents a compromise that settled a fierce and complicated debate waged from the late 1960s to the early 1980s over how to connect the loose ends of this interstate highway at either end of the notch. Environmentalists wanted a two-lane highway; the government wanted to finish the four-lane interstate. The road you drive today is a hybrid, a mini-interstate unlike any other portion of the national system of superhighways.

The White Mountain National Forest, comprising nearly 800,000 acres in New Hampshire and western Maine, was established in 1911 largely through the efforts of John Wingate Weeks (*see Drive 13*), a New Hampshire man who served as U.S. Secretary of War and as a U.S.Congressman. He was appalled to see land being destroyed by uncontrolled logging and the fires which burned, undeterred, across the barren landscape left behind. Today approximately .5% of the land is being harvested at any given time, often improving trail conditions, views, and/or wildlife habitat. More than half of the forest is closed to logging, including 112,000 acres of pristine wilderness protected by the federal Eastern Wilderness Act.

At Parkway Exit #1, head south on Rte. 3 alongside the Pemigewasset River. If the kids have grown bored with the scenery, they're bound to perk up along the next stretch through one of the state's few remaining, old-time "tourist" areas: miles of old-fashioned cottage colonies, water parks, go-cart tracks, miniature golf courses, hot dog and ice cream stands, and other related businesses, all clustered like barnacles on the narrow strip wedged between I-93 and the White Mountain National Forest.

(2) **Lincoln** owes its recent spate of development to several factors: in addition to its proximity to the Notch -- and to Cannon Mountain Ski Area -- it's at the western terminus of the Kancamagus Highway (*see Drive 11*) and the Pemigewasset Wilderness, and just a mile east of the **Loon Mountain** winter and summer resort complex.

One of New Hampshire's oldest tourist spots, **Clark's Trading Post,** was founded in 1928 for the purpose of raising and exhibiting Eskimo sled dogs. A few years later Florence and Edward Clark brought in a few trained bears as an attraction for travelers. Today, a half-hour show starring North American Black bears still draws the crowds. Descendants of the Clarks have added a host of other attractions, including the White Mountain Central Railroad, a standard-gauge wood burning locomotive which steams through a 1904 covered bridge and along the Pemigewasset; bumper boats; antique cars and motorcycles; and an antique fire station. The 120-ft.-long covered bridge, built in 1904, is the last remaining Howe truss railroad bridge.

For a different kind of railroad experience, hop aboard the Café Lafayette, a restored 1924 Pullman dining car at the **Hobo Railroad.** You'll be served an elegant, five-course meal as the train chugs its way to the station at Lake Winnipesaukee. You can also take the 1 hr. 20 min. excursion without meals in one of the restored vintage coaches.

Watch for the Riverfront Condos: a popular swimming hole on the Pemigewasset is called "The Lady's Bathtub" is on the other side of the parking lot.

(3) Although less developed than its neighbor to the north, **North Woodstock**, between Kinsman and Franconia Notches, is amply supplied with restaurants and lodgings. Stop at the venerable **Fadden's General Store** for provisions, gifts, and a whiff of nostalgia. You can order up a pint of freshly brewed ale at the **Woodstock Inn, Station & Brewery**. The **White Mountains Visitor Center** is just off the interstate.

Side Trip

(4) Waterville Valley Loop
Just south of North Woodstock, turn left onto scenic Tripoli Road (closed in winter) and continue for nine mi., through Thornton Gap (where the challenging, 6 4/10 mi. Mt. Osceola Trail climbs to the summit of 4,340-ft. Mt. Osceola) to the self-contained resort village of Waterville Valley, at the base of Waterville Valley Ski Area. Much of the activity is centered at the Town Square, a huge clapboard structure housing restaurants and shops; The Golden Eagle has overnight accommodations. Activities here include paddle boats, golf, mountain biking, and, of course, hiking. Follow Rte. 49 south back to Rte. 3 alongside the Mad River, and turn south in West Campton.

----

(5) If you've skipped the above side trip, continue south on Rte. 3 through Woodstock. If you're passing through between 8 am and 2 pm on a weekend between mid-February and the second week in April, stop in for a stack of pancakes at the **Sugar Shack** in **Thornton**. Turn left over the Thornton Memorial Bridge at Crossover Rd., and then go north on Rte. 175 for 1/4 mi. The sugar house is open year-round, selling gifts and maple items. There's also a **Mountain Bike Park** (Memorial Day-Columbus Day) and golf driving range here.

Back on Rte. 3, watch for Turkey Jim's Bridge; the original was built in 1883 to connect a turkey farm with the mainland. The present bridge, built in 1958, is one of three covered bridges in West Campton. The Campton-Blair Bridge is two mi. north of Livermore Falls; the Campton-Bump Bridge is one mi. east of Rte. 175 at Campton Hollow.

(6) Continue south on Rte. 3 to **Plymouth**. Once a thriving mill town and busy railroad junction, today its

199

economy revolves around the 4,000 students who attend Plymouth State College. The bustling downtown, with businesses like **Louis Samaha Store**, a Main St. fixture since 1917, and the 1946 Fracher's Diner, seems to have made the transition quite comfortably. The college's **Silver Cultural Arts Center** and the **New Hampshire Music Festival** concert series provide the community's 6,000 residents with a full plate of cultural events.

In front of the restored 1889 Town Hall is a British cannon believed to have been captured by General John Stark at the Battle of Bennington. On the Common, there's a bronze statue by George Borst called "Kneeling Boy Scout," and a plaque honoring Nathaniel Hawthorne. The author used to stay at the Pemigewasset House, built by John E. Lyon, president of the Boston, Concord and Montreal Railroad. Hawthorne died in the hotel on May 18, 1864, and it burned in 1909. The 5 1/2 mi. self-guided **Plymouth Heritage Trail** of 14 historically significant sights begins at the Plymouth Regional Senior Center (the former railroad depot) on Green St. (brochures are available at the beginning of the trail).

(7) Backtrack to Rte. 25/3A (Tenney Mountain Highway) and head west into the Baker River Valley, past the entrance to **Tenney Mountain Ski Area** and the **Crabapple Inn B & B** to **Polar Caves Park**. Fifty thousand years ago a continental glacier moved south over the mountains and valleys. As the ice sheet thawed, great blocks of granite cracked and loosened from Hawks Cliff and tumbled down, forming a series of caves and passages which are great fun to explore.

(8) Backtrack to Rte. 3A and head south along the eastern shore of seven-mile-long, pristine **Newfound Lake**, which is surrounded by 22 miles of mostly undeveloped shoreline. Native Americans called the lake "Pasquaney," ("place where birch bark for canoes is found"), and in 1735 Captain John Smith mentioned it as "a great pond that Indians say is three days' journey around. The land is very full of great hills and

mountains, and very rocky." Although it's the fourth largest lake in the state, for some reason (certainly not lack of scenic appeal) Newfound has remained relatively undiscovered as a tourist attraction, and as late as the 1930s was often referred to as the "hermit of New Hampshire lakes."

Watch on the right for North Shore Rd.: it's the turn-off for **Paradise Point Nature Center**, a 36-acre Audubon Society parcel with a first-rate interpretive center and several hiking trails along the lake. Trails include the one mi. Ridge/Lakeside Trail, which passes through a hardwood forest; and another footpath which wanders alongside a swamp past a stance of trees called the Elwell Hemlocks, a majestic stand dating to the 17th century. Trail guides are available at the center.

Continue on North Shore Rd. past Paradise Point for another 1 1/2 mi. to a second Audubon property, **Hebron Marsh Wildlife Sanctuary**. These 33 acres of marsh and fields alongside the Cockermouth River and Newfound Lake provide a rich environment for a large variety of waterfowl, including loons, ducks, and great blue heron. The best view is from the observation tower which looks over the marsh.

Both sanctuaries offer a series of naturalist-led educational programs.

(9) As you head south on Rte. 3A, 3,121-ft. Mt. Cardigan looms to the west. Continue along the eastern shore through **Bridgewater**, home to the **Inn on Newfound Lake,** a popular hostelry since 1840 when it was a stagecoach stop midway between Boston and Montreal. Even if you're not staying or dining here (*see "Lodging" below*), you can enjoy a cold drink or a cocktail on the broad verandah overlooking the lake. The sunsets are spectacular.

(10) Down the road apiece, at the southern end of the lake, **Cliff Lodge** offers an eclectic international menu, with seating in the lovely dining room or on the lakefront deck. The Newfound River at the southern tip

of the lake is an excellent spot to try your hand at fly fishing for salmon or brook trout.

Side Trip: Profile Falls

(11) Continue south on Rte. 3A, through the town of Bristol (once a favorite vacation spot for writer John Cheever), and watch on the left for a sign just before the bridge about 2 1/2 miles south of town. Turn here, continue to the parking area, and follow the trail to the base of scenic, 40-ft. Profile Falls.

----

(12) At the southern tip of Newfound lake, turn right at the intersection of Rte. 3A and West Shore Rd. Follow West Shore Rd. to **Wellington State Park**, one of the few places on the lake with a public beach. There's 1/4 mi. of sandy shore, and lots of protection from the sun under a dense canopy of pine trees. The Elwell Trail, which extends 10 mi. across several mountain summits to the Mowglis Trail, two mi. north of Mt. Cardigan, begins just past the park entrance.

(13) Continue north along West Shore Rd. to **Hebron**. The church on the town oval was completed in 1803 and, according to the New Hampshire volume in the 1930s *American Guide Series*, "The master-workman Benjamin Woodman was 'extended a vote of thanks and presented a bottle of brandy at the expense of the town for his generous and manly behavior while a resident of the town'." The circa 1792 **Hebron General Store** sells homemade pastries and sandwiches. There's an interesting old cemetery just on the outskirts of town.

(14) At the intersection of West Shore Rd. and Groton Rd., turn onto Groton Rd. and head north alongside the Cockermouth River to **Groton** and the turn-off for **Sculpted Rocks Natural Area**, a secluded spot where the river plunges 30 ft. into a gorge. Over eons,

stones and sediment carried along by the moving water have carved giant potholes in the rocks below, creating odd formations. Some of the deeper craters make excellent swimming holes.

(15) Continue on Groton Rd. as it twists and climbs through the Cockermouth Forest into **North Groton**, where the 1840 North Groton School House has been preserved. Turn right here onto Halls Brook Rd. and continue to the intersection of Rte. 25, and then turn west (left) onto Rte. 25, back into the Baker River Valley.

Side Trip

(16) Turn east on Rte. 25 and drive to Rumney Depot, then turn left onto Stinson Lake Rd. The road leads through the tranquil, 19th-century village of Rumney, past the Mary Baker Eddy House, to crystal-clear Stinson Lake. The lake has a reputation for fine trout fishing; there are also beaches and hiking trails. Keep an eye out for moose, which are occasionally spotted here.

On the way back trough Rumney, turn left onto Quincy Rd. to see 40-acre Quincy Bog, a rewarding spot for birders: more than 115 species have been sighted here. The bog plants at this glacially-formed peat bog bloom in May and June.

----

(17) Continue west on Rte. 25 to reach the **Clifford Memorial Rest Area,** where a plaque tells of the Honorable Nathan Clifford, a U.S. Supreme Court Justice from 1858 to 1881, who was born near here in 1803 and negotiated the Treaty of Guadalupe Hidalgo in 1848 to end the Mexican War. The Baker River, which roughly parallels Rte, 25 in this area, was named for Lt. Thomas Baker, who, with a company of 34 rangers from Northampton, Massachusetts,

destroyed a Pemigewasset Indian village while passing through in 1712. The Bay State rewarded the expedition with a scalp bounty of £40 and promoted Baker to the rank of captain.

(18) After Rte. 25 merges with Rte. 118, the road becomes Moosilauke Highway, so named for the 4,802-ft. mountain peak on the southwest edge of the White Mountain National Forest. Watch on the right for the turn-off onto Turner Lane; turn here and then turn right onto Buffalo Rd. to reach **Plummer Ledge Natural Area**, where ten glacial potholes ranging in diameter from two to more than 10 ft. have formed on the side of the Baker River.

(19) Although the village of **Wentworth** was settled in 1774-75, many of the buildings were destroyed in a flood in 1856. Several, however, including the 1829 Congregational Church with its unusual tiered steeple, and the 1815 Thomas Wipple House, survived and are clustered around the handsome common. The town's Historical Museum is housed in an old railroad depot.

(20) On the outskirts of **Warren** a small sign marks the turn-off for the **Warren Fish Hatchery**, a state-of-the-art facility for salmon rearing and management of trout broodfish populations.

Tiny Warren just may possess the most unusual "downtown" centerpiece in the state: a 68-ft. Redstone Missile. The eight-ton craft was moved here on a flatbed truck in 1971 by native son Henry "Ted" Asselin. A sign next to the missile points the way to the Jesse Bushaw Memorial Trail, which follows a defunct railroad bed past an old mica mine.

When Rte. 118 splits off from Rte. 25 just north of Warren, continue north on Rte. 118 to head back into the White Mountain National Forest. (Remember, you'll need a permit to park at any lot in the WMNF.) If you're ready for a swim, park near the iron bridge by Moosilauke Carriage Road; the Baker River runs alongside the road. Turn onto Ravine Lodge Rd. to

Dartmouth College's **Moosilauke Ravine Lodge**. One of New England's largest log buildings, it's open to the public in season for lodging and meals. At the lodge, several hiking trails begin the ascent of the southeast side of Mt. Moosilauke to the barren summit, once the site of a resort hotel called the Prospect House.

(21) At the intersection with Rte. 112, turn west onto Rte. 112 to head into the Lost River Region and **Kinsman Notch**. The notch was named for Asa Kinsman, an early pioneer who was on his way to claim a parcel of land in the town of Landaff when he discovered he'd taken a wrong turn. Rather than turn back, he and several companions used axes to hack their way nine miles through the wilderness to the other side.

The road between Mt. Moosilauke and Kinsman Ridge is one of the most dramatic and least traveled sections of the White Mountain National Forest. It winds past cascades, dramatic rock formations, and magnificent mountain vistas. At **Lost River**, the river winds through glacially-formed boulder caves and potholes -- some as large as 25 ft. wide and 60 ft. deep -- before emerging at Paradise Falls at the foot of the gorge. Visitors can take a self-guided tour along boardwalks, across bridges, and up ladders; and explore a series of rocks and caves. More than 300 varieties of native flowers, ferns, and shrubs are on display in the Nature Garden.

Two excellent hiking trails begin just past the entrance to Lost River: the rigorous but rewarding Beaver Brook Cascades, a 2.2 mi. hike almost straight up to the summit of Mt. Moosilauke alongside a series of magnificent waterfalls; and the Kinsman Ridge trail, a grueling 16.7 mi. segment of the Appalachian Trail which ends at the Old Man in the Mountain parking area in Franconia Notch.

(22) At the intersection with Rte. 116, turn north (right) onto Rte. 116 into the Easton Valley, past **Kinsman Lodge** and the **Franconia Inn**, and watch for

the turn-off to **The Frost Place.** Poet Robert Frost moved into this 1859 farmhouse overlooking Franconia Valley when he was 40 years old, and lived here for five years. Today the simple white structure is preserved as a museum. Exhibits include a rare collection of Frost's Christmas card poems, personal letters, and first editions. Throughout the summer a poet-in-residence gives readings in the barn; and visitors can follow a short Nature Trail, lined with relevant quotations, through the woods.

Continue north on Rte. 116 into **Franconia**, gateway to Franconia Notch. Nathaniel Hawthorne, John Greenleaf Whittier, and Washington Irving were among the writers who vacationed here. The **Iron Furnace Interpretive Center** on Rte. 18 preserves the state's only remaining blast furnace, all that is left of the iron industry that thrived here from 1800 to 1865. Iron ore was carted from mines in Sugar Hill, and molded into everything from kettles to heating stoves.

The handsome wooden building that dominates the Franconia townscape was built in 1884, the gift of Moses Arnold Dow, founder of the *Waverly Magazine*, who wanted to establish a model educational institution in his adopted town.

Side Trip

(23) Take Rte. 117 out of Franconia to **Sugar Hill.** It's hard to imagine that this upscale hill town -- now known for its many fine inns -- was a hotbed of religious fanaticism in the early 19th century. It was here that Baptist clergyman William Miller began to preach that the world would end on October 22, 1844. As related in the New Hampshire volume of the *American Guide Series*, "Many believed in him so firmly that they harvested no crops that year, and either sold their livestock or gave it away. They prepared themselves by six weeks of prayer and fasting and on the last day gathered either in the cemetery or at the church, clothed in white flowing robes and ready for

their ascension. ... One man went out into the field to give a final exhortation to some 'unsaved' neighbors. Worn out with fasting and prayer, he sat down on a haystack and went to sleep. The recreants then removed most of the hay and touched a match to what was left. The Millerite awoke with a start, shouting, 'Hell -- just as I expected'."

The view of the Presidential, Franconia, and Kinsman Ranges from the **Sunset Hill House** is unparalleled.

You can pick up I-93 north and south at Franconia.

Information

Appalachian Mountain Club Headquarters (617-536-0636), 5 Joy St., Boston 02108. www.outdoors.org.

Baker Valley Chamber of Commerce (764-9380), P.O. Box 447, Rumney 03266. www.pemibaker.com/bakervalley chamber.

Franconia-Easton-Sugar Hill Chamber of Commerce (800-237-9009 or 823-5661), Box 780, Main St., Franconia 03580. www.franconianotch.org.

Lincoln-Woodstock Chamber of Commerce (800-227-4191 or 745-6621), Box 358, Lincoln 03251. www.linwoodcc.org.

Newfound Region Chamber of Commerce (744-2150), N. Main St., Bristol 03222. www.newfound.org.

Plymouth Chamber of Commerce(800-386-378 or 536-1001), P.O. Box 65, Plymouth 03264. www.plymouthnh.org.

Waterville Valley Region Chamber of Commerce (800-238-2307 or 726-3804), RFD l, Box 1067, Campton 03223. www.watervillevalleyregion.com.

White Mountains Visitor Center (800-FIND MTS or 745-8720), Exit 32 off I-93, North Woodstock. www.VisitWhiteMountains.com

White Mountain National Forest (528-8721), P.O. Box 638, Laconia 03247. www.fs.fed.us/r9/white.

Lodging

(2) Comfort Inn & Suites (888-589-8112), Rte. 112, Lincoln 03251. www.comfortinnloon.com. 82 rooms and suites; fireplace and jacuzzi suites; indoor pool, whirlpool, and exercise room. Next to Hobo Railroad. $$

(2) Cozy Cabins (745-8713), U.S. Rte. 3, Lincoln 03251. www.cozycabins.com. Nine 1-2 bedroom cabins with cable TV; some kitchens. Play area. $

(2) Franconia Notch Motel (800-323-7829 or 745-2229), Rte. 3, Lincoln 03251. 12 motel units and six two-room cottages (summer) on the Pemigewasset River. $-$$

(2) Indian Head Resort (800-343-8000 or 745-8000), Rte. 3, Lincoln.www.indianheadresort.com. 98 motel rooms, 50 cabins with fireplaces; indoor and outdoor heated pools, tennis courts, and restaurant. $$-$$$

(2) The Lodge at Lincoln Station (800-654-6188 or 745-3441), Rte. 112, Lincoln. www.millatloon.com. Studios and suites with kitchenettes and balconies. Great Room with stone fireplace and sun deck; indoor and outdoor pools, jacuzzi, sauna, and tennis. $$-$$$

(3) Wilderness Inn (800-200-WILD or 745-3890), Rte. 3/Courtney Rd., N. Woodstock 03262. 1912 shingled bungalow near town has eight antiques-filled guest

rooms (two with shared bath) and a fireplaced cottage with a sleigh bed and deck. Swimming hole. $$

(3)(R) Woodstock Inn B & B (800-321-3985 or 745-3951), Rte. 3, Main St., N. Woodstock. Inn/microbrewery/restaurant has 21 rooms (13 with private bath) in the inn and two Victorian homes. $-$$

(4) The Golden Eagle (236-4551), Waterville Valley Town Square, Waterville Valley 03215. www.waterville.com. Fieldstone and shingled hotel with the feel of a turn-of-the-century mountain lodge has 139 housekeeping suites; indoor pool, whirlpool and sauna. $$$

(4) Snowy Owl Inn (800-766-9969 or 236-8383), Waterville Valley 03215. www.snowyowlinn.com. 85 rooms: some with kitchens, most with 2-person jacuzzi tubs, web bars, refrigerators,and sitting areas. Indoor/ outdoor pool, spa and sauna; access to sports and fitness center. $$-$$$

(5) The Campton Inn (726-4449), Rte. 175 and Owl St., Campton 03223. 1835 village house has five guest rooms (one with private bath). Well-behaved dogs and families welcome. $-$$

(5) Scandinavi-Inn (800-600-1689 or 726-3737), Owl St., Campton 03223. Rooms with private bath, cable, AC and some kitchens. Golf packages. Restaurant and pub. $$

(6) Crab Apple Inn B & B (536-4476), Rte. 25, P.O. Box 188, Plymouth 03246. Five guest rooms (four with private bath) with canopy beds and handmade quilts in beautifully-restored, 1835 Federal-style inn. $$

(6) Knoll Motel (536-1245), 446 Main St., Plymouth. www.whitemountainregion.com/knollmotel. Motel, cottages and seven-bedroom lodge with mountain views. $

(6) Pilgrim Inn & Cottages (800-216-1900 or 536-1319), Rte. 3, Plymouth. www.pilgriminn.com. Four-five bedroom inn; 10 motel units;and 13 cottages (some with kitchens).

(9)(R) Inn on Newfound Lake (800-745-7990 or 744-9111), Rte. 3A, Bridgewater 03222. www.newfound.com. 19 guest rooms (11 with private bath) in the inn, and 12 with private bath in the adjoining Elmwood Cottage. Private beach, restaurant (*see below*). $$-$$$

(9) Sandybeach of Newfound (744-8473), 95 Whittemore Point Rd. North, Bridgewater 03222. Year-round, lakefront housekeeping cottages with fireplaces and screened porches. Sandy beach. Weekly only in summer ($500-$900).

(19) Hilltop Acres (764-5896), East Side/Buffalo Rd., Wentworth 03282.Rooms and efficiency cottages. Pets and kids in the cottages. May-Nov. $-$$

(20) Moosilauke Ravine Lodge (in season, 764-5858; off-season, 646-1607). Bunk house or lodge bed accommodations with optional, family-style meals. $ www.dartmouth.edu/~opo/moosilauke.

(22) Bungay Jar B&B Inn (800-421-0701), Easton Valley Rd., Rte. 116, Franconia 03580. www.bungayjar.com. Six rooms (some with views and private decks) in renovated, 18th-century barn overlooking Kinsman Range. Also, one cottage. Perennial gardens and water-lily pond sauna. $$-$$$.

(22)(R) The Franconia Inn (800-473-5299 or 823-5542), Rte. 116, Franconia 03580. www.franconiainn.com. 34 rooms with private baths; Inn (fireplace and balcony), family, and honeymoon suites; tennis courts, swimming pool, stables, outdoor jacuzzi, bicycles, and lawn games. MAP only in peak season; EP and B&B available other times. $$-$$$

(22) Kinsman Lodge (823-5686), 215 Easton Rd., Rte. 116, Franconia 03580. Comfortable 1880s inn has single and double rooms with shared baths; children and small pets welcome. $

(23)(R) Sugar Hill Inn (800-548-4748 or 823-5621), Rte. 117, Sugar Hill 03580. www.sugarhillinn.com. Ten guest rooms and six cottage suites in beautifully-restored inn with original wide pine and maple flooring, stenciled walls, antiques, and great views. Some fireplaces. Gourmet breakfasts and dinners; afternoon tea. MAP available. $$-$$$

(23)(R) Sunset Hill House (800-786-4455 or 823-5522), 231 Sunset Hill Rd., Sugar Hill. www.sunsethill.com. 1882 inn on a ridge overlooking the Presidential Range has 30 lovingly-decorated guest rooms (some with jacuzzis and fireplaces), heated pool, golf course, patio, fine restaurant, and tavern. MAP available. $$-$$$

(23) The Homestead (800-823-5564 or 823-5564), Rte. 117, Sugar Hill 03585. www.thehomestead1802.com. Handed down through seven generations, the 1802 inn--one of the oldest family inns in the country--was expanded in 1898 and has 20 rooms in the inn and annex; those in the inn share baths. The inn has hand hewn virgin timbers, wide pine boards, antiques, and loads of family heirlooms. Three-course country breakfast. $-$$

Not on Drive

AMC Cardigan Lodge (744-8011), 774 Shem Valley Rd., Alexandria. www.outdoors.org. Year-round lodge and winter B &B; 3 meals, campsites, educational workshops. $

Restaurants

(2) Café Lafayette Dinner Trail (745-3500), Rte. 112, "Eagle's Nest", N. Woodstock. $46.95 includes 5-

course dinner and train ticket. Off-season, weekends and occasional week nights; July and Aug., Tues., Thurs., Sat. and Sun. Reservations rec. $$$

(2) **The Common Man** (745-3463), Pollard Rd./Main St., Lincoln. Local institution which blossomed into a popular chain NH features freshly-prepared favorites including prime rib, lobster, and pastas; grill menu available. D $$

(2) **Pycolog Bakery/Cafe** (745-4395), Main St., Lincoln. Fresh baked goodies, espresso bar, and "brown bag" lunches. $

(3) **Truants Taverne** (745-2239), Main St., N. Woodstock. Burgers, tortillas and other solid fare in a casual, fun setting. $

(3) **Woodstock Station** (745-3951), Woodstock Inn, Main St., Rte. 3, N. Woodstock. The menu at this converted train station includes everything from burritos to burgers to barbecued ribs. Beer is brewed at the Woodstock Inn brewery, which shares space. L, D. $-$$

(6) **Italian Farmhouse** (536-4536), Rte. 3, Plymouth. Common Man offshoot menu includes homemade pasta specialties, beef, bouillabaisse, and pizza. D, Sun. brunch. $-$$

(6) **Bridgeside Diver**, 175A, Plymouth. Large portions of great home cooked food. Breakfast all day; bison burger; fresh baked breads, homemade soups. B, L, D. $

(6) **Biederman's Deli and Pub** (536-DELI), 83 Main St., Plymouth (under Volpe's Market). Good sandwiches. $

(9) **Pasquaney Restaurant at the Inn on Newfound Lake** (800-745-7990 or 744-9111), Rte. 3A, Bridgewater. Continental breakfast, dinner, and Sunday brunch served in the inn's charming dining room. $$-$$$

(9 (L) Ryan's loft at the Whittemore Inn (74403517), Rte. 3A, Bridgewater. Moderately-priced fare includes fresh fish and prime beef; children's menu. Live weekend entertainment. Guesthouse and motel. $$

(11) (L) Cliff Lodge and Restaurant (744-8660), Rte. 3A, Bristol. Restaurant serves creative Continental fare; tavern menu; rustic, housekeeping cabins and beach. ($-$$). $$$

(16) Steve's Restaurant (800-786-9788 or 786-9788), off Rte. 25, Stinson Lake Rd., Rumney. Menu includes burgers, fresh fish, prime rib, and barbecue; patio. Tues.-Sat. and Sun. brunch. L, D. $-$$

(20) Calamity Jane's Restaurant (764-5288), Warren Village. Family fare, including pizza and homemade desserts served up daily. Beer and wine. B, L, D. $

(23) Polly's Pancake Parlor (823-5575), Rte. 117, Sugar Hill. Pancakes rule at this ever- popular tourist spot, housed in an 1830s restored carriage shed. Tthere are also waffles, French toast, sandwiches and homemade desserts. Mid-May-late Oct. B, L. $

Attractions

(1) Cannon Aerial Tramway (823-8800), I-93, Franconia Notch. Mid-May-Oct. $

(1) Franconia Notch State Park (823-8800), Franconia, NH 03580.

(1) New England Ski Museum (800-639-4181 or 823-7177), Cannon Mountain, Franconia Notch. Vintage ski films, ski memorabilia, and videos. Memorial Day-Columbus Day, daily; Dec.-March, Fri.-Tues.

(1) The Old Man of the Mountain Museum (745-8720), Exit 2, Franconia Notch. Historic memorabilia and photos. Mid-May-late Oct.

(2) Loon Mountain (800-229-7829), Rte. 112, Lincoln. Winter skiing, horseback and pony rides, mountain bike trails and rentals, and four--passenger enclosed gondola Skyride to the top of Loon Mountain to an observation tower, cafeteria, hiking trails, and cave walk.

(6) Plymouth Heritage Trail (536-1001), Plymouth.

(8) Hebron Marsh Nature Center (744-3516), N. Shore Rd., E. Hebron. NH Audubon Society (224-9909), 3 Silk Farm Rd., Concord 03301. Seasonal.

(8) Paradise Point Nature Center: see Hebron Marsh.

(12) Wellington State Park (744-2197), West Shore Rd., Bristol. $

(14) Sculpted Rocks Natural Area, off Groton Rd., Groton. New Hampshire Division of Parks and Recreation (271-3556).

(16) Mary Baker Eddy House (786-9943), Stinson Lake Rd., Rumney. Christian Science Church founder lived here from 1855-62. (Another of her homes is on Halls Brook Rd. in Groton).

(16) Rumney Historical Society, Old Rumney Town Hall, Buffalo Rd., Rumney. Early mill/industrial artifacts and photos.

(20) Warren Fish Hatchery (764-8593), Rte. 25, Warren. Interactive exhibits, tour, and nature trails. Hatchery open year-round; visitor center open May-Oct.

(21) Lost River (745-8031), Rte. 112, Kinsman Notch, N. Woodstock. Mid-May-mid-Oct. $

(22) The Frost Place (823-5510), Ridge Rd., off Rte. 116, Franconia. Memorial Day-June, Sat. and Sun. 1-5; July 1-Columbus Day Weekend, daily 1-5 except Tues. $

(22) Iron Furnace Interpretive Center, Main St., Rte. 18, Franconia Village.

(23) Sugar Hill Historical Museum (823-8142), Main St., Sugar Hill. Cultural development of region includes Franconia iron industry and grand hotels; 19th-century blacksmith's shop. July-mid-Oct., Thurs., Sat. and Sun. 1-4. $

Activities

(1) (L) Indian Head Resort (800-343-8000 or 745-8000), Rte. 3N, Lincoln. Tennis courts, paddleboats, swimming, hot tub, sauna, and hiking.

(1) (L) Jack O'Lantern Resort Golf Course (877-321-3636), Rte. 3, Woodstock.18-hole, par 70 course. www.jackolanterresort.com.

(2) Clark's Trading Post (745-8913), Rte. 3, Lincoln. Late May-mid-Oct.: call for schedule. Ticket includes rides, shows, and tours.

(2) Hobo Hills Adventure Golf (745-2125), Main St., Lincoln. Miniature golf. June-Labor Day, daily; spring and fall, weekends .
(2) Hobo Railroad (745-2135), Rt. 112, Lincoln. Weekends late May-early June; daily late June-foliage season. Call for schedule.

(2) The Whale's Tale Waterpark (745-8810), Rte. 3, Lincoln. Slides, wave and swimming pools, and river tubing. Late June-Labor Day, daily; Memorial Day-late June, weekends.

(3) Fadden's Sugar House (745-2406), 99 Main St., Rte. 3, N. Woodstock. Maple syrup made the old-fashioned way in 1940s sugar house.

(4) Base Camp Adventure Center (236-4666), Town Square, Waterville Valley Resort. Mountain and tandem bike rentals.

(4) Corcoran's Pond (236-4666), Waterville Valley Resort. Paddleboat, canoe and sunfish rentals; sandy beach.

(4) North Country Chamber Players (869-3154), Loon Mountain Resort. Classic chamber music.

(5) Sugar Shack/ Mountain Bike Park (726-3867), Rte. 175, Thornton. More than 15 miles of trails crisscross 240 acres; primitive, riverfront camping.

(5) Rocky Ridge Ranch (726-8067), Rte. 9, Campton. Trail rides daily except Monday (after Labor Day-Jan. 15, by appt. only).

(5) Ski Fanatics (726-4327), Campton Plaza, Campton. Mountain bike, kayak, canoe, tube rentals; shuttle service. Snowshoe and snowboard rentals.

(6) The Greasy Wheel (536-3655), 40 S. Main St., Plymouth. Bicycle rentals.

(6) Keniston-Freeman Summer Concert Series (536-1347), Main St., Plymouth. Free Wednesday evening concert series late June -Aug.

(6) NH Music Festival (253-4331), Boyd Hall, Plymouth State College. Early June-mid Aug.

(6) Pemi-Baker River Adventures (536-5652), 33 Sanborn Rd., Plymouth. Kayak, tube and canoe rentals and shuttle service; tours on Baker and Pemigewasset rivers.

(6) Rhino Bike Works (536-3919), 95 Main St., Plymouth. Mountain bike rentals.

(6) Rock Barn (536-2717), Tenney Mt. Highway, Plymouth. Indoor rock climbing.

(6) Silver Cultural Arts Center (535-ARTS), Main St., Plymouth State College. Professional and student productions.

6) Ski & Sports (536-2338), 103 Main St., Plymouth. Canoe and kayak rentals, equipment and clothing.

(6) Tenney Mountain Ski Resort (536-4125), Rte. 3A, Plymouth.

(8) Newfound Marina (744-3233), N. Shore Rd., Hebron. Boat rental.

(19) Pines Speedway (786-2115), Rte. 25, Wentworth. Seasonal dirt track racing.

(22) Glider Rides (823-8881), Franconia Airport. May-foliage season

Crafts, Galleries, and Antiques

(3) Russell Crag Gallery of Fine Crafts (745-8664), 110 Main St., N. Woodstock. Pottery, glasswork, jewelry, woodwork and artwork by regional craftspeople. Closed Tues.

(5) NH Homecraft Cooperative (726-8626), Rte. 3, Campton. Cooperative gallery sells NH crafts in 1878 one-room schoolhouse. Mid-June-mid-Oct.

(6) Downtown Artworks (536-8946), 67 Main St., Plymouth. Original art and gifts. Closed Mon.

(6) Hundelrut Studio (536-4396), 10 Hawthorne St., Plymouth. Original art, cards, pottery, quilts, and T-shirts.

(6) Karl Drerup Art Gallery (535-2614), Plymouth State College, Plymouth. Changing exhibits.

(16) Shanware Pottery (786-9835), 1819 Rte. 25, Rumney. Studio and gallery; stoneware, porcelain.

(19) The Wentworth Collection (764-9395), Rtes. 25 /25A, Wentworth. Replica 18th-century American furniture.

(20) The Village Smithy (764-5501), Rt 25, Warren. "Everything from candy to kayaks"

(23) Bowen Brook Art Center (823-7200), Rte. 117, Sugar Hill. Crafts, furniture and gifts.

(23) Colonial Cottage Antiques (823-5614), 720 Blake Rd., Sugar Hill.

(23) P.C. Anderson Handmade Furniture (823-5209), 253 Center District Rd., Sugar Hill. Handcrafted hardwood furniture.

Shopping

(2) Innisfree Bookshop (745-6107), Millfront Marketplace, Lincoln. Books, cassettes and CDs, toys, books by local authors.

(2) Mountain Wanderer Map and Book Store (800-745-2707 or 745-2594), Rte. 112, Lincoln. Hiking, biking, paddling and nature maps and guides; travel books, topo and relief maps, and gifts.

(3A) Abel's Candy & Fudge (745-6378), Main St., Rte. 3, Woodstock. Hand-dipped and sugar-free chocolates, and other homemade goodies.

(3) Fadden's General Store, Main St., N. Woodstock.

(4) Bookmonger/Toad Hall Toys (236-4544), Waterville Valley.

(5) Granite State Goodies (726-4663), Campton. NH specialty foods, ice cream shop, "make your own" gift baskets.

(6) Louis Samaha Store (536-1457), 137 Main St., Plymouth. Tobacco, harmonicas, cutlery, groceries, and sundries.

(6) Plymouth Book Exchange (536-2528), 91 Main St., Plymouth. Books, maps, NH books.

(16) Village Books (786-9300), Main St., Rumney. New, old and rare books, prints, and Paper Americana.

(16) Maple Winds Farm (786-9251), Off Halls Brook Rd., Rumney. Maple syrup, hand-spun and woven shawls. May-Nov.

(19) Atwell Hill Bison Farm (764-9041), Atwell Hill Rd., Wentworth.

(20) Foote's Sugar House (764-9929), Rte. 118, Warren. Maple syrup and products.

(22) Franconia Village Store (823-7782), Rte. 116, Franconia.

(23) Harman's Cheese & Country Store (823-8000), Rte. 117, Sugar Hill. "The World's Greatest Cheddar Cheese", maple syrup and maple products, preserves, old fashioned candies, gift baskets, and more.

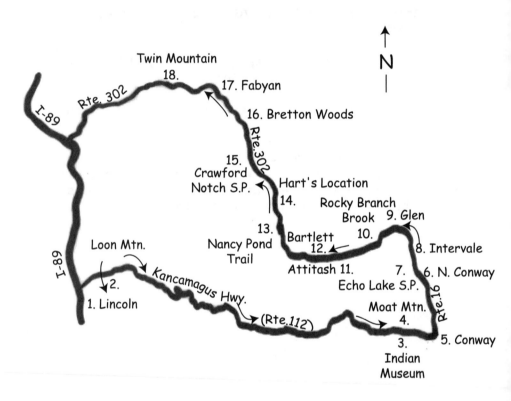

Twin Mountain
18.

Rte. 302

I-89

N

17. Fabyan

16. Bretton Woods

Rte.302

15.
Crawford
Notch S.P.

Hart's Location
14.

Rocky Branch
Brook   9. Glen

8. Intervale

I-68-I

Loon Mtn.

13.
Nancy Pond
Trail

Bartlett
12.

10.

Kancamagus Hwy.

2.

1. Lincoln

(Rte.112)

Attitash 11.

7.
Echo Lake S.P.

Moat Mtn.
4.

3.
Indian
Museum

6. N. Conway

Rte.16

5. Conway

Drive 11

Along the "Kanc" and through Crawford Notch

82 miles

Follow a spectaculaly scenic road carved through the heart of the White Mountain National Forest, then head north through a North Country mecca for skiing, shopping, and summer fun. The drive continues through Crawford Notch, centermost of the White Mountains' three great passes. Just beyond are two of the region's most famous landmarks, an Edwardian confection of a hotel and a most unusual railway.

In 1867 the state of New Hampshire sold most of the land in the White Mountains to lumber companies for $26,000, launching a period of slash-cut woodlands, forest fires, and general overharvesting of timber. In 1901, in opposition to this destruction, the Society for the Preservation of New Hampshire Forests (SPNHF) was organized. In response to the Society's urging, Congress passed the Weeks Act, creating the White Mountain National Forest, in 1911. Named in honor of John Wingate Weeks, who was instrumental in moving the legislation through Congress, the Act authorized the federal government to acquire a million acres of land at a purchase price of $6 million.

Today, the **White Mountain National Forest** covers 774,496 acres in New Hampshire and Maine, and includes five designated wilderness areas, more than 1,200 miles of hiking trails, four downhill ski areas partly or entirely on Forest land, lakes, ponds, waterfalls, 23 roadside campgrounds, and about 350 miles of trails for cross-country skiing and snowmobiling. Small portions are still harvested for timber.

Note: If you plan to leave your car in White Mountain National Forest parking areas, you'll need a WMNF parking pass. The cost is $20 for an annual pass or $5 for one seven-day Consecutive Day pass; $3 day passes are also available. There are fee tubes at many of the sites, or passes can be purchased at the Saco Ranger District Station at the eastern end of the Kancamagus Highway in Conway, at Lincoln Woods at the western end of the "Kanc," and at variety and convenience stores throughout Mt. Washington Valley.

(1) **Lincoln** (*see Drive 10*) is the western terminus of the **Kancamagus Highway** (Rte. 112), New England's first National Scenic Byway, and the only one in northern New England. The "Kanc" lies almost entirely within the borders of the National Forest, winding for 34 1/2 miles alongside the Pemigewasset and Swift rivers, climbing to almost 3,000 ft. as it crosses the flank of Mt. Kancamagus to the Saco River in Conway. Along the way there are picnic areas, swimming holes, panoramic views, and hiking trails. Stop at the **White Mountain Visitor Information Center** at the beginning of the drive for brochures and parking permits. The paved road is open all year. *(Note: More than 750,000 vehicles travel the highway each year, and traffic can be very heavy in summer and when fall foliage is at its peak. In season, the best time to drive the Kanc is early in the morning. There are no motorists' services.)*

Kancamagus (*Kan-kuh-mog-us*, "the fearless one") was the grandson of Passaconaway, a peace-loving chief who united more than 17 tribes into the Pennacook Confederacy and ruled as their first "Sagamon" until he died in 1669. Kancamagus followed his father, Wonalancet, as third and final Sagamon, trying to keep peace between his people and an increasing number of white pioneers who came to this region. Finally, in defeat, he and his followers

moved north to Quebec. Years later, he returned to lead the Indian raid on Dover (*see Drive 1*).

Side Trip

(2) Turn off the Kanc to Loon Mountain Recreation Area, a ski resort which, off season, offers rides to the summit on the Mountain Skyride Gondola, trail bike riding, horseback riding, and a skate park.

A few highlights along the Kanc, in the order in which you'll reach them traveling west to east:

-- Lincoln Woods, where a long suspension footbridge crosses the river to a swimming area.

-- Kancamagus Pass, the highest point on the highway.

-- Sabbaday Falls, where an easy 4/10- mi. trail follows a brook to a series of cascades in a narrow flume.

-- Passaconaway Historic Site, where the early 1800s Russell-Colbath Historic Homestead offers a glimpse into the lives of the regions' earliest settlers. The 1/2- mi. **Rail'n River Forest Trail** beginning at the parking lot is perfect for families with young kids: it's stroller accessible.

Ruth, the daughter of Amzi Russell, who, with his father, Thomas, built the Russell-Colbath Historic Homestead, married a carpenter named Thomas Alden Colbath and lived there with him until one night in 1891 when he left the house, saying he'd be back in a little while. Each night, for the next 39 years, Ruth put a lamp in the window to help her husband find his way home. He finally did, in 1933 -- three years after Ruth's death. When asked where he'd been, he'd

223

reply only vaguely that he'd been in California, Cuba, and Panama.

-- Bear Notch Road: this 9.3-mi. road (closed in winter) winds through the Bartlett Experimental Forest, a 3.000-acre Forest Service research project set up to study the effects of logging and disease on the WMNF. The road ends in Bartlett on Rte. 302. There are terrific views of the Pemigewasset Wilderness along the way.

-- Rocky Gorge Scenic Area, where the Swift River has worn a narrow passage through solid rock, forming a series of ponds perfect for cooling off on a summer's day (swim only in designated areas). There's a foot bridge to Falls Pond; a trail circles the water.

Many of the region's finest hiking trails begin along the Kanc. A few of the more popular include:

-- Lincoln Woods Trail (2.8 mi., easy): this footpath crosses a 160-ft.-long suspension bridge and follows an abandoned railroad grade to the beginning of the Wilderness Trail into the 75,000-acre Pemigewasset Wilderness Area, one of the largest roadless tracks in the east. A 0.4 mile turn-off from the trail goes to Franconia Falls, a massive granite ledge with a water chute which is delightful for swimming or sunbathing. (By regulating visitor traffic to the falls area to 60 people at one time, the Forest Service is attempting to reverse past impacts on this environment. Day use permits are required, and are available free at Lincoln Woods Visitor Center. To reserve permits in advance, call 536-1310).

Timber baron J.E. Henry logged the area surrounding the Lincoln Woods Trail -- and much of the Kanc -- in the late 1800s and early 1900s. In 1917 the Parker-Young company bought Henry's land and continued

224

logging. In the 1930s the firm sold the parcel to the Federal Government, with the stipulation that they be allowed to continue cutting. The sale added some 100,000 acres to the National Forest, and the company ceased operations in 1946. But today, more than a half century later, visitors can still see the remains of cutting along old logging roads (called "dugway roads" because they're dug into mountain slopes), bridge abutments, and abandoned railbeds.

-- Greeley Ponds Scenic Area and Greeley Ponds Trail (roughly 5 miles, moderately difficult) goes to Upper Greeley Pond, surrounded by old-growth timber and towering cliffs; and the shallow Lower Greeley Pond: both are good for trout fishing.

-- Champney Falls Trail (6 mi., easy), named for the 19th-century landscape artist Benjamin Champney, leads to Champney Falls.

-- Boulder Loop Hike (2.8 mi., easy - moderate): turn left and head through the Covered Bridge to the parking lot and trailhead. There are great views of Mt. Chocorua and the Swift River Valley en route.

The **WMNF Saco Ranger District** is headquartered at the eastern end of the Kanc.

(3) The **Indian Museum**, just before Rte. 112 intersects with Rte. 16, houses the eclectic collection of Treffle "Baldy" Bolduc, a French-Canadian Abenaki who also makes fine snowshoes.

Alternate Route

In Conway, immediately before the junction of Rtes. 112 and 16, turn north (left) at the traffic light onto West Side Rd. if you want to bypass the towns of

Conway and North Conway and the many shopping outlets that lie between them. This country byway paralleling busy Rte. 16 passes by two covered bridges (the 1890 Conway-Saco River Bridge, and the 1869 Conway-Swift River Bridge), Echo Lake State Park, and 54-acre Conway Dahl Sanctuary on the Saco River before it joins Rte. 302 just west of Glen. (If you choose this route, turn west onto Rte. 302 and resume the drive's main route at the Covered Bridge House, #10 below).

Side Trip

(4) Moat Mountain is a popular spot for rock hounds to gather quartz crystals. To try your hand, head north on West Side Rd. and turn onto Passaconaway Rd., then left onto High Rd. and follow the signs. At the parking lot at the end of the road, hike 3/4 mi. to the Moat Mountain Site. For information, contact the WMNF, Saco Ranger District.

----

(5) Turn north from Rte. 112 onto Rte. 16 and continue into **Conway**, tucked in an intervale between the Saco and Swift Rivers. Mt. Chocorua and the Sandwich Range are to the southwest, and Mt. Washington looms to the north. Conway and North Conway owe their growth to two principal factors: art and tourism.

By the middle of the 19th century the area was an important center for artists associated with the White Mountain School. The most famous of them, Benjamin Champney, worked here about 1850. Landscape master George Innes and the Hudson River School pioneer Thomas Cole also helped spread word of the region's beauty, which by the late 1800s was attracting an increasing number of tourists whose interests were recreational rather than artistic.

The biggest thing ever to hit the Conways was downhill skiing. In 1936, North Conway businessman Carroll

226

Reed established the country's first open-enrollment ski school at the **Eastern Slope Inn**, and hired Hannes Schneider, an Austrian émigré who had taught the Tyrolean ski troops in the army of his native country. From then on, skiers flocked to New Hampshire to sample the hell-for-leather backcountry delights of Tuckerman Ravine (*see Drive 12*), and later to patronize growing commercial areas such as Mt. Cranmore, Black Mountain, Wildcat and, in the 1960s, Attitash.

The latest chapter in Conways tourism was written in the 1980s, when the five-mile stretch of Rte. 16 between Conway and North Conway was transformed into a shopper's paradise and a sprawl opponent's nightmare. This stretch is lined with more than 200 outlet stores, including L.L. Bean, Eddie Bauer, Banana Republic, April Cornell, and Mikasa. (Don't forget: there's no sales tax in New Hampshire.)

(6) The centerpiece of the bustling town of **North Conway** is the 1874, mansard-roofed depot that marked the end of the line for the "snow trains" that brought skiers into town until 1961. Now the northern terminus for **Conway Scenic Railroad**, the yellow wooden building has its original telegraph and phone equipment and furnishings. The railroad operates seasonally, with excursions to Conway and Bartlett using antique coaches and parlor cars. If you're a true railroad buff, you might want to spring for First Class seating aboard the beautifully-restored, 1898 Pullman Parlor-Observation Car "Gertrude Emma," in service on the Conway line. The train to Bartlett crosses the Frankenstein Trestle in Crawford Notch (*see Drive 12*).

Side Trip

(7) Just past North Conway's Eastern Slope Inn, turn left on River Rd., continue for two miles, and watch for a dirt road on the left. It's an easy half-mile walk to Diana's Baths, a series of cascading falls that

plummet to potholes alongside Lucy Brook (no swimming: the brook goes into a public water supply). Continue to West Side Rd. and follow signs to Echo Lake State Park, where there's a fine swimming beach and picnic area, and a road that winds for a mile to the top of Cathedral Ledge, a 700-ft vertical wall famous among technical climbers. From here you can see hawks, falcons, and much of the Saco Valley.

----

(8) Continue north on Rte. 16 through **Intervale**. Rte. 16A, just north of the village, parallels Rte. 16 for several miles before rejoining the highway just south of Glen, and is lined with lodgings and condominiums.

For more than 20 years, Roger and Nelly Hartmann traveled the world collecting railroad items. Their collection is on display at the **Hartmann Model Railroad** -- more than 16,000 sq. ft. of space that includes Lionel and American Flyers, HO modular layouts, and handmade train and car displays.

(9) In **Glen**, **Heritage New Hampshire** artfully combines technology with a folksy approach to relate the past 350 years of New Hampshire history. There are plenty of rides, talking mannequins and fun exhibits to engage kids of all ages. Mother Goose and her gang hold court next door at **Story Land**, where there are rides and live shows.

(10) At the intersection of Rtes. 16 and 302, head west on Rte. 302 into the Saco River Valley. There's a good swimming hole ahead: a few miles down Rte. 302, turn right onto Jericho Rd. and continue 4 4/10 mi. to the Rocky Branch trailhead. Walk alongside the river back toward the highway for about 50 yds. to **Rocky Branch Brook**, a delightful spot to cool off. (See the *AMC White Mountain Guide* for details).

Note: If you took the West Side Rd. bypass from Conway, resume the drive here.

The restored, 1800s Bartlett Covered Bridge next to the **Covered Bridge House B&B** now houses the **Bridge Gift Shoppe**.

(11) At **Attitash Bear Peak Ski Area**, hop aboard the chairlift to the summit and plummet down the 3/4-mi. alpine slide on your own wheeled sled -- then cool off on the waterslide. With the **Grand Summit Hotel and Conference Center**, a golf driving range, mountain bike trials, horseback riding, and a variety of other activities, the ski area is now a year-round resort.

(12) In **Bartlett**, Bear Notch Rd. connects with the Kancamagus Highway (*see #2 above*).

(13) About 3.5 miles west, watch for the **Nancy Pond** trailhead. Trail and pond are named for one Nancy, the first woman to pass through Crawford Notch. Nancy -- her last name is lost to history -- had been working in Jefferson in the late 1700s for Colonel Joseph Whipple (*see Drive 12*), when she fell in love with one of his servants. The man promised to take her with him to Portsmouth, and she entrusted him with her savings while she went to her home in Lancaster to prepare for the journey.   Nancy soon learned that her lover had left without her.   Ignoring warnings about traveling alone in the approaching winter, she took off by herself to catch up with him. Trekking through deep snow, she made it through Crawford Notch -- but was found dead alongside a brook later named for her, her soaked clothes frozen to her body.

The trail goes to **Nancy Brook Virgin Spruce Forest and Scenic Area**, a National Natural Landmark with a 1,600-acre stand of virgin spruce, and then continues to the Pemigewasset Wilderness.

(14) Continue west through **Hart's Location**, home to the elegant, granite **Notchland Inn**, built in 1862 by

Boston photographer Samuel Bemis. The inn is on the site of Abel Crawford's Mt. Crawford House, and the restaurant was that hostelry's tavern. Hart's Location, the smallest town in the state, is the first to report its votes in national elections.

Crawford Notch, the pass used today by Rte. 302 between Bartlett and Twin Mountain, was discovered by accident by a moose hunter, Timothy Nash, in 1771. Nash immediately reported his find to Gov. John Wentworth, who was interested in developing roads into the state's interior. The governor agreed to give Nash a tract of land at the northern end of the notch if the backwoodsman could bring a horse south to Portsmouth along the route he had described. Nash and a friend named Benjamin Sawyer rode, pushed and cajoled a farm horse through Crawford Notch, sometimes using a rope sling to lower the animal over ledges and down steep banks. Nash and Sawyer got their land grant, and New Hampshire had a wilderness pass to develop through the White Mountains to the upper Connecticut Valley.

The Notch got its name from the family of Abel and Hannah Crawford, who settled on the notch road in 1792 and raised nine children. Crawford, a hunting guide for "gentlemen strangers," must have felt that his home still needed a few more people: he opened it to travelers as the Mount Crawford House in 1852. This was the first hostelry in the notch, and, in its day, one of the most famous in New England.

----

(15) Just ahead, in 6,000-acre **Crawford Notch State Park**, Rte. 302 winds for six miles through a glacially-formed notch, past some of the most magnificent scenery in the White Mountains.

Watch on the left for the Arethusa Falls Trail (2.6 mi., easy-moderate) to **Arethusa Falls**, the highest in the state, which plummets more than 200 ft. This trail connects with the Ripley Falls Trail, which continues for another 2.1 miles to 100-ft. Ripley Falls.

Just past the trailhead is the **Willey House Historic Site**, headquarters for the **New Hampshire State Park System**. Several trailheads begin here, including the easy, half-mile Pond Loop Trail.

To the left is Frankenstein Cliff, named for Godfrey Frankenstein, a Cincinnati artist who often painted in this area. Across from the Dry River Campground, the 500-ft.-long Frankenstein Trestle, built in 1905 by the Maine Central Railroad to replace the original in 1875, soars 80 ft. above Frankenstein Gulf.

Abel Crawford was working near the home of the Willey family on August 28, 1825 when a half-mile portion of the mountain behind the house roared down. He described the event in his *History of the White Mountains*: "While there they [the Willeys] saw on the west side of the road a small movement of rocks and earth coming down the hill, and it took all before it. They saw, likewise, whole trees coming down, standing upright, for ten rods together, before they would tip over -- the whole still moving slowly on, making its way until it had crossed the road, and then on a level surface some distance before it stopped. This grand and awful sight frightened the timid family very much."

The Willeys ran to a nearby shelter. The landslide split just above the house, surged past, and reunited below the house. The Willeys were killed, but the house survived intact.

Saco Lake, the source of the Saco River, is near the parking lot for the Mt. Willard and Avalon trails. Numerous cascades in the notch feed into the Saco, including the Beecher, Pearl, Flume, and Silver: several are visible from the road.

Ahead on the left is **Crawford Depot**, an Appalachian Mountain Club facility offering inexpensive lodgings and meals. The 3.6- mi., moderately difficult **Avalon Trail** begins behind the Depot and passes Beecher and Pearl Cascades on its way to the summit of Avalon Mountain.

At the northern end of the notch, there are panoramic views of the Presidential Range from **Eisenhower Memorial Wayside Park**.

(16) **Bretton Woods,** in a glacial plain at the base of Mt. Washington, is home to one of the grandest hotels in the northeast, the **Mount Washington Hotel and Resort** (pictured on the cover of this book). Celebrating its centennial in 2002, the Mount Washington is the sole survivor of the grand White Mountain resort hotels built in the days when wealthy clients arrived by railway to spend the entire summer, with steamer trunks and servants in tow.

The Mt. Washington was the creation of railroad speculator Joseph Stickney, who bought the Old Mount Pleasant House and a 10,000-acre tract and, in 1902, opened his spare-no-expense hotel. Built by Italian artisans and laborers who boarded on site throughout the two years of construction, the palatial new resort incorporated steel framework, the latest in plumbing, heating, and electricity, and its own telephone exchange. Mr. Stickney oversaw the triumphant grand opening (as did Ethan Allen Crawford III) and the first two seasons of operation before he died in December 1903. (The granite, Episcopal Joseph Stickney Memorial Church of the Transfiguration, on Rte. 302 just beyond the hotel, was dedicated to the entrepreneur a few years afterward.)

In 1944 the entire hotel was reserved by the U.S. government for the World Monetary Fund Conference, in which representatives of 44 nations shaped the economic framework of the postwar world. The summer-long deliberations resulted in the fixing of the gold standard, the adoption of the U.S. dollar as the benchmark against which other national currencies were valued, and the creation of the World Bank.

The hotel opened for its first winter in 2000, and today offers year-round activities including golf, tennis, a spa, a cross-country ski area, and alpine skiing at **Bretton Woods Ski Area**, the state's largest. The adjacent 1896 **Bretton Arms Country Inn** provides a more intimate lodging environment.

(17) **Fabyan**, a major railroad terminus during the golden era of White Mountains tourism, is home to the **Mt. Washington Cog Railway,** an improbable piece of Victorian technology whose locomotives *push* cars, clanking and wheezing, three miles to the summit of Mt. Washington. The world's "first mountain-climbing cog rail" was invented in 1869 by inventor Sylvester Marsh, who built his railway for $39,500. Dubbed Old Peppersass (because it resembled an old-fashioned peppersauce cruet), the first locomotive was shipped to Littleton and hauled piecemeal by oxen 25 mi. to Mt. Washington. The base station has a visitor center, museum, restaurant, and gift shop.

(18) Continue on Rte. 302 out of Crawford Notch, as the road veers west alongside the Ammonoosuc River, to **Twin Mountain**, a tourist center with a large number of budget-priced motels and tourist cabins. At the intersection of Rtes. 302 and 3, turn north on Rte. 3 to begin Drive 12, or south on Rte. 3 to return to I-93.

Information

Appalachian Mountain Club (617-523-0636), 5 Joy St., Boston, MA 02108. For hut reservations: 603-466-2727. www.outdoors.org.

Conway Village Chamber of Commerce (447-2639), Rte. 16, Conway.

Mount Washington Valley Chamber of Commerce (800-367-3364 or 356-3171), Box 2300, No. Conway 03860. www.mtwashingtonvalley.org

New Hampshire State Park System (374-2272), Hart's Location, Rte. 302, Crawford Notch 03575.

Twin Mountain Chamber of Commerce (800-245-TWIN or 846-5408), Box 194, Twin Mountain 03595. www.twinmountain.org

White Mountain Visitors Center (800-346-3687 or 745-8720), Exit 32 off I-93, Lincoln/North Woodstock line. www.visitwhitemountains.com.

WMNF Saco Ranger District (447-5448), Kancamagus Highway, Conway (mailing address: RFD I, Box 94, Concord 03818).

White Mountain National Forest Headquarters (528-8721), Box 638, 719 North Main St., Laconia 03246. www.fs.fed.us/r9/white.

Lodging

(4) (R) The Darby Field Inn and Restaurant (800-426-4147 outside NH; 447-2181), Bald Hill Rd., Conway 03818. www.darbyfield.com. 1826 farmhouse offers a romantic mountain retreat, with lovely guest rooms and fine candlelight, Continental dining. $$-$$$

(4) Hostelling International White Mountains (800-909-4776 or 447-1001), 36 Washington St., Conway 03818. www.angel.net/~hostel. Fully-equipped kitchen; family rates. $

(5) (R) Stonehurst Manor (800-525-9100), Rte. 16, N. Conway 03860. www.StonehurstManor.com. Circa 1900 mansion on 33 secluded acres has 24 elegant rooms (7 with fireplaces) and a highly-regarded reataurant ($$-$$$) featuring gourmet pizzas and pit-smoked prime rib. MAP available. $$-$$$

(5) The Buttonwood Inn (800-258-2525 or 356-2625), Mt. Surprise Rd., N. Conway 03860. www.buttonwoodinn.com. 1820s farmhouse on 17 secluded acres has 10 cozy guest rooms with private baths, Shaker furniture, and wide pine floors: two have gas fireplaces. Outdoor heated pool and perennial gardens; breakfast is a specialty. $$-$$$

(5) Cranmore Inn (800-526-5502 outside NH, or 356-5502), Kearsarge St., N.Conway 03860. www.cranmoreinn.com. The valley's oldest continuously-operated inn has 18 rooms and suites (14 with private bath), a fireplaced common room, and an outdoor pool. Guests have privileges at Mount Cranmore Racquet Club. Dinner features hearty, home-cooked fare. $-$$

(5) Cranmore Mountain Lodge (800-356-3596 or 356-2044), Kearsarge Rd., N. Conway 03860. www.cranmoremountainlodge.com. The one-time home of Babe Ruth is a mix of country inn, farm, and resort, with 12 inn rooms, four rooms in the barn and an independent hostel ($). Heated swimming pool (enclosed in winter), jacuzzi, tennis, farm animals, mountain bike and x-c trails. MAP available. $$-$$$

(5) Eastern Slope Resort (800-862-1600 or 356-8621), 2760 Main St., Rte. 16, N. Conway. www.easternslopeinn.com. 146 rooms, townhouses, suites and 2- and 3-bedroom units in a family-friendly resort in the heart of the village. Indoor pool, jacuzzi, and game room. $$-$$$

(6) The White Mountain Hotel and Resort (800-533-6301 or 356-7100), West Side Rd., Hale's Location 03860. www.whitemountainhotel.com. Cathedral and White Horse Ledges form the backdrop for the Valley's newest full-service resort, with 80 luxurious guest rooms with suites. There's a restaurant and English-style pub, championship golf course, tennis, and health club. $$-$$$

(7) Perry's Motel & Cottages (356-2214), Rte. 16A, Intervale. www.perrysmotel.com. Kid-friendly, with housekeeping and non housekeeping cottages, motel rooms, a heated pool and jacuzzi, toddler playground, and picnic tables and grills. $$

(10) Covered Bridge House B&B (800-232-9109 or 383-9109), Rte. 302, Glen 03838. www.coveredbridgehouse.com. Six guest rooms (four with private bath) in a lovely Colonial Revival house overlooking the Saco River. Outdoor hot tub. $-$$

(12) The Country Inn at Bartlett (800-292-2353 or 374-2353), Rte. 302, Bartlett 03812. www.bartlettinn.com. Informal, family accommodations set in a stand of pines surrounded by the WMNF. Inn and housekeeping cottages; some fireplaces. Outdoor hot tub. $$

(12) The Grand Summit Resort Hotel and Conference Center (888-554-1900), Rte. 302, Bartlett. www.attitash.com. 143 deluxe and condominium-style rooms; health club, outdoor heated swimming pool, full-service restaurant. $$-$$$

(14) (R) The Notchland Inn (800-866-6131 or 374-6131), Rte. 302, Harts Location 03812. www.notchland.com. On 100 acres: five suites, seven doubles, all with private bath; two suites in 1852 schoolhouse. Five-course dinner candlelight dinner($35 pp before tax and tip). MAP available. $$$

(15) Crawford Depot (see AMC in "Information").

(16) The Mount Washington Hotel and Resort and The Bretton Arms (800-258-0330; in NH 278-1000), Rte. 302, Bretton Woods 03575. www.mtwashington.com. MAP

(18) Carlson's Lodge (846-5501 or 800-348-5502), Rte. 302, Twin Mountain. Spacious rooms with color TV, and private baths; large living room and balcony lobbies; game room; mountain views. $-$$

(18) Northlander Motel (800-272-4284 or 846-5520), Rte. 3, Twin Mountain. www.musar.com/northlander. Standard rooms, suites, efficiencies, and cottages. Heated pool, playground. $-$$

(18) Patio Motor Court (846-5515), Rte. 3, Twin Mountain. www.thepatio.com. One- and two-bedroom housekeeping cottages; pool, lawn games. $-$

Restaurants

(5) Bellini's (356-7000), Seavey St., N. Conway. For more than 50 years serving Tuscan Italian specialties such as focaccia, lobster ravioli, and homemade desserts. D, closed Tues. $-$$

(5) Conway Scenic Railroad (356-5251), N. Conway. Lunch and dinner on the 47-seat, refurbished dining car, *Chocorua*.

(5) Bloomer's Delicatessen (356-3030), Main St., N. Conway. New York-style deli. $

(5)(L) Scottish Lion Inn and Restaurant (356-6381), Rte. 16, N. Conway. Scottish, American and European specialties include prime rib, Scottish steak and mushroom pie, and Finnan Haddie. Sun. brunch recommended. Eight tastefully-decorated rooms with private bath and AC. ($$). L, D. $$-$$$

(5) Elvio's Pizzeria and Restaurant (356-3307), Main St., N. Conway. Excellent pizza, subs, sandwiches, pasta, and daily specials. L, D. $

(7)(L) The 1785 Inn (800-421-1785 or 356-9025), Rte. 16, Intervale. www.the1785inn.com. Cozy rooms and award-winning dining in an historic inn overlooking the Saco River. Extensive appetizer menu including a tableside Caesar salad and crab Imperial; entrées include beef, poultry, and fresh fish. Extensive wine list. B, D. $$$

(8) (L) The Bernerhof (800-548-8007 or 383-39132), Rte. 302, Glen. www.bernerhofinn.com. European-style inn with luxurious, antiques-furnished guest rooms ($$) has long been famous for its fine contemporary and middle European cuisine. Taste of the Mountains Cooking School holds classes here. $$$

(8) Red Parka Pub (383-4344), Downtown Glen. Steaks, ribs, and poultry and other hearty, New England fare in a casual, family environment. The bar has live entertainment. $-$$

Attractions

(4) Indian Museum (447-5287), Rte. 112, Conway. Afternoons or by chance. $

(4) Conway Historical Society (447-5551), Eastman-Lord House Museum, 100 Main St., Conway. Twelves period rooms from 1820 to 1945. Memorial Day-Labor Day, Tues. and Thurs. 6-8 pm, Wed. 2-4.

(5) Conway Scenic Railway (800-253-5251 or 356-5251), Rte. 16, N. Conway. One- to five-hr. excursions; lunch and dinner excursions. Weekends mid-April-mid-May and Nov.-mid-Dec., daily mid-May-late Oct. $

(5) Conway Dahl Sanctuary. A 54-acre property with 1,800 ft. of unspoiled shoreline on the Saco River. NH Audubon (224-9909), 3 Silk Farm Rd., Concord 03301.

(5) Weather Discovery Center (356-2137), Rte. 16, N. Conway . Mt. Washington Observatory project has interactive exhibits and lots of weather information.

(7) Hartmann Model Railroad (356-9922), Rtes. 16/302, Intervale. Daily. $

(8) Heritage New Hampshire (383-4186), Rte. 16, Glen. Memorial Day weekend-Father's Day, weekends; Fathers Day-Columbus Day, daily. $

(8) Story Land (383-4293), Rte. 16, Glen. Daily mid-June-Labor Day; wknds Labor Day-Columbus Day. $

(16) Bretton Woods Ski Area (800-232-2972), Rte. 302, Bretton Woods. $

(16) Mt. Washington Cog Railway (800-922-8825 or 846-5404), off Rte. 302, Fabyan/Bretton Woods. Weekends in May, daily until Nov. Advance reservations highly recommended. $

Activities

(1) Loon Mountain Resort (800-229-LOON or 745-8111), Rte. 112, Lincoln. NH's longest gondola skyride, glacial caves, mountain biking, horseback riding, skate park and train rides.

(5) Northern Extremes (877-SACORIV or 383-8117), Rte. 302, Glen, and Main St., N. Conway. Canoe and kayak rental, shuttle, and white water instruction on the Saco River.

(5) Mt. Washington Valley Theater Company (356-4747), Eastern Slope Playhouse, Main St., N. Conway. Venerable repertory theater features professional actors, directors and designs from around the country.

(5) (L) The Stables at The Farm by the River (356-4855), 2555 West Side Rd., N. Conway. Horseback riding; pony, horse-drawn sleigh, and wagon rides.

(5) Pirate's Cove Adventure Golf (356-8807), Rte. 16, N. Conway. 18 creative holes of miniature golf. May-mid-Oct.

(5) Horse n' Around (356-6033). Horse-drawn wagon rides to Echo Lake and Diana's Baths from Schoeller Park in N. Conway; in winter, sleigh rides from Mount Cranmore and the White Mountain Hotel in Hale's Location.

(5) Mt. Cranmore (374-2368), Kearsarge Rd., N. Conway. Ski area.

(5) International Mountain Climbing School (356-7064), 2733 Main St., N. Conway. Rock and ice climbing, family climbs, Mt. Washington ascents.

(11) Attitash Bear Peak Alpine Slide and Waterslides (374-2368), Rte. 302, Bartlett. Wknds May-mid June & Labor Day-early Oct.; daily mid-June-Labor Day. $

Not on Drive

Saco Bound & Downeast Company (447-2177), Box 119, Center Conway. Canoeing and rafting expeditions; boat rentals.

Tours

Brake for Moose Scenic Tours (745-0919), Main St., Lincoln. Bus tour through the White Mountains.

Privatours, Inc. (447-1010), Mountain River Village, Rte. 16, Conway. Three-hour cassette tape tours of the central New Hampshire mountains. Rent or buy at the Saco Ranger Station and lodgings throughout the area.

Crafts, Galleries, and Antiques

(5) Handcrafters Barn, Rte. 16, N. Conway. N.E.-made crafts, clothing, and gifts.

(5) League of New Hampshire Craftsmen (356-2441), Rte. 16, N. Conway. Handcrafts by juried artisans.

(5) North Conway Antiques and Collectibles (356-6661), Rte. 16/302, N. Conway. 80 dealers display collectibles and antiques.

(5) Richard M. Plusch Antiques, Main St., N. Conway. Period furniture, glass, sterling, Oriental porcelains, rugs, jewelry, paintings, and prints.

Shopping

(5) Bye the Book (800-491-2665), Main St., N. Conway. Excellent inventory of new books.

(5) Tanger Outlet Centers (800-407-4078), N. Conway: three locations on Rte. 16.

(5) White Birch Booksellers (356-3200), 2568 S. Main St., N. Conway. New England and general travel books, children's books, and best sellers.

(5) Eastern Mountain Sports (356-5433), Eastern Slope Inn, Main St., N. Conway. Outdoor gear.

(5) International Mountain Equipment (356-6316), Main St., N. Conway. Technical climbing and outdoor gear; canoes, kayaks, and camping gear.

(5) North Country Angler (356-6000), Rte. 16, N. Conway. Fishing equipment and advice.

(5) Scottish Lion (356-3229), Rte. 16, N. Conway (across from Memorial Hospital). British imports include coats, crystal, blankets, and foods.

(7) Peter Limmer and Sons (356-5378), Rte. 16A, Intervale. Superbly-crafted custom hiking boots.

(7) Ragged Mountain Equipment (356-3042), Rte. 16 & 302, Intervale. Factory store with outdoor equipment clothing and fabric, including their own "Made in Intervale" clothing, packs and luggage.

(10) Bridge Gift Shoppe, (800-232-9109 or 383-9109), Rte. 302, Glen.

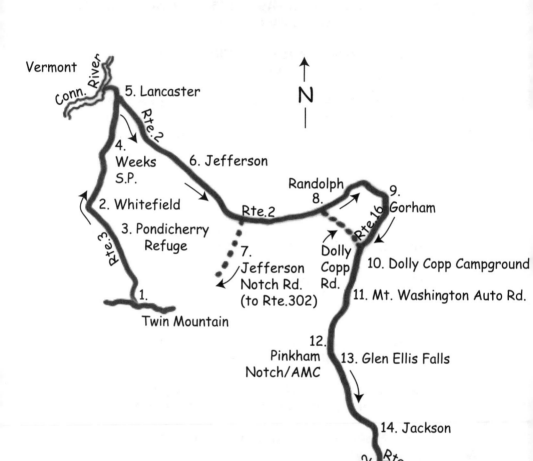

Vermont

Conn. River

5. Lancaster

Rte. 2

4. Weeks S.P.

6. Jefferson

Randolph
8.

9. Gorham

Rte. 16

2. Whitefield

Rte. 3

3. Pondicherry Refuge

Rte. 2

Dolly Copp Rd.

10. Dolly Copp Campground

7. Jefferson Notch Rd. (to Rte. 302)

11. Mt. Washington Auto Rd.

1. Twin Mountain

12. Pinkham Notch/AMC

13. Glen Ellis Falls

14. Jackson

Rte. 302

Rte. 16

N

Drive 12

The Northern Approach to Mt. Washington

67 miles

This route loops around the northern fringes of the Presidential Range, lofty heart of the White Mountains, then drops south beneath the steep walls of Pinkham Notch. Climb Mt. Washington by car or on foot; explore a famous string of hikers' huts; then descend to the cozy inns of Jackson, at the foot of the notch.

(1) Head north on Rte. 3 out of **Twin Mountain** (*see Drive 11 for Twin Mountain information*). The **Twin Mountain Hatchery and Wildlife Center** just north of the intersection is open to the public.

(2) **Whitefield**, in the valley of the Johns River at the northern edge of the White Mountains, was named by colonial Governor Benning Wentworth for his friend George Whitefield, a popular 18th-century Methodist evangelist who had died recently in Exeter.

For many years, beginning in 1866, the town was home to the **Mountain View House**, which grew to be one of the finest resort hotels in the White Mountains. Luminaries such as Babe Ruth and Bette Davis vacationed here; and President Eisenhower came to play at the nine-hole golf course. The grand hotel closed its doors in 1986 but was recently purchased by Massachusetts developer Kevin Craffey, who has undertaken the immense task of renovation. The golf course has been expanded to 18 holes and is now open; the full service resort and spa, being restored to Victorian splendor, is scheduled to open in May, 2002.

The **Weathervane Theatre** is the successor to the country's oldest summer theater, the Chase Barn Theater, which burned in the 1960s. The 1875 bandstand in the center of the village is the venue for summer band concerts.

Side Trip

(3) The 312-acre National Natural Landmark Pondicherry Wildlife Refuge is the jewel of the Audubon Society of New Hampshire's properties. One-hundred-acre Big Cherry Pond is home to a wide variety of birds including loons, three-toed and pileated woodpeckers, several kinds of ducks, and blue- and green-winged teal. The views of the presidential range are magnificent.

You can paddle by canoe from Big Cherry Pond to Little Cherry Pond, and then continue into the Johns River. To get to the refuge, follow signs for Whitefield Airport. Past the airport, continue south on Hazen Rd. for 3/10 mi. to a wood-fired power plant. About 1/10 mi. beyond the plant, on the north side of the road, watch for the abandoned railroad grade. Park near the small foot bridge and walk northeast along the grade for 1 1/2 mi. to the pond.

----

(4) In 1913 Lancaster native John Wingate Weeks, who sponsored the White Mountain National Forest Bill (*see Drive 11*), bought several farms on Mt. Prospect, including land at the 2,958-ft. summit. He cut a 1 1/2 mi. road through stands of white birch, past rugged rock outcroppings, ferns and wildflowers, to the top, where he built an estate overlooking the Connecticut River Valley and the White Mountains. Today, visitors can drive up the Prospect Mt. Road Scenic and Cultural Byway to the Weeks State Historic Site at 420-acre **Weeks State Park.** Exhibits in the summit lodge

include a bird collection, historic photos, and furniture. There's also a stone observation tower.

(5) Continue north on Rte. 3 to **Lancaster**, bordered by the Kilkenny Mountain Range on one side, and the Connecticut and Israel Rivers on the other. It's the county seat of Coos County, nearly a million acres of mostly wooded and sparsely populated land. There are two theories about the origin of the Abenaki word: it either derives from "coo-ash" meaning "pine"; or from "cohos," in reference to the great bend in the Connecticut River. In any event, it's pronounced as a two-syllable word, "Co-os," and not like a plural of the sound doves make.

A manufacturing center in the 1800s and early 1900s, Lancaster is today a typical northern New England town, a mix of large, handsome homes, restored historic structures, and tired-looking buildings left behind when the mills closed. Coos County's first two-story building, the 1780 **Wilder-Holton House**, is reputed to have been a stop on the Underground Railroad. Today it houses the collection of the **Lancaster Historical Society**. Be sure to poke into the beautifully-preserved second-floor courtroom at the 1886-87 Old Historic Courthouse on Main St. The unusual fox statue in Centennial Park honors "the brave men and women who redeemed Lancaster from the wilderness."

There are two fine covered bridges in the area: head west toward Vermont, where the 1911, 266 ft. 3 in. Howe truss Mt. Orne Bridge crosses the Connecticut River. The 94 ft. 3 in. Mechanic Street Bridge, built in 1862, spans the Israel River. A life-size "iron horse" sculpture is just past Israel River Bridge on Main St.

Each Labor Day weekend Lancaster hosts the 130-year-old Lancaster Fair (for information, 788-4531).

There are many theories as to how the settlement of Lost Nation, northeast of Lancaster, got its name.

According to the most creditable, an itinerant preacher arrived one Sunday only to find a single soul in his congregation. He closed his service by asking God to forgive "this poor Lost Nation."

Head east out of town on Rte. 2. Known as "The roof of New England," this U.S. highway stretches nearly 300 miles from Burlington, Vermont to Bangor, Maine.

(6) Two fairly low-key attractions up ahead are sure to catch kids' eyes: **Santa's Village**, home to Santa and his elves and a variety of kiddy rides; and **Six Gun City,** with frontier shows, rides, a horse-drawn-vehicle museum, and water slides within the walls of an elaborate western "town."

Jefferson, on a ridge above the Israel River Valley, has spectacular views of the Franconias to the southwest, the Whites to the south, and Cherry Mountain in the distance. It's at the base of Mt. Starr King, named for Rev. Thomas Starr King, an enthusiastic early visitor to the White Mountains whose 1859 book, *The White Hills*, sparked tourism in the region.

The town was settled in 1773 by Colonel Joseph Whipple, a wealthy Portsmouth merchant who bought the land in the township for about $4,200, built roads and sawmills, and encouraged development. He was also the employer of the doomed Nancy (*see Drive 11*), and a passionate Jeffersonian Democrat. He had the town's named changed in 1796, four years before Thomas Jefferson was elected as the nation's third president.

At **Jefferson Highlands**, the road dips south to skirt the northern boundary of the White Mountain National Forest. As you head into the Randolph Valley, there are fine views to the south of Twin Mountain and Mt. Washington.

Side Trip

(7) About two miles out of town, watch on the right for the turn-off onto **Valley Rd.**, which leads to Jefferson Notch Rd. The winding gravel road (closed in winter) climbs to 3,008 ft. at Jefferson Notch -- the highest elevation of any public through road in New Hampshire --- before it winds south to the Mt. Washington Cog Railway Base Station Road and Rte. 302.

---

(8) On Rte. 2 in **Randolph**, the **Randolph Mountain Club** oversees an extensive trail network in the northern Presidential Range. Most of these trails begin along the main road, including the moderately difficult 9 6/10 mi. Lowes Path to the summit of Mt. Adams, which starts by **Lowe's Store** in town. The store sells copies of the Club's trail guide. The guide is also available by mail: RMC, Randolph 03570; or at the Androscoggin Ranger Station (466-2713), 80 Glen Rd., Gorham 035811.

Alternate Route

Just east of town, on the right, the Dolly Copp Rd. (also known as Pinkham B Rd.) cuts through the wilderness, skirting Snyder Brook Scenic Area and the base of Mt. Madison before it emerges at the Dolly Copp Campground off Rte. 16 (see #10 below). There are several hiking trails along the way.

---

(9) **Gorham**, in a valley at the confluence of the Androscoggin and Peabody Rivers, has been a gateway to the northern White Mountains since 1851, when the Atlantic and St. Lawrence Railroad first brought tourists here. Moderately-priced motels and fast-food restaurants line Main St.

(10) From Gorham, head south on Rte. 16 alongside the Peabody River into the heart of the White Mountain National Forest, with the Presidential Range to the west, and Carter and Wildcat ridges to the east. The road south through the notch (named for Joseph Pinkham who settled here in 1790), winds alongside the eastern flank of 6,288-ft. **Mt. Washington**, New England's highest peak, called "Agiochook" (the dwelling place of the Great Spirit) by native Americans. It passes by campgrounds, trailheads, and the glacially-scoured **Great Gulf Wilderness**, framed by some of the highest of the Presidentials. Several hiking trails begin at the **Dolly Copp Campground**, one of the largest in the National Forest system. The "Imp Profile" of Imp Mountain, one of the peaks of the Carter Range to the east, is visible from here.

Dolly Copp Campground is on the site of a farm owned by pioneers Dolly and Hayes Copp, who came here as newlyweds in 1831. Dolly was known throughout the region for the fine linen and woolen articles she produced and sold to tourists staying at the nearby Glen House. On the day of the couple's golden anniversary, she proclaimed, "Hayes is well enough. But fifty years is long enough for any woman to live with a man." That day, the two divided their possessions and she moved to Auburn, Maine, where she remained until her death.

According to legend, the peaks of the Presidential Range got their names one day in 1820, when Ethan Allen Crawford of the mountains' famous Crawford clan ascended Mt. Washington with seven friends and a keg of rum. At the summit, the party dipped into the rum and began naming the surrounding peaks, each with a toast: Madison, Adams, Jefferson, Monroe. Those were all the presidents there had been so far, so they next honored Benjamin Franklin. They named another peak Mt. Pleasant, which is how they felt, but it has since been renamed Mt. Eisenhower.

----

(11) Continuing south on Rte. 16, look on the right (just past the viewing area) for the turn-off for the **Mt. Washington Auto Road**, the world's first mountain toll road. It was completed in 1861 after seven years of off-and-on labor involving horses, oxen, and human muscle. The eight-mi. route to the top was originally traversed by stout Concord coaches, pulled by eight horses each, which left from the **Glen House**, across from the entrance. Today, hired vans leave from the same spot in spring, summer and fall; in winter, sightseeing tours leave from the nearby **Great Glen Trails Outdoor Center**. Private auto travel began in 1908. In 1912 the company operating the road began using gasoline-powered coaches to carry passengers disinclined to trust their own driving skills, and hotel guests who had left their Pierce-Arrows at home.

Today the Auto Road is safe and smoothly graded, and open between mid- May and October (weather permitting). While nosing heavenward at your stately, careful pace, think about Frank Sprongl. In 1998, he set the speed record in the annual Audi Mt. Washington Hill Climb: 6 minutes, 41.99 seconds, from the base of the mountain to the summit.

The oft-repeated cliche is that 6,288-ft. Mt. Washington has the "worst weather in the world," and in terms of sheer dramatic changeability this is probably true. The South Pole just stays consistently miserable; nobody freezes there because they dressed for a lark in 70º weather and got caught in an ice storm. This can easily happen on Mt. Washington.

If there is a single instance that has contributed more than any other to Mt. Washington's reputation for climatic extremes, it is the one that occurred on Thursday, April 12, 1934. On that day the instruments at the summit's Observatory recorded a wind speed of 231 mph, the greatest ever documented on the planet. Although the wind speed since then has never exceeded 200 mph, the mountain's reputation is safely entrenched.

P.T. Barnum called the view from the top "the second greatest show on earth". If you're fortunate enough to be at the summit on a clear day, you'll be able to see Portland Harbor, 75 mi. to the east, as well as Mt. Mansfield in Vermont, and Whiteface and Mt. Marcy -- an astounding 139 mi. distant -- in the Adirondacks.

The Observatory is in the Sherman Adams State Park Building, part of **Mount Washington State Park**. In addition to a snack bar and gift shop, the building also houses the **Summit Museum**, with exhibits on the natural and human history of the mountain. Be sure to visit the restored Tip Top House, the oldest building on the mountain, which opened in 1853 as a hotel.

Want to become a member one of New Hampshire's most exclusive -- and least formal -- clubs? All you have to do is climb to the top of each of the state's 48 mountains which are 4,000 ft or higher. Then send your name to the Appalachian Mountain Club (*see "Information" below*), and they'll send you a certificate of membership in the Four Thousand Footer Club.
----

(12) Continue south on Rte. 16, past **Wildcat Mountain Ski Area**, to **Pinkham Notch Visitor Center** and the **Appalachian Mountain Club Pinkham Notch Camp**.

The Appalachian Mountain Club (AMC) was founded in 1876 by a group of Bostonians interested in hiking, climbing and the natural history of the mountains at their northern doorstep. (Despite the organization's name, its prime focus always has been the White Mountains). In 1888 the Club built the first of its huts at Madison Springs, in a col, or saddle, above the walls of Madison Gulf between Mt. Madison and Mt. Adams. Madison Springs, replaced after a fire in 1941, remains the northernmost in what became a string of eight AMC huts, not counting the base camp and

North Country headquarters of the Club at Pinkham Notch. The others, completed between 1904 and 1964, are Carter Notch, east of Pinkham between Wildcat Mountain and Carter Dome; Lakes of the Clouds, at the 5,000 ft. level on Mt. Washington; Mizpah Spring, on Mt. Clinton; Zealand Falls and Galehead, on the northern fringes of the Pemigewasset Wilderness; and Lonesome Lake, in Franconia Notch below the Old Man of the Mountains. The huts are between three and six miles apart -- approximately a day's mountain hiking -- and all offer meals and bunk space.

The AMC quite naturally found itself involved in maintaining the network of trails that links the huts; over the years the Club has evolved an informal yet important role of co-stewardship with the Forest Service in the White Mountains. It is involved in environmental research and occasional lobbying, in the training of volunteers, and in instructional programs ranging from rock climbing to telemark skiing to whitewater canoeing. The AMC maintains a search-and-rescue staff of trained volunteers: the core of this group is the "notchwatchers" on 24-hr. duty at Pinkham.

Parking at Pinkham Notch Visitor Center is free, and several trails begin here. These include the 3/4 mi. hike from the parking lot to **Crystal Cascade**, a lovely mountain waterfall (follow the Tuckerman Ravine Trail until you see steps on the right leading to the Cascade overlook); and the moderately difficult, 4 1/10 mi. (one way) Tuckerman Ravine Trail to the summit of Mt. Washington via **Tuckerman Ravine**. Every year this large glacial cirque, famous for its spectacular scenery, collects an average of 55 ft. of snow which blows off the Presidential Range, making it a prime destination for backcountry skiers who come to challenge themselves at the 40-ft. freefall drop over the headwall from late March through May. The trail is one of the most heavily traveled in the White Mountains: up to 3,000 people may visit the ravine on a spring day. Be sure to check avalanche conditions before hiking or skiing here in the spring. Inquire at the lodge about overnight accommodations.

(13) South on Rte. 16, at the **Glen Ellis Falls Scenic Area**, a short trail passes through a tunnel under the highway and down a stone walkway and stairs, built by the CCC in the 1930s, to the 66-ft. waterfall. A steep, 3 2/10 mi. hike up the Glen Boulder Trail goes to the base of Glen Boulder, a huge glacial erratic visible from the highway.

A local Indian legend tells of a chief's daughter who promised her hand in marriage to a brave even though she had fallen in love with another. To set things right, the chief proclaimed that his daughter would go to whichever brave could shoot an arrow closest to the center of a target. When her lover lost the contest, the two fled. Unable to escape, they held hands and jumped into Glen Ellis Falls. Today, some say that when the conditions are right they see the star-crossed lovers, still holding hands, in the mist.

----

(14) Continue alongside the Ellis River to the turn-off for **Jackson,** a tidy little settlement with comfortable inns, built around a green at the foot of the Wildcat Brook rapids. The Jackson Covered Bridge into town, also known as the Honeymoon Bridge, was built in 1876, widened in 1939, and rebuilt in 1965.

The town is home to the highly-regarded (and very popular) non-profit **Jackson Ski Touring Foundation**, a cross-country skiing center with 154 km of finely groomed trails which connect many of the area's inns and shops. **The Wentworth**, a small resort in the village center and on the trail network, has been one of the area's premier inns for more than 150 years.

Back on Rte. 16, continue to Glen (*see Drive 11 for Glen Information*).

See Drive #11 for information about other facilities in the region.

Information

Appalachian Mountain Club Pinkham Notch Visitor Center and Lodge (466-2727), Rte. 16, Gorham 03581. www.outdoors.org

Gorham Information Booth (466-3103), Main St., Gorham. Memorial Day-June, weekends; July-Columbus Day weekend, daily.

Jackson Area Chamber of Commerce.(800-866-3334 or 383-9356), P.O. Box 304, Jackson 03846. www.jacksonnh.com. Serving Jackson, Glen, Bartlett and Intervale.

Lancaster Visitor Center (788-3212); Chamber of Commerce (788-2530), 25 Main St., Lancaster 03584.

Mt. Washington Valley Visitors Bureau (800-367-3364 or 356-3171), Box 2300, N. Conway 03860. www.mtwashingtonvalley.org

New Hampshire Audubon Society (224-9909), 3 Silk Farm Rd., Concord 03301. www.nhaudubon.org.

Northern Gateway Chamber of Commerce (788-2530), P.O. Box 537, Lancaster 03584.
Northern White Mountains Chamber of Commerce (800-992-7480 or 752-6060), 164 Main St., Box 298, Berlin 03570. www.northernwhitemountains.com.

White Mountain National Forest Headquarters (528-8721), 719 N. Main St., Laconia 03246. www.fs.us/r9/white.

Androscoggin Ranger Station (466-2713), 300 Glen Rd., Gorham 03581. To reserve campsites: 800-280-2267

Lodging

Country Inns of the White Mountains (800-562-1300 or 603-356-9460).

White Mountains B&B Assoc.: www.wmbandbs.com.

****

(2)(R) The Inn at Whitefield (837-2760), Rte. 3N, Whitefield . Twelve newly-renovated rooms (eight with private bath), restaurant, lounge with entertainment, outdoor pool, and tower library. Near Mountain View Country Club. $-$$

(2) The Mountain View House (837-2100), Mountain View Rd., Whitefield. www.mountainviewhouse.com. Golf course open; hotel scheduled to open May, 2002.

(2) The Spalding Inn (800-368-8439 or 837-2572), Mountain View Rd., Whitefield. www.spaldinginn.com. Turn-of-the-century estate on 200 acres has one- and two- bedroom cottages with fireplaces, refrigerators; some kitchens. Rooms in 1750 Carriage House; and rooms and family suites in main house. Heated pool, clay tennis courts; next to Mountain View Country Club. Pets welcome in cottages. B&B or MAP. $$-$$$

(5) Coos Motor Inn (788-3079), 209 Main St., Lancaster. Two-story in-town motel has 41 spacious and nicely furnished rooms. $-$$
(R) Cabot Motor Inn & Restaurant (788-3346), Rte. 2, Lancaster 03584. 55 rooms with cable TV and direct dial phones; indoor pool, sauna, jacuzzi, fitness and game rooms. $-$$

(5) Twin Maple B&B (788-3936), 185 Main St., Lancaster 03584.   Village Victorian has three rooms with shared bath; antique shop. $-$$ www.greatnorthwoods.org/twinmaples.

(5) The Olde Morse Lodge (788-4600), 39 Portland St., Rte. 2, Lancaster 03584. Six bedrooms with antique beds and period furnishings on upper two floors of

1858 carriage house; sitting room has a handsome fieldstone fireplace. Small pets welcome. $-$$

(6) The Jefferson Inn (800-729-7908 or 586-7998), Rte. 2, Jefferson. www.jeffersoninn.com. 1896 Victorian has 11 antiques-filled guest rooms and suites with private baths and antique tubs. Across from spring-fed swimming pond and Waumbek Golf Course. Afternoon tea. $$-$$$

(6) Jefferson Notch Motel & Cabins (800-345-3833 or 466-3833), Rte. 2, Jefferson. www.jeffnotchmotel-cabins.com. Pleasant motel and 1-room efficiency cabins; hot tub, pool, gas grills; pets welcome. $$

(8) Grand View Lodge (466-5715), Rte. 2, Randolph. Housekeeping cottages and rooms with private baths and color TV; heated pool. $-$$

(9) Royalty Inn (800-43-RELAX or 466-3312), 130 Main St., Gorham 03581. www.royaltyinn.com. 90 rooms and suites; indoor and outdoor pools, jacuzzi, sauna, exercise facility. Restaurant. $-$$

(9) Town & Country Motor Inn (800-325-4386 or 466-3315), Main St., Gorham 03581. www.townandcountryinn.com. 160-unit motel with indoor heated pool, hot tub, jacuzzi and health club, and restaurant. $-$$

(10) AMC Huts and Pinkham Notch Lodge (466-2727), Rte. 16, Gorham. www.outdoors.org. $

(14) (R) Eagle Mountain House (800-966-5779 or 383-9111), Carter Notch Rd., Jackson 03846. www.eaglemt.com. Grand historic National Register of Historic Places hotel has 93 rooms and suites, a 9-hole golf course, tennis courts, heated pool, and a wraparound verandah overlooking Wildcat River and Carter Notch. B&B, MAP, and packages. Dining room serves classic New England fare. $$-$$$

(14) (R) Inn at Thorn Hill (800-289-8990 or 383-4242), Thorn Hill Rd., Jackson. www.innatthornhill.com. Romantic, 1895 Stanford White-designed Victorian inn overlooking the village has 19 rooms in several buildings, and fireplaced common rooms. The highly-regarded dining room specializes in New England fusion cuisine and has an award-winning wine list. B&B or MAP. $$$

 (14) (R) The Wentworth (800-637-0013 or 383-9700), Rte. 16, Box M, Jackson 03846. 62 rooms and suites (some with fireplace and/or jacuzzi), golf course, tennis courts, and heated outdoor pool. MAP includes five-course dinner. B&B or MAP. Also, condominium rentals. $$-$$$ www.thewentworth.com.

(14) Inn at Jackson (800-289-8600 or 383-4321), Thorn Hill Rd., Jackson 03846. Landmark B&B designed by architect Stanford White has 14 spacious rooms with bath (5 with fireplaces), and a hot tub/jacuzzi. $$-$$$

Not on Drive

Philbrook Farm Inn (466-3831), North Rd., Shelburne 03581. 18 rooms and a variety of efficiency cottages (summer only) with fireplaces and porches at one of New England's oldest hostelries, surrounded by mountains. A wonderful spot for families. MAP. $-$$

Restaurants

(6) The Water Wheel Breakfast and Gift House (586-4313), Rte. 2, Jefferson. Generous portions of buttermilk pancakes, Belgian Waffles, and homemade soups and sandwiches; the gift shop features local crafts. B, L. $

(9) La Bottega Saladino (466-2520), 125 Main St., Gorham. Homemade pastas, pizzas, and other Italian specialties. L, D (closed Sun.)

(14) (L) Wildcat Inn and Tavern (800-228-4245 or 383-4245), Rte. 16A, Jackson. Creative country cuisine features dishes such as sauteed shrimp with artichoke hearts, sun dried tomatoes, and fresh basil over linguine. The tavern serves lighter fare (closed Sat.). 14 family-friendly Colonial, antiques-filled rooms (eight with private bath), with TVs and VCRs; two-bedroom cottage. D, L daily in summer; weekends and holidays in winter. $$-$$$

(14) The Red Fox Pub & Restaurant (383-6659), Rte. 16A, Jackson Village. Hearty appetizers, sandwiches, and entrees. Sports bar, microbrews, and all you can eat Sun. Jazz Breakfast Buffet. $-$$

Attractions

(1) Twin Mountain Hatchery and Wildlife Center (859-2041), Rte. 3, Twin Mountain.

(2) Forest Lake State Beach, off Rte. 116 S, Whitefield. One of the state's original parks built 1935, has 50 acres, a 200 ft. beach, bath house, and picnic sites. $

(4) Weeks State Park (788-4994 or 788-3155?), Rte. 3, Lancaster/Mt. Prospect Ski Area. Seasonal. $

(5) Wilder-Holton House, Lancaster Historical Society (788-3004), jct. Rtes. 2 and 3, Lancaster. By appt.
(6) Jefferson Historical Museum (586-7004 or 586-4488), Rte. 2, Jefferson. Memorial Day-Columbus Day, Sun. 1-5 or by appt. $

(9) Gorham Historical Society Railroad St., Gorham. Railroad, tourism and logging history.

(9) Moose Brook State Park (466-3860), off Rte. 2, Gorham. Campground with pool. June-Labor Day. $

(10) Wildcat Mountain Ski Area (800-255-6439 or 466-3326), Rte. 16, Pinkham Notch. Alpine ski area

has off season gondola ride to observatory summit; hike along part of Appalachian Trail. Late May-early June, weekends; mid-June-mid-Oct. daily. $

(11) Mt. Washington Auto Road (466-3988), Rte. 16, Great Glen. Mid-May-late Oct., weather permitting. $

(11) Mt. Washington Summit Museum (356-8345), P.O. Box 2310, N. Conway 03860. Seasonal. $

(11) Mount Washington State Park (466-3347), P.O. Box D, Gorham. Seasonal. $$

(12) Pinkham Notch Visitor Center and Lodge (466-2727), Rte. 16, Gorham 03581. www.outdoors.org

Activities

(2) Weathervane Theatre (837-9010), Rte. 3, Whitefield. Theater; children's concerts and other productions. Call for schedule.

(5) Crystie's Maple Farm (800-788-2118), Rte. 2 N, Lancaster.

(6) Santa's Village (586-4455), Rte. 2, Jefferson. June-mid-Oct. and Christmas season. $

(6) Six Gun City (586-4582), Rte. 2, Jefferson. Daily Father's Day-Labor Day; wknds until Columbus Day. $
(9) Mt. Washington Sky Adventures (888-353-2893 or 456-5822), Gorham Airport, Rtes. 16/ 2, Gorham. Sightsee in a vintage three-seat Schweizer glider, a 1942 Sterman biplane, or a six-passenger twin-engine Piper Aztec.

(11) Great Glen Trails Outdoor Center (466-2333), Rte. 16, Pinkham Notch. Year-round recreation, including mountain biking, canoeing, kayaking and fly fishing, x-c skiing, snowshoeing, snow tubing, and sighting tours up the Mt. Washington Auto Road.

(14) Jackson Ski Touring Foundation (800-927-6697 or 383-9355), Rte. 16A, Jackson.

(14) Nestlenook Farm Recreation Park (383-0845), Dinsmore Rd., Jackson. Horse drawn sleigh rides, ice skating, snowshoeing.

Not on Drive

White Mountain Adventures (466-2363), Rte. 2, Shelburne. Hiking, backpacking and snowshoeing guide service.

Tours

(9) Moose Tours (800-992-7480 or 466-3103), Gorham Information Center, Main St., Gorham. Twilight, moose-viewing van tours. Memorial Day weekend-foliage season.

(11) Mt. Washington Auto Road at Great Glen (466-3988). Guided van, from 8:30-5, take approximately 1 1/2 hrs., with a half hour at summit. Tours leaving before 9:30 a.m. include an hour stay at the summit.

Antiques/Crafts/Shopping

(5) CMW Emporium (788-2421), 18 Middle St., Lancaster. Candles, stuffed animals, music boxes, Salmon Falls and Great Bay pottery; gourmet foods.

(5) Coos Canoe & Snowshoe (788-2019), 64 Portland St., Lancaster. Birch bark canoes and baskets, hand-crafted paddles, snowshoes, and quill boxes.

(5) Israel River Trading Post (788-2880), 69 Main St., Lancaster. Antiques and auctions.

(5) Two Nations Native American Herb & Gift Shop (788-0948), 22 Middle St., Lancaster. More than 200 medicinal and culinary herbs, oils, mandalas, dream catchers, and jewelry.

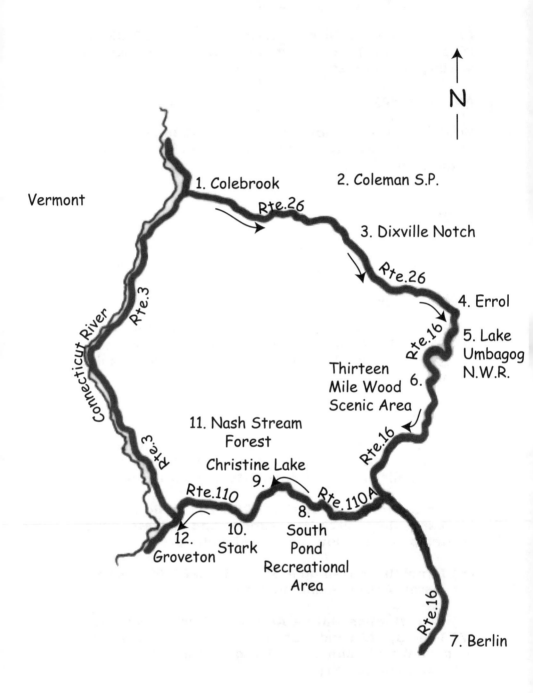

N

Vermont

1. Colebrook

2. Coleman S.P.

Rte.26

3. Dixville Notch

Rte.26

4. Errol

Rte.16

5. Lake
Umbagog
N.W.R.

Connecticut River

Rte.3

Thirteen
Mile Wood   6.
Scenic Area

Rte.16

Rte.3

11. Nash Stream
Forest

Christine Lake

9.

Rte.110

Rte.110A

8.

12.   10.   South
Groveton Stark   Pond
                   Recreational
                   Area

Rte.16

7. Berlin

Drive 13

Coos County Wilderness

85 miles

Follow this route north of the White Mountains to find one of New Hampshire's most secluded corners, a place where wilderness trails, loggers' legends, and the cry of loons along the unsullied shores of Lake Umbagog summon the spirit of the North Country as it once was -- and often still is. In the midst of it all is a grand hotel, a surprise at a bend in the road.

"The people of Coos County they are poor, and for aught that appears to the contrary, must always remain so, as they may be deemed actual trespassers on that part of creation, destined by its author for the residence of bears, wolves, moose and other animals of the forest."

> -- John Farmer, *Gazette of New Hampshire*, 1823.

*****

Although the forest products industry has largely taken the sting of inevitability out of this prophecy of eternal poverty, Mr. Farmer's observations about Coos County residents seeming like "trespassers" in a primeval realm is as true as it was 175 years ago. New Hampshire's largest county -- more than 1,000,000 acres -- encompasses the state's most undeveloped lake, one of its most pristine rivers, a 40,000-acre state forest, and a resort nestled amidst 15,000 acres of largely undeveloped woodlands.   With roads that wind through miles of wilderness, Coos indeed feels like country that was created for "animals of the forest."

(1) Begin the drive in **Colebrook** (*see Drive 14*).   Head east out of town on Rte. 26, a "Scenic and Cultural Highway" which follows alongside the Mohawk River.

A group of dedicated volunteers has been working hard to develop Cohos Trail, a footpath that extends for some 160 mi. from near the town of Bartlett to the Canadian Border.   Many sections have been completed, and offer some of the state's finest wilderness hiking. Information: www.cohostrail.org

----

(2) In **Kidderville**, turn left on Diamond Pond Rd. and continue four mi., past **Diamond Sportsman's Lodge**, to **Coleman State Park** on Little Diamond Pond.   Both Little Diamond and Diamond Pond, just up the road, offer excellent trout fishing.

(3) Continue on Rte. 26 to **Dixville**, home of the **Balsams Grand Resort Hotel** in **Dixville Notch.**   The resort, overlooking man-made Lake Gloriette in the 15,000-acre Balsams Wilderness, is an outpost of old-style mountain hotel luxury.   It began in 1861 as Dix Farm, where passers-by could get a room and a meal for $2 a night.   Today the resort, with more than 200 guest rooms, offers a full roster of activities including downhill skiing, golf (at one of the country's most scenic courses), tennis, hiking, and live entertainment. Dixville Notch has another claim to fame: along with the town of Hart's Location, it's one of the first two communities to vote in New Hampshire primary and presidential elections.   The midnight rituals of casting and counting ballots take place in a meeting room in the Balsams' main building.

Visitors are welcome to tour the hotel and grounds even if they are not registered guests. Abenaki Mountain, which rises behind the hotel, is a prime nesting spot for peregrine falcons.

By the post-WWII era most of the great hotels of the White Mountains and the North Country had become anachronisms, and the Balsams ended up on the block in a federal foreclosure auction in 1954. The integrity of the resort and the property were preserved, though, when a Massachusetts rubber products manufacturer named Neil Tillotson purchased the land and buildings and set about proving that at least here in Dixville Notch, the old traditions could survive. The rubber business still operates out of a cluster of unobtrusive buildings right behind the hotel, turning out latex medical examination gloves and toy balloons. Tillotson's first novelty balloon, "Tilly the Cat," has been a company staple since 1931.

Several hiking trails begin on or near the hotel grounds, including a steep, rocky trail to Table Rock, a stark cliff formed of vertical slabs which is less than 10 ft. wide at its narrowest point. The views from the top are spectacular. A second, easier trail to Table Rock begins just up the road. The Mount Sanguinary Trail, which begins at the Flume Brook Picnic Area in Dixville Notch State Wayside, climbs through a balsam and spruce forest to a rocky pinnacle overlooking the hotel. Ask at the hotel desk for a trail map.

A short distance east of the hotel turnoff is the official entrance to **Dixville Notch** and 137-acre **Dixville Notch State Park**. Dixville is the northernmost of New Hampshire's four great notches, or mountain passes. It slices through the height of land separating the Connecticut Valley from the Androscoggin basin.

The steep, craggy walls of the notch, formed eons ago when the bedrock folded, keep the narrow highway in near-perpetual shadow. The park, with a gorge, waterfalls, and meadows that rise 2,500 ft. above sea level, is home to much of the state's moose population.

(4) Rte. 26 continues east alongside Clear Stream through tiny Millsfield to **Errol**, on the Androscoggin River in the Upper Androscoggin Valley. This is the heart of the Northern Forest, a vast swath of hardwood trees such as maple and beech, and the boreal conifers spruce and pine. The tiny logging and farming village has a motel, a few restaurants (plan to eat dinner early), and an airplane sightseeing service.

(5) At the junction of Rte. 26 with Rte. 16, turn north (left) and drive a short distance to the headquarters of the 13,000-acre **Lake Umbagog National Wildlife Refuge**. The country's newest wildlife refuge, created in 1992 to conserve wetlands and protect migratory birds, encompasses the 8,700-acre lake, and is home to the state's only breeding pair of bald eagles, as well as a wide variety of other birds, including ospreys, loons, 25 species of warblers, kingfishers, and blue herons. Mink, otter, and moose are just a few of the refuge's year-round residents.

Umbagog, which laps across the border into Maine, is named for an Abenaki word meaning "clear lake or water." One of its most unusual features is Floating Island, a mass of vegetation which moves according to wind direction. As the source of the Androscoggin River, Umbagog was for many years the collecting point for logs awaiting shipment to downcountry mills. When the melting snows raised the water levels, the timber gathered here would be herded down the Androscoggin by men with caulked boots using the long, jam-breaking peaveys or "cant dogs."

Jigger Johnson, a logger's logger and northern New Hampshire legend, went into the woods at the age of 12. Just 5 feet 6 inches tall, he fought his way up to the position of boss and threatened to kill anyone who

didn't do his job right. In his book *The Great White Hills of New Hampshire,* Ernest Poole described him:

"When stripped, his whole body showed the scars left by scores of calked boots; but men left his head alone, for his bite was swift and his teeth were strong. He is said to have bitten off a man's ear and spit it out when the fight was done. When once with his crew he went into Berlin and got thoroughly soused, some of his men laid for him on the dark road back to camp and 'calked' him well and, with both his arms and legs broken, left him for dead. But Jigger managed to wriggle and roll to a neighboring pigsty, rolled into manure to keep warm and so slept off his drunk, was found by a forest ranger and taken to a hospital whence a month later he emerged limping a bit but still going strong."

----

(6) Head south on Rte. 16, as the road hugs the west bank of the Androscoggin. This section, from the lake south to Dummer, is part of the Northern Forest Canoe Trail, a 700-mile stretch of water which begins in Old Forge, New York and ends in Fort Kent, Maine. It's based on historic and prehistoric travel routes, and crosses all of the Northeast's major watersheds.

Thirteen Mile Wood Scenic Area offers some of the finest trout fishing and white water canoeing in the state.   Androscoggin Wayside Park, on a bluff overlooking the river, is a delightful spot for a picnic.

"They learned to eat green apples and green cucumbers, dried salt pork, boiled potatoes. They ran barefoot, often times until old enough to earn a pair of calfskin shoes. Their clothing was thin, but they had an abundance of exercise. They climbed about the barn after hen's eggs, up an apple tree after fruit like squirrels, and over fences like dogs ... They paddled about in the neighboring brook and never thought of catching cold ... They learned to spin and weave. They attended school, but usually did not learn much for it was thought that they did not need to know much to become wise mothers. To go through the simple rules of arithmetic, to be able to read their bible and hymn book, and write a poorly spelled letter were their usual accomplishments. There were no organs or pianos those days to torment them. Their music consisted chiefly of the spinning wheel with the loom as an accompaniment, and the noise of half a dozen children. ... They became mothers of large families and grew to a good old age after seeing their children all settled in life, and sank to rest and sleep with the hope of a better life in the future."

   -- The Gorham Mountaineer, August 25, 1882, on the subject of what life had been like for Coos County girls 60 years earlier.

Side Trip

(7) Detour south on Rte. 16 for 10 miles to Berlin, "The City that Trees Built," at the confluence of the Dead and Androscoggin Rivers. Along the way, watch for boom piers in the river: a series of them -- chains of logs linked end to end, from pier to pier -- permitted log drivers to divide the logs and channel them to paper companies in Berlin.

Berlin continues to thrive as a paper mill town. Its civic legacy includes some wonderful buildings, including the onion-domed Eastern Orthodox Church of the Holy Resurrection on 20 Petrograd St.; the Stick-style Congregational Church of Christ on Main St.; and St. Anne's Church at 58 Church St. Northern Forest Heritage Park, "celebrating the working forest," encompasses the Historic Brown Company House, an operating blacksmith shop, Visitor Center, and riverside amphitheater for concerts, ethnic festivals, and logging competitions.

Just north of the city limits is Nansen X-Country Ski Touring Center, founded in 1872 by Scandinavian

immigrants who helped pioneer Nordic skiing in America. Nansen Ski Jump, erected in 1936, is the second highest steel tower jump in the country.

----

(8) At the junction of Rte. 16 and Rte. 110A, turn right onto Rte. 110A and head past Cedar Pond (where you can take a dip at the privately owned beach for just 50¢) to Rte. 110. Turn right onto Rte. 110, and head west for roughly 3 mi. to the left-hand turn onto South Pond Road, leading to the **South Pond Recreation Area**, a picnic and swimming spot (note: the gate, a mile from the pond, is generally open in summer from 9 a.m. to 8 p.m.). Here is the northern terminus of the Kilkenny Ridge Trail, and the beginning of Devil's Hopyard Trail, which parallels the Kilkenny Ridge Trail before splitting off to the Devil's Hopyard, a picturesque, boulder-lined gorge. The 2.4-mile hike is moderately difficult and the rocks can be slippery. According to a 1930s guide, "the trees hereabout are covered with hanging gray moss, giving a fancied resemblance to a hop-yard with its poles covered with heavily laden vines, which accounts for the name."

(9) In tiny **Percy**, turn right and head a 1/2 mi. north to **Christine Lake**, tucked in a mountain basin in the shadow of the twin Percy Peaks (see below). The lake is a good spot to fish for brown trout.

Continue through the Ammonoosuc Valley along Rte. 110. Watch on the left for a roadside marker which commemorates the area where, in the spring of 1944, four guard towers transformed a CCC camp into Camp Stark, New Hampshire's only WWII Prisoner of War Camp. Two hundred and fifty Germans and Austrians were interred here for two years, cutting pulp in the forest. Many returned for a reunion in 1986.

(10) The handsome village of **Stark** stands on the Upper Ammonoosuc River at the foot of a sheer, 700-foot cliff called the Devil's Slide. The town is named for General John Stark, a hero of the American Revolution (*see Drive 2*). At the center of the village is the 1853 Union Church, and, next to it, a 134-foot,

two-span, Burr-type covered bridge with walkways on both sides. The gracious **Stark Inn** is just on the other side. Whitcomb Field is the venue for the town's annual Fiddlers' Contest in June.

(11) Continuing west toward Groveton, watch on the right for Emerson Road -- it's the turn-off for **Nash Stream Forest**, 40,000 acres of woods, wetlands and ponds, including 6,000-acre Stratford Bog. The forest, which contains South and North Percy Peaks within its boundaries, is managed jointly by public and private agencies. Although some logging is permitted, the forest is mainly reserved for public use.

Take the 3.4 mile hike to the scrubby summit of 3,418 ft. North Percy Peak for spectacular 360°views. To get to the trailhead, continue on Emerson Road for 2.2 miles and turn left onto Nash Stream Road. Continue for 2.7 miles to a sign and a small parking area. Other forest highlights include Little Pond Bog, a fine area for fly fishing; and Pond Brook Falls, a series of cascading falls.

(12) **Groveton,** near the junction of the Upper Ammonoosuc and Connecticut Rivers, has long been a paper mill town. The Burr-type Groveton Bridge, built in 1852, is open to foot traffic only.

Note: see Drive 14 for additional Colebrook area listings.

Information

Northern White Mountain Chamber of Commerce (800-992-7480 or 752-6060), 164 Main St., Box 298, Berlin 03570. www.northernwhitemountains.com.

Umbagog Area Chamber of Commerce (482-3906), Errol 03579. www.umbagogchambercomerce.com.

White Mountain National Forest Androscoggin Ranger Station (466-2713), 80 Glen Rd., Gorham 03581.

Lodging

(1) Rooms with a View (800-499-5106 or 236-5106), Forbes Rd., Colebrook 03576. B&B in a new home in a meadow overlooking Connecticut Valley and Dixville Notch. $

(2) Diamond Sportsman's Lodge (237-5211), Diamond Pond Rd., Colebrook 03576. $

(3) The Balsams Grand Resort Hotel (800-255-0600; in NH 800-255-0800), Rte. 26, Dixville Notch 03576. www.thebalsams.com. Mid-May - mid-Oct., and mid-Dec. - March. $$$$

(4) Errol Motel (482-3256), Rte. 26, Erroll. Basic accommodations and housekeeping units. $

(4) Magalloway River Inn (482-9883), Rte. 16, Wentworth Location, Errol 03579. Comfortable and homey accommodations--all with private baths--in an 1800s country inn with a fireplaced living room. $

(4) Umbagog Lake Campground and Cottages (482-7795), Rte. 26, P.O. Box 181, Errol 03579. Housekeeping cabins and primitive camp sites on lakeshore and islands; family campground. Late May-mid Sept. $

(7) Traveler Motel (752-2500 or 800-365-9391), 25 Pleasant St., Berlin 03570. www.budget-inn.net. Clean, basic accommodations. $

(10) Stark Village Inn (636-2644), Stark 03582. Three guest rooms with private baths in a fireplaced B&B near the covered bridge. $

Restaurants

(3-4) Log Cabin Campground, Restaurant and Lounge, Ret. 26, Millsfield. Pizza, home cooking, and a pub with entertainment. $

(4) Errol Restaurant (482-3852), Main St., Errol. Sandwiches include the house special "mooseburger" and *poutine* (French fries with melted cheese and gravy). $

(4) Bill's Seafood and Country Cooking (482-3838), next to the airport, Errol. Seafood, homemade soups and desserts. BYOB. $

(7) Northland Dairy Bar and Restaurant (752-6210), Rte. 16, Berlin. Fresh seafood, sandwiches, and homemade ice cream. $

Attractions

(2) Coleman State Park (53-6965), off Rte. 26, Stewartstown. Primitive camping, swimming, boat launch, fishing. $

(3) Dixville Notch State Park (482-3373), Rte. 26, Dixville. Scenic gorge, waterfalls, brooks. $

(5) Lake Umbagog National Wildlife Refuge (472-3415), P.O. Box 240, Rte. 16e, Errol.

(6) Mollidgewock State Park (482-3372), Rte. 16, Errol. Primitive campsites; boat launch. $

(7) Moffet House (752-7040), 119 High St., Berlin. C. 1892 Victorian home is the headquarters of the Berlin & Coos County Historical Society.

(7) Nansen Cross Country Ski Touring Center (752-1573), Rte. 26, Berlin.

(7) Northern Forest Heritage Park (752-7202), 961 Main St., Berlin.

Not on Drive
Milan Hill State Park, Rte. 110B, Milan. Auto road to summit of Milan Hill; hiking. $

Activities

Great North Woods Wilderness Adventures (800-992-7480 or 752-6060). Bus tours through the Northern Forest; moose-viewing tours.

Saco Bound/Northern Waters Canoe & Kayak Sales, Rentals & Instruction (447-2177).

Umbagog Outfitters Kayak Touring & Whitewater School (356-3292).

(3) The Balsams Mountain Bike and Nature Center (255-3921 or 255-3400), Dixville Notch. 60 km of trails through 15,000 acres. Rentals; guided tours.

(4) Mountain Rain (482-3323), Errol Airport. Airplane rides, and seaplane transportation to remote areas.

(4) Northern Waters Canoe and Kayak (447-3801), Errol Bridge. HQ: Box 119, Conway 03813. Guided tours of Magalloway River; canoe and kayak rentals.

(4) Umbagog Outfitters (356-3292), Box 268, Errol. Guided flatwater and whitewater kayak tours.
(7) Moriah's (466-5050), 101 Main St., Gorham. Biking, hiking, and paddling tours; boat and bicycle rentals.

Shopping
(4) L.L. Cote's (482-7777), 76 Main St., Errol. North Country staples, including rainwear, guns, fishing equipment, and camping supplies.

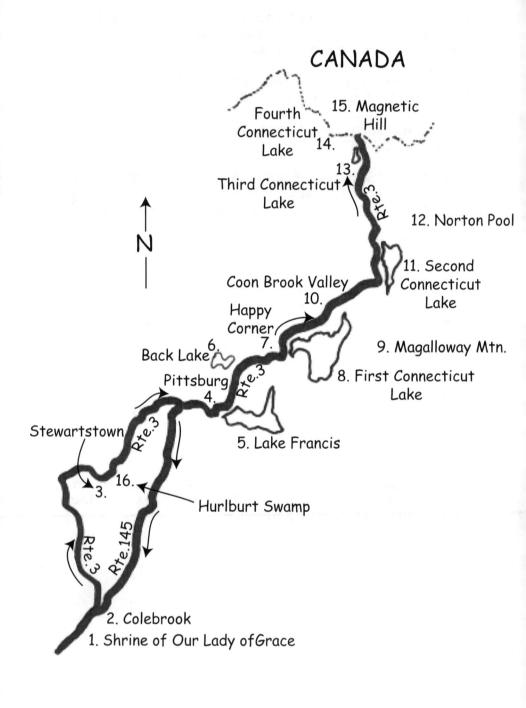

CANADA

15. Magnetic Hill

Fourth Connecticut Lake

14.

13.

Third Connecticut Lake

12. Norton Pool

Rte.3

Coon Brook Valley

10.

11. Second Connecticut Lake

Happy Corner

7.

9. Magalloway Mtn.

Back Lake 6.

N

8. First Connecticut Lake

Pittsburg

Rte.3

4.

5. Lake Francis

Stewartstown

Rte.3

16.

3.

Hurlburt Swamp

Rte.3

Rte.145

2. Colebrook

1. Shrine of Our Lady of Grace

Drive 14

The Connecticut Lakes

83 miles

This drive takes in some of the state's least-visited wilderness, traversing what was once a bitterly contested no-man's land and ending at one of the world's most peaceful frontiers. It's also a journey to the source of the stream the Abenaki called Quinn-attuck-auke, "The Long Deer Place" -- New England's longest river.

If you're approaching this drive from the south along Rte. 3, watch on the left in Columbia (just south of #1, below, and the town of Colebrook) for Columbia Covered Bridge. This 145 ft. 9 in. span across the Connecticut River, built in 1912 to replace one that burned the year before, is the northernmost covered bridge between Vermont and New Hampshire. It's unusual in that it is sheathed in open latticework for nearly half its length on its upstream side, while the downstream side is fully enclosed.

Note: if you're planning to explore the logging and old roads in this region, be sure to pick up the map "Roads and Trails, Connecticut Lake Region" at one of the local stores.

(1) The drive begins, oddly enough, with a look at the only stone motorcycle in New England. It's just south of Colebrook, in **Columbia**, on the grounds of the Oblate fathers' **Shrine of Our Lady of Grace**. Called "Motorcyclists in Prayer," the statue, by sculptor John M. Weidman, Jr., is a life-size depiction in granite of a man and a woman kneeling in devout contemplation beside their bike, a bible lying open before them.

The rest of the site, with its well-kept lawns, fountain, votive-lighted altar and benches, is pretty though not out of the ordinary -- but the shrine attracts hundreds of motorcyclists from throughout New England in late spring for the blessing of the bikes. The origins of this ritual are lost in the mists; however, it always takes place here, and here is where cycling enthusiasts of a religious turn of mind decided to place the statue. We're not sure if it's serendipity that Rte. 145, which runs between Colebrook and Pittsburg, has all the dips and turns of a first-rate motorcycle route.

(2) **Colebrook**, situated where the tiny Mohawk River joins with the Connecticut, grew up as a logging center and market town for outlying farms. Although its population is barely above 1,000, it has the busy main street of a town 10 times its size, if only because those living in the hinterlands of northern Coos have nowhere else to shop. Beyond the **Colebrook House and Motel** -- providing lodging since 1830 -- the houses and stores thin out quickly and Rte. 3 meanders on, with the infant Connecticut on its left. The river can't be more than 50 ft. across here, and the Vermont cows on the other side seem as if they could casually wade across and change their citizenship. Vermont's Mt. Monadnock, a 3,140 ft. namesake of the slightly taller peak in southern New Hampshire (*see Drive 3*), is the dominant feature of the surrounding landscape.

(3) Continue past **Stewartstown,** a scant collection of houses where a bridge crosses the Connecticut to Canaan, Vermont. A roadside marker identifies **45° North Latitude**, the line halfway between the Equator and the North Pole.

This was the latitude chosen in the 1842 Webster-Ashburton Treaty as the boundary between Canada and the United States, to a point as far east as Hall's Stream, a south-flowing tributary of the Connecticut.

From there (a spot in the forest just west of Rte. 3, where Quebec, Vermont and New Hampshire meet), the frontier follows Hall's Stream north, allowing New Hampshire to reach a higher latitude than straight-bordered Vermont. (This arrangement wrote *finis* to a thorny little chapter in the history of the North County, as we'll see when we get to Pittsburg.)

If you look west across the river, however, that's not Canada but Beecher Falls, Vermont that you see. Surveying was a less exact science back when the line was drawn, since Canada actually starts about a mile north of here.

George Van Dyke, born in Canada to a poor family, moved to Stewartstown and became a lumber baron and president of the Connecticut Valley Lumber Company. When trouble brewed during the very dangerous lumber drives from the North Woods down the Connecticut, his slogan was "To hell with the man, save the cant dog" (poles used to keep logs apart in river drives).

One day as he was passing by Turner Falls, he asked his driver to back up so he could get a better look. The car rolled over the bank, killing him.

----

(4) The Connecticut threads alongside Rte. 3 to **Pittsburg**, unsurpassed in acreage (and close to dead last in population) among all of New Hampshire's municipalities. There are more than 300,000 acres of forests, mountains, lakes and streams within its boundaries, but hardly much of a settlement: a few general stores, a school, a gas station, a handful of houses, and an information center make up the village of Pittsburg.

A plaque in the center of town tells about the Republic of Indian Stream, established in 1836 by local residents who tired of the inability of American and

British diplomats to agree on which stream was the northwesternmost of the sources of the Connecticut. It was accepted that that waterway would form the boundary between New Hampshire and Canada, but the two nations couldn't reach an agreement on which one it was to be. The Americans lobbied for Indian Stream, actually the next-to-northwestern most; the British wanted the boundary to be the fledgling river that links what we now call the Connecticut Lakes. Each side tried to extend political control over the disputed area and the lives of the farmers and backwoodsmen who lived there, so these inhabitants set themselves up as an independent nation.

The dispute continued, however, and residents began to take sides, some wanting to join with Canada, and others with New Hampshire. The "Indian Stream War" started and ended, without fatalities, when a Coos County sheriff's deputy was seized by Canadian sympathizers and nearly carted off across the border before being rescued by the New Hampshire faction. Finally, the Indian Stream legislature, in its last official act, opted to join New Hampshire. The matter came to a formal close with the adoption of the Webster-Ashburton Treaty.

Several annual August events draw crowds to Pittsburg: the Pittsburg Guides' Show (538-6984) in the middle of the month; and, in the last week, the North Country Moose Festival (237-8939), with parades, barbecues, auto shows, and moose watching.

At any point between Pittsburg and the border you're likely to pass a heavily-laden logging truck, a reminder that farming long since has been eclipsed by timber harvesting in this region. The forest holdings amassed by the great paper companies over the past century comprise a swath of Vermont, New Hampshire and Maine so vast as to constitute a nation within a nation that would dwarf the Republic of Indian Stream, and which in its way is far more

autonomous. Ownership and maintenance of this territory for its logging potential has paradoxically assured the survival of much of it as a wilderness, and corporate policy has generally been favorite to campers, hikers, hunters, and fishermen. But the paper companies in recent years have been divesting themselves of much of their landholdings, raising the possibility that forest lands previously off limits to development may be subdivided for vacation homes. Extensive backcountry acreage has recently been preserved through private and public purchase and easement arrangements in Maine and Vermont, although a region-wide solution remains elusive.

----

(5) The first lake you come upon is proof that the rise and fall of farming and logging have by no means been the only major influences on the lay of this lonely land. Hydro power is another shaper of geography. Lake Francis (not one of the Connecticut Lakes) was created by damming the Connecticut between the points where Perry Stream and Indian Stream join the river proper, itself no more than a stream above and below the man-made lake. The 2,000-acre **Lake Francis State Park** at the northern tip of the lake offers primitive lakefront camping, stream and lake fishing (trout, salmon, and pickerel), picnicking, and boating.

(6) Continue north on Rte. 3 past turn-offs for tiny **Back Lake**, home to several comfortable fishing lodges and other accommodations.

Side Trip

(7) Up ahead, in Happy Corner, turn right onto Hill-Danforth Rd. to the 60 ft. 6 in. Happy Corner Bridge, which spans Perry Stream. According to Thedia Cox Kenyon in her book *New Hampshire Covered Bridges*, it "derived its name from the number of happy young

people who lived in its vicinity at one time." The New Hampshire volume in the 1930s *American Guide Series*, however, says that the name derives from the fact "that its store was a rendezvous for a group of men in the vicinity who whiled away the hours with cards and jovial fellowship." Although the exact year it was built is unknown, this Paddleford truss bridge (with an added arch) is recognized as one of the oldest in northern New Hampshire. To see the 57-ft.-long Queenpost truss River Road bridge, continue on Hill-Danforth Rd. to the first left, Dan Day Road, then continue north on River Rd. back to Rte. 3.

----

(8) The Connecticut Lakes obviously were numbered by settlers moving from south to north; logically, the "first" should be the northernmost lake in the chain, which is the true source of the Connecticut River. But the actual **First Connecticut Lake**, at 2,807 acres the largest of the "Connecticuts," is the first on our route and a splendid place to picnic or launch a canoe and try to catch one of the region's famous lake or rainbow trout, or landlocked salmon. The western shore is home to **The Glen**, a handsome cluster of lakeside cabins set among birches and pines, with a big, rambling main lodge where guests' meals are served (the public is welcome by reservation).

As you leave First Connecticut Lake you enter the 1,548-acre Connecticut Lakes State Forest, known unofficially as "Moose Alley." The area is appro- priately named: watch out for the beasts as you drive!

Side Trip

(9) Just past First Lake, watch for the turn-off for Magalloway Mountain and its summit fire tower. Continue eight miles on an often muddy dirt road, following signs to the right to the Bobcat Trailhead for a 1.6 mi., moderately difficult hike to the top of 3,360 ft. Magalloway Mountain. Climb the fire tower

for fabulous views of the Connecticut lakes, Maine's Rump Mountain, and the Middle Branch of the Dead Diamond River.

----

(10) Haven't seen a moose yet? Back on Rte. 3, just past the Magalloway Mountain turn-off, watch for a road on the left. It goes a short distance into **Coon Brook Valley**, a marshy region which is a favorite dining spot for the behemoth herbivores.

(11) The 1,286-acre **Second Connecticut Lake**, in the George O. Roberts State Park, also offers good salmon and trout fishing, although the picnic area is nicer on the First Lake.

Side Trip

(12) The only remaining lowland virgin spruce/fir forest in the state is in the New Hampshire Nature Conservancy's 427-acre Norton Pool property, an isolated wilderness of ponds, marshes, and bogs.

At the northern tip of Second Lake, watch on the right for the turn-off for East Inlet Rd. (just past Deer Mountain Campground). Drive over the Connecticut River and East Inlet Stream and continue 2.8 miles from the East Inlet Dam to where the road bends. The parcel, donated to the Conservancy by Champion Paper Company in 1987, is one of the few in the North Country never to have been cut, and is one of the region's premier animal and bird watching areas.

Among species sighted: ring-necked and black ducks, black-backed woodpeckers, common snipe, hoary comma butterflies (with black, white, and rust-colored wings), moose, otter, and mink. Scott Bog, to the left on the dirt road, is another prime spot for wildlife watching.
----

(13) It wasn't until 1939 that a crew from the Civilian Conservation Corps completed the road from the southern tip of Second Connecticut Lake to the last two lakes and the border. The 278-acre **Third Connecticut Lake** has a boat ramp and teems with brown and lake trout.

(14) Great oaks from little acorns grow: tiny (two-acre), secluded **Fourth Connecticut Lake**, nestled in the woods smack on the border, is the ultimate source of the Connecticut River. From here, it's a 407-mile canoe ride (with portages around dams) to Long Island Sound.

Fourth Connecticut Lake is part of a 78-acre parcel of land donated to the Nature Conservancy by Champion Paper in 1991. The tract also encompasses a floating bog that is a fertile habitat for insectivorous plants. At the border, park at the patrol station, sign in at the U.S. Customs, and follow the trail to the west to the preserve entrance.

Side Trip

(15) If you've never coasted uphill in your car, cross the border and continue just over a mile to the bottom of Magnetic Hill (*Côte Magnétique Observation Phénomè Optique*) in Chartierville, Quebec. At the first house on the right, turn your car around so it faces south, and drive to a sign which tells you to put your gearshift in neutral. You'll experience a startling optical illusion as your car seems to roll uphill!

Note: the border station here is open 8 a.m.-4 p.m., December to April; until 8 p.m. through mid-June; and to midnight through November. If you cross back into the U.S. when the station is closed, you must drive immediately -- without stopping -- to the customs station in Beecher Falls, Vermont to avoid a penalty. To cross the border you'll need your vehicle registration and I.D. (your driver's license will do).

Return to Pittsburg village on Rte. 3 and turn left onto Rte. 145. Over the 15 miles between here and Colebrook, the road loops, rises, and drops through a series of magnificent vistas -- rolling dairy lands in the foreground (be careful of farmers taking their cows across the road at milking time), and the remote peaks of Vermont's Northeast Kingdom in the distance.

Side Trip

(16) About five miles south of Pittsburg, turn right off Rte. 145 onto West Rd. and continue for about 1 1/2 miles to a dirt road on the left. Turn there (at a small, artificial pond) and drive 1 1/10 mi. to Hurlburt Swamp, a 284-acre Nature Conservancy property that encompasses a northern white cedar swamp and several rare wildflowers, including the endangered yellow lady slipper.

----

(17) Back on Rte. 145, watch on the left for **Beaver Brook Falls Natural Area**, where waters cascade more than 60 ft. This is a delightful spot for a picnic before you arrive back in Colebrook.

Information

Connecticut Lakes Tourist Association (538-9900), Box 38, Pittsburg 03592.

The Nature Conservancy (Hurlbert Swamp; Fourth Connecticut Lake, Norton Pool), (224-5853), 2 1/2 Beacon St., Suite #6, Concord 03301.

North Country Chamber of Commerce (800-698-8939 or 237-8939), Colebrook 03576.

New Hampshire's Connecticut Lakes Region (538-7118), PO Box 400, Pittsburg 03592.

New Hampshire Information Center, Rte. 3, Colebrook. Memorial Day-Columbus Day.

Lodging

(2) (R) Colebrook House and Motel (800-365-9391 or 752-2500), 132 Main St., Colebrook. www.colebrookhouse.com. Simple but comfortable rooms; entertainment in lounge Thurs.-Sat. $

(2) Monadnock B&B (237-8216), Bridge/Monadnock sts., Colebrook 03576. Friendly and reasonably priced accommodations in a 1916 home Three guest rooms (one with private bath); four in the basement. $

(2) Northern Comfort Motel (237-4440), Rte. 3, Colebrook 03576. Just outside town and set well back from the road, the motel has clean, comfortable rooms, a pool, and a hot tub. $$

(2) Room with a View (237 5106), Forbes Rd., Colebrook 03567. B&B with seven guest rooms (two with private bath) has spectacular views, an outdoor hot tub, and miles of hiking trails. $

(4) Magalloway Cabins (538-6353), RFD #1, Box 50-B, Pittsburg 03592.   One and two-bedroom housekeeping units overlook First Lake. Boat rentals. $-$$ www.northcountrychamber.org/magalloway.

(6) (R) Tall Timber Lodge (800-835-6343 or 538-6651), Back Lake, Pittsburg 03592.   Small, traditional waterfront sporting camp has lakeside log cabins, lodge rooms, and luxury cottages with whirlpool baths and fireplaces. $-$$$ www.talltimber.com.

(7)(R) The Glen (800-445-GLEN or 538-6500), First Connecticut Lake, Pittsburg 03592.   The region's premier resort, down a mile of private road, is a full-service lodge with spacious rooms with private bath, or rustic log cottages -- all with maid service. Hiking, boats, motors, and guides. Open May-Oct. FAP. $$$

(8) Lopstick Lodge and Cabins (800-538-6659, First Connecticut Lake, Pittsburg 03592. www.Lpstick.com. 1,2 or 4-bedroom cabins in a quiet, picturesque setting overlooking the lake. Flyfishing and bird hunting guide service. $-$$$

(8) Timberland Lodge & Cabins (800-545 6613 or 538 6613), First Connecticut Lake, Pittsburg 03592. Resort complex of 20 one-four bedroom log cabins, some directly on lake with private beaches and docks. Also, Metallak Lodge, a four-bedroom log home with cathedral ceiling, fieldstone fireplace, and private beach. Boat rental. $-$$$

Restaurants

(2) Sutton Place (237-8842), 152 Main St., Colebrook. Dinner nightly, except Sun. in winter. $-$$

(2) Howard's Restaurant (237-4025), Main St., Colebrook. Where the locals and fishermen chow down on three meals daily (open at 5 a.m. Mon.-Sat., Sun. at 6). $

(4) Moriah's Restaurant, Main St., Pittsburg. Breakfast and lunch daily. Homemade baked goodies, soups, and sandwiches. $

(6) The Rainbow Grille at Tall Timber Lodge (800 83-LODGE or 538-6651), Back Lake, Pittsburg. Specializing in trout of every description, char-grilled venison and elk, and prime beef; also hearty breakfasts. $$-$$$

Attractions

(1) Shrine of Our Lady of Grace (237-5511), Rte. 3, Columbia. Gift shop across the street.

(2) Colebrook Area Historical Society (237-4528), Colebrook. May-Oct., Sat. 10-2.

(4) Pittsburg Historical Society (246-7233), Town Hall, Main St., Pittsburg. July-Aug., Sat. 1-3.

(5) Lake Francis State Park (538-6965), River Rd., Pittsburg. Mid May-Columbus Day.

(15) Magnetic Hill (800-217-8111), Chartierville, Que.

Activities

(2) Osprey Fishing Adventures (922-3800), Box 121, Colebrook. Mid- June-Labor Day. One- to three-day fly fishing trips in a three-person drift boat.

(2) Yankee Sportsman (246-3675), Rte. 1, Box 304, Colebrook.

(4) Magalloway Cabins (538-6353), RFD #1, Box 50-B, Pittsburg. Boat rentals.

(4) Northern Enterprises (538 6352), Rte. 3, Pittsburg. Snowmobile rentals.

(8) Lopstick Outfitters (800-538-6659), First Connecticut Lake. Guided fly fishing, canoe rental, fishing equipment, maps, housekeeping cabins.

(8) Timberland Lodge (800-545 6613 or 538-6613), First Connecticut Lake. Boat rental.

Not on Drive:

River Excitement (802-457-4021), Box 65, Hartland Four Corners, Vermont 05049. Guided drift-boat and wading trips on the Connecticut. Fishing equipment and gourmet lunches included.

Shopping

Young's Store, Rte. 3, Pittsburg: "we sell generally everything."

INDEX

Recommended Reading

AMC White Mountain Guide. Boston: Appalachian Mountain Club. 26th ed., 1998.

The Connecticut, by Walter Hard. (Rivers of America Series) New York: Rinehart, 1947.

The Great White Hills of New Hampshire, by Ernest Poole. Garden City, NY: Doubleday, 1946.

Let Me Show You New Hampshire, by Ella Shannon Bowles. New York: Knopf, 1938.

Natural Wonders of New Hampshire, by Suzi Casanave. Castine, ME: Country Roads Press, 1994.

New Hampshire: An Explorer's Guide, by Christina Tree and Christine Hamm. Woodstock, VT: The Countryman Press. 4th ed., 1999.

New Hampshire: A Guide to the Granite State (American Guide Series). Boston: Houghton Mifflin/ The Riverside Press, 1938. (Part of the celebrated 1930s "WPA" series of state guides; look for it in second-hand stores.)

New Hampshire: Off the Beaten Path, by Barbara Radcliffe Rogers and Stillman Rogers. Old Saybrook, CT: Globe Pequot Press. 3rd ed., 1998

New Hampshire's Covered Bridges: History and Legends, by Thedia Cox Kenyon. Sanbornville, NH: Wake-Brook House, 1957.

A Treasury of New England Folklore, edited by B.A. Botkin. New York: Bonanza Books, 1965.